Customizing Indigeneity

Customizing Indigeneity

Paths to a Visionary Politics in Peru

Shane Greene

Stanford University Press
Stanford, California

Stanford University Press
Stanford, California

Printed in the United States of America on acid-free, archival-quality paper

Library of Congress Cataloging-in-Publication Data

Greene, Shane, 1971–
  Customizing indigeneity : paths to a visionary politics in Peru / Shane Greene.
    p. cm.
  Includes bibliographical references and index.
  ISBN 978-0-8047-6118-5 (cloth : alk. paper) — ISBN 978-0-8047-6119-2 (pbk. : alk. paper)
  1. Aguaruna Indians—Politics and government. 2. Aguaruna Indians—Ethnic identity.
3. Indians of South America—Peru—Politics and government. 4. Indians of South America—
Peru—Ethnic identity. I. Title.
  F3430.1.A35G74 2009
  985'.01—dc22
                              2008050865

Typeset by Bruce Lundquist in 10/14 Minion

*For Adolfo, who taught me much of
what I know. And Samik, who might
want to know it too someday.*

Contents

Illustrations

Tables

Acronyms

AIDESEP (Asociación Interétnica de Desarrollo de la Selva Peruana)

CAAAP (Centro de Antropología y Aplicación Práctica de la Amazonía Peruana)

CAH (Consejo Aguaruna Huambisa)

CART (Central Ashaninka del Río Tambo)

CCP (Confederación Campesina del Perú)

CECONSEC (Central de Comunidades Nativas de la Selva Central)

CIPA (Centro de Investigaciones y Promoción Amazónica)

CISA (Consejo Indio Sudamérica)

CNA (Confederación Nacional Agraria)

COCONASEP (Comité de Coordinación de Comunidades Nativas de la Selva Peruana)

COICA (Coordinadora de Organizaciones Indígenas de la Cuenca Amazónica)

CONACAMI (Coordinadora Nacional de Comunidades Afectadas por la Minería)

CONAM (Consejo Nacional del Ambiente)

CONAP (Confederación de Nacionalidades Amazónicas del Perú)

CONOAP (Consejo de Comunidades Nativas Nomatsguenga y Asháninka de Pangoa)

COPPIP (Coordinadora Permanente de los Pueblos Indígenas del Peru)

FAD (Federación de Comunidades Aguarunas del Domingusa)

FECOHRSA (Federación de Comunidades Huambisas del Río)

FECONADIC (Federación de Comunidades Nativas del Distrito
 de Cahuapanas)

FECONARIN (Federación de Comunidades Nativas Aguarunas del Río Nieva)

FECONAU (Federación de Comunidades Nativas del Ucayali)

FECONAYA (Federación de Comunidades Nativas Yanesha)

FECONAYY (Federación de Comunidades Nativas Yine Yami)

FEDECOCA (Federación de Comunidades Nativas Cocama-Cocamilla)

FEMAAM (Federación de Mujeres Aguarunas del Alto Marañon)

FENAMAD (Federacion Nativa del Río Madre de Dios)

FENARA (Federación Nativa Awajun del Río Apaga)

FERIAM (Federación Regional Indígena del Alto Mayo)

FORMABIAP (Formación de Maestros Bilingues de la Amazonia Peruana)

Grupo DAM (Desarrollo del Alto Marañon)

ICBG (International Cooperative Biodiversity Group)

IMF (International Monetary Fund)

IWGIA (International Work Group on Indigenous Affairs)

JAARS (Jungle Aviation and Radio Service)

MRTA (Movimiento Revolucionario Tupac Amaru)

NIH (National Institutes of Health)

OAAM (Organización Aguaruna Alto Mayo)

OCCAAM (Organización Central de Comunidades Aguarunas del
 Alto Marañon)

ODECINAC (Organización de Desarrollo de las Comunidades Indígenas
 Numpatkaim y Alto Comaina)

ODECOFROC (Organización de Desarrollo de las Comunidades Fronterizas
 del Cenepa)

ONAPAA (Organización Nativa Aguaruna de la Provincia de Alto Amazonas)

ORASI (Organización Regional Aguaruna de San Ignacio)

ORIAM (Organización Regional Indígena del Alto Mayo)

PETT (Proyecto Especial de Titulación de Tierras)

SIL (Summer Institute of Linguistics)

SINAMOS (Sistema Nacional de Apoyo a la Movilización Social)

WBT (Wycliffe Bible Translators, Inc.)

Acknowledgments

I now realize there is a reason for writing the acknowledgments section last. The paranoia created by the idea of leaving someone off the list is overwhelming. So, if you should have appeared here and didn't, I beg for your forgiveness.

Mentors, colleagues, and co-conspirators from the University of Chicago are at the top of the list: Jean and John Comaroff, Manuela Carneiro da Cunha, John Kelly, and Terry Turner were all an inspiration at multiple points. There's also little chance I could have found my way in (or back out of) the University of Chicago without the help of John MacAloon and the MAPSS program; and no anthropologist could get anywhere without Anne Chien. Among the many memorable friends and colleagues at Chicago, the following all had a hand in shaping my thinking about life as an anthropologist, whether they realize it or not: Paul Liffman, Jessica Jerome, Kathleen Lowrey, Michael Cepek, Jeff Martin, Alex Dent, Alan Durston, and Joshua Kaplan.

Beyond Chicago a number of people have actively contributed to providing intellectual feedback on this project or just the occasional memorable words of wisdom about academic life in general: María Elena García, Jose Antonio Lucero, Michael Brown, Laura Graham, Jean Rahier, and Jean Jackson are certainly among them. So, too, are Quetzil Castañeda, Anya Royce, Rick Wilk, Eduardo Brondizio, and Jeff Gould, all at Indiana University.

A number of people in Peru were indispensable in making my work there possible and more enjoyable. I'd like to recognize the frequent help of Richard Chase Smith, Carlos Mora Bernasconi, Gisela Cánepa-Koch, Raul Romero, James (Jaime) Regan, and Marcos Cueto in particular. Life simply would not have been the same in Moyobamba without the constant laughter and discussion with Patricio Zanabria, Helene Collongues, Carlos Palomino, and the absolutely unyielding generosity of José Carmona, Bertha Tulumba, and their two kids (Eberth and Lisseth)—oh, and of course, the famous "Tío Pachuro" (Heribert Schlebbe).

There are so many people who helped me forge my path through Aguarunia worth mentioning here it boggles the mind. But I can never forget the support and guidance provided by the following individuals over the years: Adolfo Juep, César Sarasara, Jorge Sarasara, Abel Chumap, Ricardo Apanú, José Lirio, Evaristo Nugkuag, Gil Inoach, Albertina Nanchijam, Celestina Cahuaza, Noé Cahuaza, Elias Peas, Martín Reátegui, Eduardo Gomez, Román Tsamajain, Pijuch and Chimpa (who need no last name), Kjersti Juep, Vossler Juep, Victor Juep, Nestor Juep, Francisco Shajian, David Caicharo, and Jaime Pijuch. I've also had a number of memorable contacts with Aguaruna university students in Lima over the years, all eager to exchange ideas. I remember especially conversations with Diógenes Ampam, Anfiloquio Paz, Fermín Tiwi, Abel Uwarai, and Isaac Paz (special thanks to Abel and Isaac for first introducing me to the complexity of the Aguaruna language). It is with extraordinary sadness that I must thank the following persons for all they did for me perhaps long after I should have, indeed after they have departed from this world and found their path to the next: Majik, Henning Juep, Pablo Bazán, Jeremias Juep, Zacarias "Chuncho," and José Catip.

Finally, what can one say about my close family except that they put up with a lot from an anthropologist. Perhaps instead of thanks I should offer apologies to my mother for making her constantly worry about what her son the traveler might not be telling her about his travels. Thanks to my father for coming around to the slightly weird idea of me going into debt to pursue the path of an intellectual in the first place. And thanks to my stepfather for his constant intellectual curiosity and my sister for her remarkably unconditional support. And, finally, a deeply felt thank you to Mamais and Samik for, well, you know, all that mushy stuff that goes without saying.

Customizing Indigeneity

A Path In . . .

After an enchanting trip up-river, I had certainly found my savages. Alas! they
were only too savage. . . . There they were, all ready to teach me their customs
and beliefs, and I did not know their language. They were as close to me as a
reflection in a mirror; I could touch them, but I could not understand them. I had
been given, at one and the same time, my reward and my punishment.

Claude Levi-Strauss, *Tristes Tropiques*, 1955

Gringos only come here to steal our customs. We want to know with what
authorization you have arrived here.

Remark made to the author by a bilingual teacher
from the Aguaruna community Achu, 1999

While doing fieldwork in Peru's *selva alta* (high jungle), a transitional zone fixed between the lowland Amazonian forest and the highland Andes, I was repeatedly struck
by the importance of paths. Motorboats, rafts, and canoes are the main form of river
transport. And over the past half century or so the Aguaruna native communities
that I was working in have grown accustomed to the presence of a national highway
system that leads to Peru's urbanized coast. Despite these various veins of transport,
footpaths cut from dense jungle vegetation still represent a customary and quotidian
form of travel.

One occasion in particular proved to be an unforgettable lesson in the importance
of paths. After several months of work in the Aguaruna native community Bajo Naranjillo on the Upper Mayo River in the Department of San Martín, I decided to begin
work in another community, Cachiyacu, after gaining permission from the community
chief and the Organización Aguaruna Alto Mayo (OAAM), with which I had signed a
research agreement. The change in field site was deliberate since Bajo Naranjillo and
Cachiyacu represent a kind of microcosm of the extremes found in Aguarunia. Located
alongside the main provincial highway, Bajo Naranjillo is almost indistinguishable
from the rural, commercially oriented agricultural settlements populated by mostly
Spanish-speaking migrants from the Andes whom Aguaruna speakers refer to as *apach*,

a term they usually translate as *mestizo* (person of mixed blood or culture). By contrast, Cachiyacu was a two-day hike into the forest and populated by a mere fifty people. Most of them are monolingual Aguaruna speakers and depend on their more bilingual kinfolk in places like Bajo Naranjillo for transactions with the region's emerging markets and Andean migrants.

During a brief excursion to a provincial town the day before my departure, I bumped into an Aguaruna man from the native community Shampuyacu (just up the highway from Bajo Naranjillo) whom I had met several months earlier. When I mentioned my imminent departure for Cachiyacu, he reintroduced himself by formal title as the newly elected president of the Organización Regional Indígena del Alto Mayo (ORIAM), a rival Aguaruna organization in the area. Switching to a more confrontational tone, he clarified that no gringos should visit Cachiyacu without his organization's express approval. A little uneasy, I responded I would consult with OAAM leaders about my plans. I did so. But José Catip, then president of OAAM, and Adolfo Juep, a retired bilingual teacher and longtime OAAM organizer, counseled me to ignore the offhand remarks of ORIAM's president. So the following morning, just before dawn, I set out for Cachiyacu in the company of Evaristo Nankai (the community's vice-chief), his wife, nephew, and a frighteningly scrawny hunting dog.

In contrast to the smoothly asphalted highway from which we set out, the dirt road to the Mayo River was just one impassable mud pit after the next. We crossed the Mayo with a large raft and pulley system and then had to pass several mestizo settlements on paths where the mud came midway up the calf thanks to the seasonal rains and the constant traffic of livestock. After we forged a small creek, there was an abrupt turn onto another, different kind of path that we traveled for the rest of the day. This path went up and down semivertical inclines and required that every few steps we assure our footing on a root, a rock, or some other solid object in the otherwise loose, damp earth. We rested for the night at one of the little palm-leaf shelters that are always staggered along the paths in Aguarunia.

Day two of the journey proved equally exhausting. We had to cross at the crest of a waterfall by placing one foot in a rock channel about 1.5 meters across just before the rushing water crashed downward another 10 meters or so. Further along the trail we happened upon a troop of red uakari monkeys. Evaristo couldn't resist the easy prey. No longer forced to push on out of hunger, we stopped early at another palm-leaf shelter to enjoy the fresh game with a little bit of toasted manioc Evaristo's family had brought along. Finally, the following morning we arrived in Cachiyacu. Evaristo, having already suffered three days of gringo duty, deposited me in the house of Pijuch, the eldest member of the community.

My second day in Cachiyacu forced an entirely new level of intercultural negotiation into the anthropological endeavor. That afternoon I wandered down to the river and perched myself on a rock to watch the cascading water. My brief absorption into the Thoreauvian landscape was cut short by a much uglier reality—one brought on by my own naïveté and the intensity of politics in Aguarunia. Pijuch's wife, in a state of virtual panic, appeared out of nowhere beside me. She had broken away from masticating manioc, the essential step in the preparation of manioc beer. As a result she arrived with her mouth still full and began inadvertently spitting bits of manioc out at me as she tried to get her message across: "*Umajú, Achunmaya aents mininawai!! Irinkun maátjai, tuinawai!! Juu kaya nui uumkáta!! Juwi pujustá!! Juwi pujustá!!*" (Brother, the people from Achu are coming!! They say they are going to kill the gringo!! Hide here behind this rock!! Stay here!! Stay here!!)

That's all I understood, and then suddenly she was gone. I immediately recalled my uncomfortable conversation with the president of ORIAM four days earlier. And just as the panic was starting to set in, two young boys, ages six or seven, arrived at the river to fill me in further. The older one informed me, "Brother, the people from Achu arrived. They say we have to talk. There is a meeting in the schoolhouse." And then the little one added, "Brother: Speak strong! Speak strong!" Finally, Aurelio, the youngest household head of Cachiyacu, appeared in his finest slacks and shirt to assure me the threats of violence had subsided, but we did have to face the men from Achu in dialogue to resolve the dispute.

Upon our return to Pijuch's house, it was evident he was absolutely enraged, shouting all sorts of things I imagined to be Aguaruna obscenities. He jumped on his bed, pulled down a small plastic suitcase from a rafter, and removed five or six shotgun shells from it. After loading his 16-gauge, and still apparently cursing in Aguaruna, he disappeared.

Although utterly confused during the heat of the moment, I later learned Pijuch responded to the aggressive arrival of the men from Achu with his own war tactic. He scouted out a sniper's position nearby on the return path to Achu and awaited any identifiable sounds of conflict in order to exact immediate retaliatory action. Meanwhile, Evaristo and Aurelio ushered me into the small thatch-roofed schoolhouse where we awaited the men from Achu. They filed in one by one, and all the signs of a confrontation became apparent. Two wore head adornments made from monkey hides. Several others had painted their faces red and black with the seeds of *ipák* (achiote) and *suwa* (huito).

The discussion that ensued was long and anything but reconciliatory. The conversation centered on my presence, but it was mostly a conversation among the men from Achu in a language I have never fully learned. I was left to endure the massive loss in translation provided by a bilingual teacher accompanying the men from Achu. However, the spirit of their complaint seemed clear. They wanted to know who authorized an *irinku*, "gringo" in Aguaruna phonetics, to enter Cachiyacu, which in reality pertained to the state-titled native community of Achu. Implicit in their anti-gringo critique was another criticism aimed at their Cachiyacu kin. They had yet to make good on a projected resettlement within their own recently titled community bordering Achu's territory.

Most frustrating was my inability to provide a locally meaningful or, at least, circumstantially satisfactory justification for the anthropological enterprise in the precise moment it was most needed. The only strategy that came to mind was to stereotype myself as the liberally empathetic global citizen, which in disciplinary terms translated into a self-portrait as a politically engaged anthropologist. I tried to make clear that I was in full support of indigenous rights campaigns that protest the world's evil imperial forces. The reader will excuse my self-caricature here. But in all honesty, when it really mattered—which is to say when progressive anthropological empathy was faced with the life of cultural and historical difference on the ground—some version of that was all I could really muster. And in that moment, in that context, these ideas just weren't very convincing. So far as I could tell, the whole point was that I, the engaged anthropologist, was, for them, a part of evil imperial forces. This made my own denunciation of the empire rather questionable. The men from Achu expressed their disbelief in my engagement through constant invocations of a place and a power called *irinkunum*, meaning something like "where gringos are." I have come to learn it is laden with a profound sense of ambivalence, simultaneously communicating feelings of awe and admonition, envy and enmity. At a certain point in this two-hour-long dialogue the meeting came to an abrupt end. By that point I wasn't even sure if anyone had agreed on a plan for resolution of the dispute. And the Achu war party immediately left Cachiyacu despite the approach of nightfall.

After the meeting, Aurelio took me to his house, where I would sleep for the night. Shotgun slung over his shoulder, Evaristo came by just after dark and suggested we talk to Pijuch, who had returned from his sniper duties. Exiting the house, I noticed that Aurelio picked up his shotgun on the way out. As we walked single file down the path toward Pijuch's house, it dawned on me that they were not about to go hunting. I was the subject of an armed escort.

Almost the entire community was packed inside Pijuch's house to discuss the day's events. Pijuch sat near the fire on his *chimpui* (a carved stool reserved for elder men). Everyone listened intently to his long list of complaints about the people from Achu, delivered in his characteristically raised and agitated voice. As I sat down, several of the young boys of the community crowded around me. Leaning against me, they grabbed my hands, patted my back affectionately, and whispered over and over, *"Yatsujú, pujamek? Pujamek?"* (Brother, how are you? Are you ok?) The sudden sensation of emotional solidarity provided a momentary elation. But it was immediately deflated by the obvious realization that in my unwitting personification of the globally destructive reach of "where gringos are," I was a central figure in an Aguaruna house of war.

That night Evaristo and Aurelio discussed taking me back to Bajo Naranjillo via a forest detour route on older, rarely used paths to avoid surprise attacks. But Evaristo postponed the return three days in a row, first due to a swollen river after a night of heavy rain and then twice due to his counsel to wait for Adolfo Juep, my translator, who was due to arrive to assist in my research efforts. On the third day Adolfo finally did arrive and had anticipated what had happened. Rumors had circulated between the two Aguaruna organizations ORIAM and OAAM. Before leaving for Cachiyacu, Adolfo went to a nearby provincial town and sent a fax to the Lima offices of the Confederación de Nacionalidades Amazónicas del Perú (CONAP), the national-level Amazonian organization that facilitated my entrance into OAAM-affiliated communities. The fax alerted César Sarasara, Aguaruna president of CONAP, that my "physical integrity" was in danger and advised him to call CONAP's national-level rival in Lima, the Asociación Interétnica de Desarrollo de la Selva Peruana (AIDESEP). Remarkably, Sarasara did just that. He asked AIDESEP's president, yet another Aguaruna leader named Gil Inoach, to communicate with ORIAM at the local level and call off the heat.

Adolfo's arrival also allowed me a final retrospective reckoning of all that was going on. Apparently, ORIAM's leader communicated with Achu via two-way radio to alert them to my arrival and instructed them to take me hostage to ORIAM's headquarters. According to the Cachiyacu version, although mobilized long distance by ORIAM, the Achu men actually intended to drag me off to a completely different Aguaruna organization in the Department of Loreto with which they are also affiliated. Not even the simple dyadic rivalry between OAAM and ORIAM was enough to explain the complexity of Aguaruna loyalties in times of crisis. The men from Achu were rather surprised to find that their close relatives in Cachiyacu acted so strongly in my defense. Adolfo gathered from local commentary that several of the older women of Cachiyacu seized the opportunity to insult the aggressors' intelligence and argued that whatever knowledge of their way of life I might acquire, the way of life itself would continue as long as they were around to practice it.

We decided to stay in Cachiyacu after another member of Cachiyacu arrived and brought news that ORIAM had radioed again to call off the war mission. Despite encouragement to stay on, I never reexperienced the tranquil atmosphere present when I first arrived. Latent tensions persisted in the imagination. One day during a communal work effort, a light drizzle fell from scattered white clouds without blocking out the bright light of the tropical sun. Rain mixed with sunshine was a bad sign, Pijuch said, a sign of an enemy reorganizing. A few days later, Adolfo woke from a bad dream. The threat of a bite from an aggressively barking dog was not random dream imagery, he said, but a symbol of an enemy planning a next assault. He suggested we move our return trip to Bajo Naranjillo forward several days, and I agreed.

Emerging from this particularly intense journey in Aguarunia, I decided to take a short trip to Lima. While there, I met with César Sarasara, who encouraged me to find the meaning and moral of the story. I arrived at his Lima office late one afternoon; he pulled me aside into the small conference room to solicit the details of the confrontation. He nodded now and again during my story but expressed no particular alarm. Instead, his response was a simple, straightforward one: "Shane, you have to understand that this experience is also part of your research. That's all I can say."

Thus began my search to extract from this confrontation a lesson. I latched on to one when I reflected a bit more on a conversation Adolfo Juep had with Pijuch shortly after his arrival in Cachiyacu just three days after the intimidating arrival of the men from Achu. Pijuch knew Juep to be one of the first *profesores bilingues* (bilingual teachers) of the Alto Mayo Aguaruna communities, so he invited him to see the one-room schoolhouse. Seated on tree trunks the children use as desk chairs, under the palm-leaf roof, the two men engaged in a close, face-to-face, and intensely competitive dialogue.

Despite my limitations in the Aguaruna language, I do clearly recall the beginning of Adolfo's carefully crafted response to Pijuch's agitated discourse about Achu's aggression: "*Yatsuju, Awajunik yaunchuk tuu chicha ajakui jintá weta. Yambaik, tuinawai papi ausata.*" (Brother, before the Aguaruna said, "Follow the path." Now they say, "Talk to paper.") But such a literal translation does not do justice to the force of these words. A freer one might read: "Brother, customarily the Aguaruna said, 'Follow the example set by your elders and seek your vision for war and well-being.' Now they say, 'Get an education.'"

It is to this task of following paths while also talking to paper that I dedicate myself in this book.

Site I   Projects of Customization

Customizing Indigeneity

Arrival at Site I: On Ethnographic Arrivals

The opening section, "A Path In . . . ," is easily recognizable as an ethnographic arrival story. It deploys some fiercely criticized anthropological tropes that range from the dangerous intercultural encounter in the jungle to an implicit desire to establish anthropological authority over the natives. Yet the "writing culture" critique of the canonical ethnographic entrée is itself so canonical by now that it has reached the point of cliché.[1] Rather than focus solely on my purported proposal for old-style ethnography, this Path In also entails a dizzying array of institutional acronyms, phones, radios, and fax machines, all of which are being administered by natives in and outside the jungle. Whatever authority I invoke is surely less interesting under the lens of this well-known scholarly critique than that of the indigenous activists in the story who have their own postcolonial critique to offer.

My Path In is only one of many possible points of ethnographic entry. So, why did I choose this one? Where does this particular path lead? I chose this path because it directs our attention to a dialogic encounter between two notable men. They sit on schoolhouse tree stumps, eye-to-eye, face-to-face, engaged in an aggressive debate. And they deliberate the past, present, and future of Aguarunia and the politicized layers of indigeneity found there.

At first glance these two notable men appear to represent two opposite extremes. Pijuch, the visionary warrior, represents the past of indigenous custom. Juep, the bilingual indigenous organizer, symbolizes the inevitable approach of Euro-American modernity. If my Path In were interpreted in this way, it would also mark the entrenched conceptual divide between culture and history and, as a matter of course, the disciplinary boundaries between the fields of anthropology and history. There is some kind of before and after implied in Juep's statement. Perhaps he means to suggest that global modernity, symbolized by the act of "talking to paper," inevitably replaces indigenous custom, symbolized in the act of "going down the path." That would also imply that Juep, in the very act of talking to Pijuch, is in the act of displacing him: that Juep's past represents Pijuch's future.

There is an element of truth to this interpretation that can't be denied. The post–World War II investment in Third World development and all that came before it—colonial officials called it civilization; mid-twentieth-century social scientists renamed it modernization—has clearly had an impact throughout Aguarunia. But I interpret the before and after of Juep's statement as indexing something considerably more complex than simply his false consciousness of a customary modernization narrative—a master narrative that announces the historical arrival of a global capitalist modernity as the inevitable defeat of local customs. After all, if Juep gave in entirely to the old ideology of modernization, he would ultimately also have to give up on the idea of being Aguaruna. Indeed, he would have to trade in Aguarunia's multiple converging and diverging paths for the single, unilinear path ending in an imagined telos called modernity.

In fact, this dialogic invocation of paper and paths is intended to connote something substantially less unilinear than the single path proposed by modernization. Notice that Pijuch self-consciously acts as he acts within the bounds of a native community. This is the land-tenure institution, crafted for indigenous Amazonians by the Peruvian state in the 1970s, that frames the conflict I experienced in Cachiyacu. The fact that in 2001 Pijuch decided to relocate his house within the territory demarcated by the state as Cachiyacu to avoid further boundary tensions with Achu is evidence enough that he, too, talks to paper even though he doesn't know how to read. Notice, too, that Adolfo Juep does more than promote educational advancement and indigenous organization building. He also dreams like an Aguaruna warrior. In fact, on a separate occasion, in reference to his long career in indigenous organizing, Juep once told me matter-of-factly: "In my mind I am still a warrior, just of a different kind."

What is one to make of these distinct paths that simultaneously intersect and diverge from the single path leading toward the homogeneous time and space of global modernity? And what does trying to follow such paths—while trying to avoid making too many enemies or, at least, trying to make a few crucial allies en route—demand of an anthropologist writing in the new century? This is a problem I address by considering Aguaruna activists' ethnic politics in Peru as projects to customize indigeneity. Specifically, I seek to understand the experience of these notable men who have been absolutely central in building Peru's pan-Amazonian movement over the last half century. The book analyzes how these men struggle to represent—if only partially—the experiences found in Aguarunia. They do so working both within and well beyond Peru and in the face of considerable historical constraints. Over the long haul the book became my own personal vision quest of sorts. In that quest I follow diverse paths of thought to arrive at distinct sites of analysis. The objective of the journey is to attempt a reconciliation of anthropological representations with contemporary indigenous realities and representations of indigeneity with the contemporary realities of anthropological practice. Engaged in a journey along these paths and through these sites, I attempt to customize my particular mode of talking to paper by making it speak about the visionary importance of paths.

Seeking an Academic Vision

When I first began this text, I sought an academic vision that might help articulate this problem of paths and paper that Adolfo Juep once aptly described. It began in the library, the site on which every path that involves talking to paper eventually converges. I wondered what alternative paths exist to the straight and single path symbolized by modernization theory. What postmodern paths—a controversial periodization—have already been forged?

Given developments in social theory over the last couple of decades, I see there are already several alternative paths to follow. I could represent indigenous activists as creatively adapting to their very own "alternative modernity" (Gaonkar, 2001). Or I might interpret their actions in terms of an indigenization of their conjuncture with modernity through a complex mytho-praxis (Sahlins, 1993). Or, for that matter, I could read their indigenous politics as a process of "glocalization" through which they make global capitalism just a little more locally familiar (Robertson, 1995).

Each of these alternative paths is preferable to the unilinear path invoked by classical modernization and the social evolutionary theory on which it was predicated. Choosing among them seems to depend quite a bit on where one wants to place the final analytical emphasis. Will it be on the postcolonial problematic of trying—always trying if never quite succeeding—to recover the silenced voice of subaltern difference? On the drive toward dialectical resolution of the culture-versus-history, structure-versus-action, ideology-versus-practice dichotomies of social theory? Or on the political economics of global capitalism and localized resistance or, at a minimum, adaptation to it? Each path presents a plausible alternative theoretical vision for explaining indigenous activism in Aguarunia. Yet choosing one entails accepting some assumptions that I find problematic. Indigeneity in such accounts becomes an almost automatic synonym for difference, mythic culture, and locality. The relevant dialectical counterparts—the implied sameness, the factual history, and the emergent globality of modernity—seem to constantly hover in the background.

What can the alterity of subalterns be, other than generic difference, if the primary point of contrast is always modernity's ostensible drive toward generic sameness? The idea of alternative modernities doesn't make much sense unless alterity is conceptualized as that which must perpetually, and thus generically, differentiate itself from modernity's equally generic and perpetual singularity (cf. Knauft, 2003). Perhaps this explains why Dilip Gaonkar (2001: 1) can devote an entire discussion to the ways in which alternative modernities represent pluralization only after his opening confession: "To think in terms of 'alternative modernities' is to admit that modernity is inescapable and to desist from speculations about the end of modernity." The slippage between the plural and the singular is telling. To insist we look for modernity's alternatives everywhere is also to insist we not look for alternatives to modernity anywhere, as John Kelly (2003) warns us. The iron cage, newly partitioned to suit multicultural times and lingering postcolonial anxieties, still rattles a lot like the old one.

If, on the other hand, I were to choose to "explode the concept of history by the anthropological experience of culture," as Sahlins (1985: xvii) once forcefully suggested we do, I am left with a slightly different problem. Does mytho-praxis—Sahlins's dialectical synthesis of *langue* and *parole*; structure and action; American and French anthropology—resolve the culture-history opposition once and for all? And Levi-Strauss's division of the world into "cold" and "hot" societies along with it? Or does it not also resymbolize it in other forms? For all Sahlins's convincing rereadings of Captain Cook's arrival in Hawaii, I am still left with one impression. The Hawaiian Islands appear to be lying in wait, all ritually equipped and mythic structures set perfectly in place, right up until the moment when Captain Cook's ship sails into the harbor. That's when the mytho-praxeological action really seems to begin.

Finally, what can one say about a term like "glocalization"? Without theories that assert the economic reality of Europe's global capitalist expansion, and the accompanying assumption that capitalism is filtered through European-styled nation-states inherited from the Peace of Westphalia, neither globality nor locality makes much sense. The "global" in "globalization" is often used as a euphemism for "capital." "Local" is used as a euphemism for "everything else" that already has been or soon will be overrun by it. The hybridized term "glocalization" seems doomed to replicate the idea that the local is always a non-Europeanized nation, or a less Europeanized segment within a European-ized nation, which has "not yet" (to invoke Chakrabarty's [2000] phrase) been absorbed by capital but necessarily will be. How does one speak about capital-ism without setting it up as this eternal contrast between the globalized Euro-pean nation-state form and localized non-Europeanized nation-states' degree of conformity to it? How does one talk about capitalism without seeing global capital's past as local people's future?

My sense of doubt about these alternative paths to that of modernization is what leads me in search of an alternative to the alternatives, other paths lead-ing toward a slightly different vision. At first, it occurred to me to try the exact opposite starting point. I might start from the assumption that indigeneity, rather than representing an opposite, is in reality a synonym for sameness, for history, and for the global. Here, too, appear a series of possible paths, as in the following examples.

Subjected to European colonization, lamented through post–World War II modernization, indigeneity is now revitalized through multiculturalization. In Africa indigeneity appears to be simultaneously the essential obstacle and a possible solution to that continent's historical struggle with decolonization (Hodgson, 2002; Mamdani, 2001). In Australia aboriginal populations repre-sent the paradoxical presence of an unrecognizable past from the point of view of the multicultural state (Povinelli, 2002). By all accounts, Latin America is experiencing an indigenous awakening of regional and revolutionary propor-tions, redefining citizenship, neoliberal capitalism, and the region's utopian futures in the process (Albó, 1991; Brysk, 2000; Hale, 2002; Rappaport, 2005; Warren and Jackson, 2002; Yashar, 2005). Marisol de la Cadena and Orin Starn (2007) note how today's indigenous experiences, seen from a more explicitly cross-regional perspective—from those of Maori parliamentarians to Mapuche punk rockers—couldn't be any more cosmopolitan. One might add, as John and Jean Comaroff (in press) do, that indigeneity increasingly takes on incor-porated forms, morphing into ethnic firms that both internalize and contest today's neoliberal market values (cf. Greene, 2004b).

But perhaps we might reconsider indigeneity not just in terms of geopolitical space but also in terms of historical time. We might think of indigeneity not as continuous with the prehistorical past but as a full member, indeed a constituent element, of the historical present. Indigeneity is not that which comes before but that which derives from the stage of modernity: Walter Benjamin's empty homogeneous time that intellectual critics constantly fill up with an analysis of the rise of nation-states, science, narratives of progress, experiences of alienation and urbanization, and, of course, the all-pervasive logic of the commodity form.

There seems to be more than enough evidence for this. The United Nations has now officially declared indigeneity. The International Labor Organization now consults it. The World Bank operationalizes indigeneity into international development policies and procedures. One can't even begin to summarize the ways in which it is legally constituted and institutionally arranged through multicultural reforms, land-titling initiatives, language-recognition policies, and nongovernmental advocacy networks around the planet. Yet, counter to Niezen's (2003) focus on "indigenism" as a product of the United Nations era, we might start by recognizing that it has existed in a legally sanctioned, institutionalized form since European coloniality began.[2] The Spanish Crown sanctioned its existence via the creation of the Republica de Indios in the early stages of Iberian expansion to the Americas. By some accounts this was the first experiment with modern techniques of governmentality and certainly the process of colonial racialization that attends to them (Silverblatt, 2004). Importantly, as de la Cadena and Starn (2007: 7) note, the institutionalization of indigeneity occurred not only via the processes of colonial bureaucratization but also in critical dialogue with multiple indigenous and pro-indigenous intellectuals. In colonial Peru indigenous writers like Guaman Poma de Ayala and mestizo intellectuals like the Inca Garcilaso de la Vega were already writing protest letters to the king and comparing Peru's highland indigenous civilization to the best Europe had to offer at the turn of the seventeenth century.

Indigeneity also turns up in modernity's bad habits and eternal hopes, accompanying suburban sprawl and constantly haunting guilty white imaginations. It's in Native American casino chips, DNA databases, the tour packages to Amazonian eco-lodges, and World Music bins at the CD store. It's in the latest pathbreaking drug at the pharmacy and on the alternative medicine shelf at the health food store. Indigeneity also finds its way into all those houses equipped with cable TV and a subscription to the Discovery channel. And it was just recently repopularized into a new form to make the *New York Times* Notable Books list (Mann, 2005).

The point—or, rather, one alternative vision to a vision of alternative modernities—is that indigeneity doesn't merely "creatively adapt" (Gaonkar, 2001) to the space-time of the modern, global, capitalist world in order to fragment it into pieces of localized generic difference. Indigeneity is what keeps the modern, global, capitalist world going! It is a form of generically modern difference constructed on the model—and in the mirror—of generically modern sameness. It doesn't emerge as an alternative path to modernity but as a path that begins and ends with modernity. One might even go so far as to say (with apologies to Bruno Latour) that indigeneity has always been modern. Indeed, in many ways it is more modern than modern Europe (with a nod to Charles Mann and a footnote to Guaman Poma).

In short, indigeneity joins the ranks of those other equally vacant, essentially empty, and yet universally theorized terms like "nation," "citizen," "capital," "history," "commodity," and "science." One must at least be willing to admit that indigeneity's ostensible cultural locality, much like modernity's ostensible globality, is incredibly generalizable. It is so overgeneralized and so abstracted that it becomes essentially indefinable, indeed, sublime. I have no idea at what moment it became academic custom to add the suffix "-ity" to the term "indigenous"—and thus formally enunciate the abstracted state and virtual space-time of being indigenous. But a suffix like that one, a suffix connoting the fixity of an inherently shifty term, in many ways gives it all away (Kelly, 2003).

An excellent example of the ways in which indigeneity is thoroughly abstract and globally modern comes from a recent special issue of *American Anthropologist* on indigenous movements in Africa and Latin America. Indeed, using the language of indigeneity as a means to link these two vastly different and diverse continents would be the first sign of this. Further, in the introduction to the issue Dorothy Hodgson (2002) cites all the most current literature and then summarizes the contemporary politics of indigeneity under four, alliteratively revealing rubrics: representation, recognition, resources, and rights. What better summation of indigeneity's inherently modernizing impulse could there be? The correspondences seem impossible to avoid. For "representation" there is democracy; for "recognition," liberation narratives; for "resources," capitalism; and for "rights," citizenship.

The problem with envisioning indigeneity as synonymous with modernity is that here, too, one immediately encounters some real problems. The synonymic relationship between indigeneity and modernity always resonates with a certain amount of dissonance: the two terms' obviously synonymic qualities always reverberating off their otherwise antonymic nature. One risk therefore is that of reconstituting indigeneity in a primarily ironic, possibly caricatured, and potentially even theoretically irreconcilable form. Yet irony, caricature, and theoretical irreconcilability are things that modernity, especially in its post-postmodern form, knows well. In the case of indigeneity one runs the risk, for example, of beginning to speak in terms of the existence of a "hyper-real" indigenism (Ramos, 1998), of indigenous movements largely in terms of "strategic essentialism" (Warren and Jackson, 2002), or, what is worse still, of indigenous activists as recent invitees to a "global cocktail circuit," as Friedman (1999) once put it.

We have learned much from these accounts of indigenous activists' sometimes ironic engagements and strategic practices of self-representation with the nation-state, nongovernmental organizations (NGOs), development institutions, and all the other arenas in which contemporary indigenous politics are practiced. I do not mean to make light of them. But they also potentially leave one with the opposite problem as that encountered on the paths toward alternative, indigenized, or glocalized modernities. Taking these paths as another alternative to alternative modernities leads us to their logical end point: How do we account for indigeneity without retreating too far into the luxurious space of critical intellectual distance that we associate with the scholar who values knowledge production above all else? The danger is embarking on a path that leads us to an overly ironic sense of self-awareness, staking out essential scholarly claims on unessentializable indigenous identities. Here I invoke a word frequently heard in certain circles of current anthropology. How exactly does one engage with the complexity of indigeneity in its various ideological and practical forms, including its more ironic and essentializing expressions, while also pursuing a politics of scholarly "engagement" with actually existing indigenous activists? In short, I believe that Jean Jackson's (1989) important question from two decades ago—"Is there a way to talk about making culture without making enemies?"—still begs for other possible answers. I am back where I started, once again pondering what paths might lead toward a vision that will prove most effective.

Thus, I decided to follow a different series of paths leading to different sites of analytical vision. To avoid the traditional modernization narrative, I will not focus on alternative, indigenized, or glocalized modernities. To avoid the potentially dangerous detour into indulgent academic self-awareness, neither will I focus on indigeneity's ironic strategic essentialisms. I will instead focus on the projects, logics, and politics of customizing indigeneity. To understand what it might mean to speak of customizing indigeneity thus requires a deeper examination of the two terms at the center of such a vision. I leave an explanation of how I have customized my anthropological engagements for the Epilogue.

Envisioning Customization (and Getting Accustomed)

Throughout the text I intend the concept of customization to refer both to specific acts and to a structural process of constrained creativity. To avoid having the reader wonder where exactly this path might be leading, I provide a summary sketch of what this vision of customization entails.

Customization first has to do with the interdependent nature of social values and social actions, which are in turn dependent on the dialectic of structural repetition and practical transformation. In essence, it indexes the dynamic relation between those things we do without thinking and those things we do with purpose.[3] The dynamism I imagine hinges on a theory of habitualized social actions that I will call custom. Such actions correspond to socially produced values—the logics of custom—that in turn reinforce the apparent validity of the actions. The logics of custom are the ideological references that make the practices appear meaningful, so meaningful that they seem logical, and so logical that they become implicitly unquestionable. Although repetitive if left unconfronted, custom and its logics are routinely found in spaces of confrontation with the custom and corresponding customary logics of others. The result is a process of articulation with what at first appears to be a foreign object, be it a person, a practice, a place, a thing, or an entire social group.

The second order of significance is the phase of articulation. This is a stage of *getting accustomed* to something that at first appears to be foreign but becomes a bit more familiar over time. Articulation is thus also a process of domestication in which social actors are both forced into and desirous of establishing a proper relationship with a foreign object that has appeared or imposed itself on them. Beginning to customize that object then unfolds from first getting accustomed to it. Indeed, the aim of the struggle to redefine one's relation to what at first appears foreign is to reduce the tension found in the original confrontation: to make more familiar that which began as something foreign. Part of the project to customize involves social actors thinking more purposefully about what previously they had done without thinking. It involves them seeking to defend, even while being forced to redefine, that which they customarily do from that which they customarily don't.

This brings me to the third significant analytical dimension of customization. The degree of purposeful creativity achieved through acts of customization depends heavily on the structures of power that inevitably constrain it. All social actors are also political actors, and some political actors are considerably more powerful than others. Projects of customization not only creatively redefine forms of practice and value but also reveal which modes of practice and realms of value are dominant in these articulated spaces of confrontation between one custom and the next. Thus, cross-cutting the dialectic of doing without thinking and thinking about what you are doing is another that is equally central. Social actors are always free to act, but their actions are never entirely free. This is another way of saying that projects of customization are rooted in my Herderian-inflected vision of what Marx once called material history, and perhaps a Boasian-influenced vision of what Gramsci called hegemony. Any project of customization is thus constrained by the politics of customization in which it is enmeshed.

To begin the discussion of these three major points, I admit that a vision of customization immediately indexes the rather controversial root word "custom." One risks deploying custom with both its older disciplinary and dominating connotations. Kroeber and Kluckhohn (1952: 67) noted in the 1950s that the "specifically anthropological concept" of culture derives from anthropology's older concern with custom. Relatedly, the term "custom" in some contexts continues to index a hierarchical system of two-tiered citizenship and thus an evolutionary colonial mentality (Mamdani, 2001). I say relatedly because anthropology as a discipline is implicated in the forms of domination on which European colonial practices and social evolutionary thinking were predicated (Asad, 1973; Trouillot, 1991).

Despite these risks, and following several decades of the postcolonial critic, it might be time to recall that early anthropology's interest in custom was actually quite complex, for example, Edward Sapir's (1984) work from the early twentieth century. Sapir viewed custom as a particular group's "diffused or socialized habits." The link to Bourdieu (1977) is clear. And his renowned work on the habitus, those "practices regulated without express regulation" (17), is still routinely taught as contemporary social theory. Furthermore, Sapir states that "the impermanence of custom is a truism" (367). This impermanence results, he says, from any number of factors that include technological innovations (material history?), the "rise of new values" (ideology wars?), and "influences exerted by foreign peoples" (colonial domination?) (368).

The collective meaningfulness of such habituated practices, and thus the ability to form a collective consciousness around that meaningfulness, is precisely what makes custom both continuous and constantly open to change. Social groups do not merely enact customs through everyday practice. They also fight over custom in the ideological abstract both among themselves and in response to threats, real and perceived, that come from the outside, that is, from other, foreign social groups. The link to the currently fashionable discourse about the "cultural politics of identity" should also be clear. Custom is simultaneously practiced and politicized, routine and revolutionary, habitual and historical, continuous and creative action. What constitutes custom in the ideological abstract—the logics of custom—is determined by the ways in which social actors slip in and out of a collective consciousness about who they are as a group: generating new and re-creating old ideas about what their customs are, what they were, what they might be, and what they should be. Needless to say, the ideas and lived experience of groupness remain highly relative to context, and any one social actor is likely to claim allegiance to or reject alignment with multiple groups at any given time.

Custom's simultaneously continuous and creative capacity has a corollary principle in the fact that structures of power are neither entirely fixed nor completely flexible. Instead, relations of power consist of dominated peoples who alternately capitulate to power and contest it and dominating peoples who alternately enforce power and cede it. In this respect there is ample room to think in terms of contemporary meanings of the term "custom" without continually fretting over its past colonial connotations.

References to custom, customary law, and customary practices are widespread in the ideological discourse of those who self-represent as the colonized, and particularly in the arena of indigeneity. This is a crucial point not to overlook: Those once subject to colonial domination—and subjects of an earlier anthropology—have historically appropriated some of the very terms used to justify their subjection, including not only terms like "custom" but also the term "indigenous" itself. Yet, in so doing, they prove that capitulation to another's terms does not always mean capitulation to the circumstances under which such terms were initially used. And noncapitulation to the circumstances is often precisely what gives rise to the struggle to subversively appropriate the terms, thus giving them new meaning.

RECLAIMATION of terms once used to subjugate indigenous peoples.

Another crucial point is that by endlessly emphasizing the associations between a term like "custom" and formerly colonized populations, we risk overlooking the way such a term has been used self-referentially within the very
centers of colonial modernity. We risk missing the point that this term not only
has been historically used as a means to evolutionarily demote an imagined
colonial other but continues to be used as a means of talking about the intrica-
cies of nation-state capitalism. Thus, my use of the term "custom," as part of a
vision of customization, is a direct intervention into this multivalent discursive
space: a space where colonial languages that the colonized have reappropriated
confront idioms of the market that capitalists have long employed.

It is in this sense that the language of customization appears to be a perfect
place to start. It is an alternative to both modernization's pretensions to forge a
path leading to a single site of infinite sameness *and* to alternative modernization's pretensions to forge multiple paths toward a single horizon of inevitably
modernized, generic difference. My aim is to theorize things more openly. A customized modernity might be one, but only one, of the possible outcomes along
the various paths of customization. To engage in a project of customization is
not only to recall past practices of customization but also to leave open future
possibilities for further customization: if and when the need arises and if and
when structures of power are permitting. The more general theoretical point
is not that people everywhere *make themselves differently modern* despite (or, to
spite) modernity's purported attempt to make people the same but that people
everywhere *make themselves* despite whatever structures of power they face.

Stating the case as such is tantamount to rethinking a very basic dialectical
idea: "Men make their own history, but they do not make it just as they please"
(Marx, 1978 [1852]: 595). If one can pardon the gendered nature of Marx's language, and invert the logic a bit, something of general importance does arise.
Social actors not only "do not make it just as they please"; they also "make their
own history." From the vantage point of projects of customization one merely
has to go one step further. By making their own history, people are also engaged
in a struggle to make history their own.

At another level I envision the idea of customization as an active intervention into the culture-versus-history debates. The critiques of history as an academic discipline are by now well known. It has been variously debunked as
too empiricist, too unilinear, too acultural, and just too obviously European
(Chakrabarty, 2000; Trouillot, 1995; Poster, 1997; Novick, 1988). The critique
of history is so thorough that at some point a new noun apparently had to be

invented: "historicity." Derived from Heidegger, it is now meant to establish a line. The line is supposed to demarcate a particular notion of European time dominant within Enlightenment ideals and the multiple, essentially infinite, notions of temporality that constantly rupture European time (Chakrabarty, 2000; cf. Koselleck, 1985). The awkwardness of a term like "historicity" appears rather obvious to the average undergraduate. Yet an emerging generation of dedicated researchers interested in problematizing the past appears to have grown accustomed to it.

For its part, anthropology has grown noun shy and adjective friendly when it comes to the topic of culture, presumably the discipline's biggest claim to fame (see Knauft, 2003). The various internal critiques of culture are well known (Abu-Lughod, 1991; Gupta and Ferguson, 1992; Kuper, 1999). It's too reified. It's too spatially bounded. It's too ahistorical. Or, in essence, it's just too essentialized. As a result anthropologists grow increasingly weary of referencing "culture" as a noun but continue to use "cultural," the adjective, to modify what they hope to be less loaded nouns (Knauft, 2003). Thus, anthropologists routinely speak of cultural politics, cultural identity, cultural conflict, and, in their dialogues with the official representatives of the past across campus, cultural history.

This problem of how anthropologists don't speak about culture even when they do speak about things cultural appears odd in an era in which ordinary citizens, multinational corporations, and even institutions of governance all claim to possess cultures (Sahlins, 1993). The paradox is striking: Anthropologists confront "culture" the noun everywhere they go in the field and then feel compelled to shy away from it the minute they make it back to the office. Perhaps we are in need of a less paranoid way of talking.

Resorting to awkwardly modified nouns and hiding behind less loaded adjectives seem like piecemeal solutions at best. To establish the necessary interdisciplinary correspondence requires a feat of dubious rhetoric management. What is it that anthropologists interested in the past and historians interested in different experiences of temporality should claim to be doing? Are we to narrate cultural history or do an ethnography of culturicity? And would those be the same thing or something different?

"Customization," a processual noun, derived directly from the active verb "customize" and found in common usage strikes me as interesting terminology with which to start a different conversation. This is not simply a matter of semantics. Have you ever noticed how difficult it is to talk about culture in an active, historical voice? Scholars inside and outside anthropology have long employed the words "acculturation," "enculturation," and, thanks to Fernando Ortiz, "transculturation." But none of these satisfies the requirement. Even though such terms certainly refer to history, they do so by indexing processes that imbue social actors with passivity rather than a capacity for action. Actors are acculturated. They don't acculturate. If they do acculturate, they do so less as promoters of culture and more as representatives of imperial forces: as those who are actively engaged in stamping out the culture of others with the weapons of civilization. Anthropologists began to invoke the words "enculturate" and "transculturate" in part to adopt a less assimilationist tone. But the usage of these terms indexes similarly passive processes. One is more likely to hear that someone was enculturated or is transcultured, not that someone, somewhere is out there actively enculturating or transculturating. The implication is that historical action occurs via a transition from being outside of culture to being inside it or as a movement between one culture and the next. This leaves us in doubt as to how exactly to describe the practical historical actions associated with those movements as also cultural—as "culture in practice," to borrow a well-known phrase from Marshall Sahlins.

To think of things in terms of processes of customization—and to speak of social actors in terms of their actions to customize—is thus to do away with more awkward rhetorical maneuvering. In fact, it might even allow us via Herder (via Cicero) to reconnect with culture's own historical roots, to that uniquely grounded form of enlightenment and enlightened form of groundedness that Herder once imagined:

> But the imitator must have powers to receive what is communicated or communicable, and convert it into his own nature, as the food by means of which he lives. Accordingly, what and how much he receives, whence he derives it, and how he uses, applies it, and makes it his own, must depend on his own, the receptive powers. . . . Whether we name this second genesis of man *cultivation* from the culture of the ground, or *enlightening* from the action of light, is of little import: the chain of light and cultivation reaches to the end of the Earth. (Herder, 1803: Book 9, 409–410; emphasis in original)

Finally, a vision of customization is already well equipped to speak about capitalism. Importantly, it does so in a way that does not assume that capital always references the inevitable globalization of Westernized economies, housed by European-derived nation-states, for which the only adaptable alternative appears to be the glocalization of other, non-European localities. It seems curious that in seeking to emphasize the Japanese importation of Western business, apparently the first model of glocalization, and even linking it to contemporary practices of micro- or niche marketing, Robertson (1995: 28) completely overlooks its more obvious counterpart in the English-speaking capitalist world.

Anglo market actors are already quite accustomed to speaking about customization in reference to capitalist practices. When used in this sense, customization speaks to the way each sphere of a market—production, consumption, and exchange—is open to specialized modification. It invokes an inherent tendency of heterogenization that emerges from within the center of European capitalism, not from its eternally non- or less European satellites. Producers are always, at least in theory, and oftentimes in practice, potential customizers. They can and do choose to make otherwise homogeneous commodities into something more distinctly recognizable as custom-made products.

Historically speaking, capitalist production's tendency toward homogeneous massification has always been offset by a considerable degree of niche and locally responsive specialization. This is in no small part because capitalist consumers continually demand it. And this is a lesson we should have learned already. The current impulse of neoliberal consumptive habits is undoubtedly structured to reinforce capitalist consumption of some kind. But this does not make of consumption a completely mindless act. By defining specific patterns and defying certain modes of consumption, consumers also struggle to enact their own creative desires and voice their own political concerns even when faced with the overwhelming odds of "free" market expansion (García-Cancilini, 2001; Miller, 1998).

Customers can and do purchase commodities "custom made" especially for them. True: It is usually for them and every other consumer like them who holds, or rejects, similar consumer tastes. But if still not satisfied, consumers can take virtually any commodity, even of the most mundane and massified sort, and customize it for themselves when they return home to that other "hidden abode" about which Marx wrote little: the sphere of consumption. As Dick Hebdige (1981) already taught us a long time ago, such creative acts of capitalist consumption are a significant part of how consumer subcultures in fact become subversive actors of anticapitalist protest.

In this sense there is some other, less frequently remarked upon but equally added value that is created in the act of exchange between producer and consumer. Capitalist consumption—one particular mode of customization—is also an act of production, one also rooted in the artful practice of constrained creativity. Does this result in antisystemic action or just more shopping malls with different kinds of products? In reality, it's a bit of both, not a simple either/ or kind of answer. It's as if the Anglo corporations, retailers, and everyday middle-class consumers that come to symbolize the neoliberal assumptions surrounding contemporary capitalism already speak freely about capitalism's open secret. You don't have to go to Tokyo to locate the glocal so that you can then destabilize the global. The glocal has always already been on sale locally in New York and London.

To the important insight provided by the Anglo consumer we would have to add here that of the customs officer. This is the person—backed up by an entire sovereign apparatus—who defines nation-state boundaries as a matter of regulating the flow of commodities from one point on the planet to the next. The use of custom in this context—as a duty levied on goods transported across the boundaries of a given sovereign territory—has a genealogy that connects the modern capitalist age with one rooted in the Middle Ages, according to the *Oxford English Dictionary*. In current geopolitics it reveals what exactly is at stake in the economic regulation of today's global commodities. In acting as a customs officer the person is quite literally officiating custom. This person engages not only in the daily act of redrawing the boundaries between foreign and domestic goods but, more fundamentally, the collective meaningfulness of the "us" and "them" attached to such goods as they cross and, by crossing, reconstitute national borders.[4]

The emphasis the customs official places on the boundaries between the domestic and foreign, the us and the them, makes explicit that to speak in terms of customization is to engage not only in practices of collective cultivation but also in that which is prior to it: the collective act of domestication. This brings me to my final point. My invoking customization in this broad sense—of making something one's own through acts of domestication that lead to practices of cultivation—logically presumes the existence of something that is the object of these actions. By implication it is at least initially some foreign thing. In this sense, the move from domestication to cultivation is simply another way to talk about the transition from getting accustomed to some foreign thing to then customizing that thing in accord with one's own dominant practices and values. This is a simple acknowledgment of the fact that social collectives are everywhere intent on continually defining certain objects, and of course people, practices, and values, as foreign in order to define others as domestic. Strictly speaking, that's what makes these groups think and act as social collectives.

In sum, to speak of getting accustomed and customization is to acknowledge that in recognizing something as foreign, one has already begun to develop a new practical habit and with it potentially meaningful new values. In the act of recognition emerges a structured practice of establishing a relation with that foreign something. By defining an object as foreign, a social group finds itself in a position of being forced to and simultaneously desirous of establishing a proper relationship with that object. I mean proper in the Latin sense of *proprius*, in the sense of trying to establish a relationship of one's own. I mean it in the sense of making the foreign, under whatever conditions of power it appears, just a little more familiar. Indeed, the exact balance between the degree of force and the measure of desire matters a great deal. Getting accustomed to something, and then beginning to customize it, depends significantly on the specific structures of power that bring the foreign and domestic, them and us, this object and that, into relation with one another in the first place.

Envisioning Indigeneity in Peru

If this is how I envision customization and I seek to apply it to Aguaruna activist politics in Peru, another rather obvious question immediately arises. To what foreign object are actors in Aguarunia getting accustomed? And in what ways—by means of which paths—are Aguaruna activists working on projects of customization? If it weren't for the multiple reservations stated previously, I would be extremely tempted to declare Aguaruna activists' primary foreign object as the modern history of global capitalism. But how could I then take account of the fact that Aguaruna actors at multiple levels pronounce themselves as modern, know history better than I do, and appear more than willing to be global capitalists? How could I take account of the fact that they have already thoroughly customized modernity, history, and capitalism to the point they consider them their own?

In reality, I think there is one foreign object in particular to which Aguarunia has grown accustomed but which Aguaruna activists still work tirelessly to customize. That object is the abstracted condition that the modern history of global capitalism continually imposes on them: the condition of indigeneity. It is an equally homogenized, equally intangible space-time of *generic difference*—in theory always different from but in practice always moving in direct

parallel to modernity's history of global capital. Their struggle is thus to establish a proper relationship with it, a relation they can call their own.

In the course of this book I seek to explore their attempts to customize
indigeneity as part of three concentric layers of indigenous identification. The
first and broadest layer revolves around what it means for Aguarunia to be part
of Amazonia in Peru. This is essential, as Aguaruna activism has been central
to the emergence of the pan-Amazonian indigenous movement over the last
several decades. The second layer of indigeneity—a bit of a bridge between the
first and third—has to do with Aguaruna activists' appropriation of the term
"Jivaro." It is meant to describe their association with a larger ethnolinguistic
family spanning Peru's northern Amazonian border with Ecuador. The third
layer of indigeneity—framed in terms of what it means to customize oneself
specifically as Aguaruna—is the one I explore in the most detail throughout
the book. I do so because in my estimation this category of indigeneity most
closely approximates the actual lived experiences of Aguarunia as I came to
know them. And this is a crucial point: Although each of these layers of indigenous identification is an abstract and partial representation of a more complex
reality, none of them is as ideologically abstracted as indigeneity itself. Nor, in
the minds of the Aguaruna activists at the center of my account, are these layers
of identification equally prioritized. I conclude that identification as Aguaruna
entails a deeper sense of social belonging, emotional attachment, and political
commitment than the other layers of identification because of its closer reflection of lived experience.

To place this overview in context, we must remember that Peru is the site
of very old and very new, both pre-Columbian and post-Incaic, dimensions of
indigeneity. Before the Spanish arrived, highland Quechua speakers referred
to lowlanders as *anti,* a reference to Antisuyu, the Inca quadrant northeast of
Cuzco that included many groups whose descendants now identify as Amazonian. The term *anti* was even used specifically to reference the Aguaruna.
Earlier anthropologists used *Antipa* until about the mid-twentieth century to
refer to a certain segment of what I now call Aguarunia (see Greene, 2008).
Another Andean term, *chuncho,* is still widely employed as a form of depre-
cation aimed at the native inhabitants of Peru's eastern forests and tropical
Andean foothills. With the arrival of the Spanish, the term *chuncho* became
essentially interchangeable with the widely influential concept of the *indio
salvaje,* or wild Indian, a central trope throughout colonial South America
(see Taussig, 1987).

Quechua terms like *anti* and *chuncho* originally connoted the lowlanders' ostensible backwardness, lawlessness, and ferocity compared to the ostensibly civilized and rational order of the highland Inca (see Santos-Granero, 1992; Varese, 1973). This is crucial for understanding the contours of indigeneity in Peru because such ideas existed before the Spanish and Portuguese even began to imagine the place we now call Amazonia. As Slater (2002) reveals, the colonial legacy of Amazonia entails a series of complex ideological entanglements. Centuries of European thought about the region combine Judeo-Christian images of Eden, Greek figures of warlike women, paradigms of social-cum-biological evolution, and, more recently, the charged symbols of global environmental panic. Yet, seen from the vantage point of Peru, as in other Andean countries, the Inca had already laid their own foundation for how indigenous Amazonians were imagined before Europeans arrived. The Inca quest to consolidate a highland civilization entailed mapping an indigenous hierarchy of human difference onto differing geographic regions. That Andean hegemony continues to tower above Amazonia in Peru. Peru's Andean self-image—which entails a long-standing national ideology about the centrality of the Andes—is deeply intertwined with Europe's colonial imaginary. This dynamic persists even today in the country's politicized language and everyday practice and is something this book also seeks to reveal (see Greene, 2007).

The Spanish creation of the Viceroyalty of Peru in 1542 proved to be an early testing ground for a multilayered system of indigenous ranks and denial of indigenous rights by degree. Colonial realities complicate the abstract racialized contrast between *español* (Spaniard) and *indio* (Indian), invader and indigene, that otherwise defines the ideological conditions of global indigeneity today. The inequality between Indian and Spaniard was made more complex by indigenous forms of social inequality that Spaniards recognized and then institutionalized in Peru: hence the Crown's differentiation between noble Indians and common Indian subjects under the colonial regime. The indigenous nobles consisted essentially of royal Inca lineages and *kuraka* (noble Indian intermediaries). They enjoyed considerably better treatment, as well as a series of economic privileges and royally sanctioned rights guaranteed by the Crown (see Stern 1982; Rasnake 1988; Abercrombie 1998). The indigenous commoners, who were also the noble Indians' subjects, consisted primarily of the various Andean and coastal ethnic groups. The people indigenous to what we now consider the Amazonian region of Peru were certainly present in colonial missionary and military chronicles. Indeed, the frequent depictions of their wildness helped to justify the underlying logic of colonial occupation. But in Peru at least there were virtually no attempts to enact indigenous legislation for Amazonians or institutionalize their indigeneity until the twentieth century. And when the Peruvian state finally did so, it, unsurprisingly, used the past history of the common Andean Indian as its ideological and institutional model. It is a model that has repeatedly proven inadequate for interpreting Amazonian realities.

Despite this long-standing Andean-Amazonian dynamic there exists a widespread tendency to treat Andean history as isolated from that of Amazonians, particularly prominent among Peruvian and Peruvianist academics and ideologues (see Greene, 2006). This entails a certain lack of recognition about the hegemonic role that Andeans have played in Peru's indigenous legislation. And it is the result of a long-standing narrative that places the Inca past and by logical extension the Andean region at the center of the nation. Yet the actual peoples in question, those identified as Andean and Amazonian, have been exchanging things and ideas and moving across these artificial boundaries for centuries. These boundary crossings not only predate the seemingly total rupture scenario represented by the Spanish conquest but also continue to play a tremendous role in the development of Peru's contemporary politics.

Perhaps then it is necessary to acknowledge here the divergent profiles of indigeneity that exist just within the Peruvian nation. By multiple accounts the privileged and powerful image of the Inca—this enduring utopian idea of the noble Andean—has governed Peru's transition from the colonial period through its early independent nation-building project and into the present (see Flores Galindo, 1988; Degregori, 1998; Mendez, 1996; de la Cadena, 2000; Greene, 2007; Pagden, 1998). The long-standing fascination with the Incaic patrimony—by no means exclusive to but certainly very concentrated in Peru—constitutes the very fabric of a shared national history forged out of the colonial encounter. What makes this situation a bit exceptional is the long tradition of colonial Spaniards and American-born creoles who repeatedly expressed their own deep admiration for the Inca past. Everyone from Spanish *encomenderos* (those "entrusted" by the Crown to bring Spanish civilization to the natives) and creole nationalists to *indigenista*-era intellectuals sought to appropriate the Incaic patrimony as their own even when actively denigrating the everyday "common" Andean. This utopian aspiration is still part of Peru's mainstream political horizon, noticeable for example in the 2001 rise of President Alejandro Toledo, who famously was inaugurated as Peru's new Pachacútec (see Greene, 2006,

2007). According to the well-known Peruvian historian Alberto Flores Galindo (1988), it is this utopian figure of the returning Inca that explains Peru's peculiar national history. It rests not on an idea of *mestizaje*, the political language of racial and cultural mixture used by elites in many parts of Latin America as a means to whiten indigenous peoples; instead, in Peru what predominates among the elite is a seductive idea about the glory of an ancient indigenous aristocracy, a lost Inca sovereign who will one day return to rule.

Over the long term repeated elitist appropriations of the Inca image have had considerable impact on actual Andeans. In a country where the elite have effectively already appropriated the Inca "essence" and yet continue to degrade everyday "common" Andean Indians, outwardly self-identifying as indigenous doesn't necessarily look so attractive. Instead, they customize a multiplicity of other forms of being indigenous in the Peruvian present. In the 1960s following General Juan Velasco's military takeover, the state began to officially consider Andeans as "peasants." The state thus replaced their original designation as members of "indigenous communities" by the indigenista-influenced government of Leguia in the 1920s. As a result many community-based Andeans belong to nationwide networks of agrarian unions, packing their indigeneity inside a peasant cover (see Chapter 5).

Migration also plays a significant role in Peru's regionalized forms of identification. Since the 1960s Peru has also witnessed a mass movement of Andeans to Lima, which is now home to a third of the Peruvian population. In Lima these migrants are known as *cholos*. Their urbanization results in a broad identification with the Peruvian poor without ever fully shedding provincial mountain roots (see Nugent, 1992). In smaller but still significant numbers many impoverished Andean and a few coastal migrants now look for cultivable land in the more accessible parts of the upper Peruvian Amazon.

According to Marisol de la Cadena (2000), in places like urban Cuzco there is a dynamic of indigenous mestizaje. There, she says, urban Quechua have customized the ideology of mestizaje so that it encompasses rather than opposes indigeneity. In provincial Cuzco, Quechua villagers express indigenous demands in a seemingly self-effacing manner by rejecting the state's bilingual education programs that aim to promote the preservation of highland indigenous languages. As García (2005) demonstrates, this is the result of an ongoing critique of the Peruvian state and its NGO contractors that, despite the turn toward multiculturalism, continue to operate in familiarly racist and paternalistic ways from the point of view of Quechua villagers.

Finally, during the 1980s to mid-1990s many community-based Andeans consolidated themselves into *rondas campesinas* (self-defense patrols). Organizing these patrols became a crucial method to negotiate a way out of the massive violence between the Peruvian military and the Maoist Shining Path guerrillas that shaped Peru into a landscape of fear for over a decade (see Starn, 1999). Even though Peru's dirty war has been officially over since the mid-1990s, it extended from the southern Andes into many parts of the country, including certain parts of the upper Amazon and metropolitan Lima. Many reminders of the conflict still exist. The most symbolic is the Truth and Reconciliation Commission set up in 2000. It sought to painstakingly document and publicly account for the horror of nearly seventy thousand deaths, the majority of which were attributed to Shining Path activities.

Whereas many Andeanist scholars describe the relative difficulty in outwardly identifying as indigenous in the Andes, a different scenario has arisen in most parts of the Peruvian Amazon. Unlike what García (2005) describes for rural Andean communities, most Amazonian groups have grown accustomed to bilingual education as the normative mode of state education. Bilingual education is an accepted part of native community life. And it has also become a critical site of struggle for the creation of a pan-Amazonian consciousness as well as more specific acts of customization within Aguarunia (see Chapter 4). Unlike what de la Cadena describes for Cuzqueños who identify as indigenous mestizo hybrids, Aguaruna actors typically draw somewhat sharper ethnic lines (see Chapter 2).[5] In Aguarunia, and from within the pan-Amazonian politics Aguaruna activists direct, mestizo is a catch-all category used to refer to multiple groups not considered indigenous to Peru's tropical forested region, such as recently arrived migrants in search of land, including those of Andean peasant or coastal background. It also commonly includes long-established Spanish-speaking residents of the Amazonian region with historic connections to towns like Yurimaguas, Pucallpa, and Iquitos, or those more directly connected to Aguarunia like Rioja, Moyobamba, Santa Maria de Nieva, Jaén, and Bagua.

Finally, the political violence witnessed in 1980s and 1990s Peru was relatively rare in Aguarunia even while severe in the central Peruvian Amazon, particularly among the Ashaninka ethnic group. Aside from a few memorable incursions by the Movimiento Revolucionario Tupac Amaru (MRTA) in the Mayo River area in the early 1990s, mention of Peru's decades of political violence do not figure prominently in Aguaruna narratives of the recent past. The MRTA, made famous by its dramatic takeover of the Japanese ambassador's residence in 1997, was a rival of the Shining Path and operated on a much smaller scale. Aguaruna discourse about life during the time of *terrucos*, Peruvian Spanish for "terrorists" and usually in reference to the Shining Path, periodically emerges. But in my experience it appears as truly anecdotal compared to the kinds of systematic infiltration that others describe in the central Amazonian region or in many parts of the Andes (Starn, 1999). Most of Aguarunia was spared the violence and intimidation of those years.

Accounting for Aguarunia's incorporation into Amazonian indigeneity thus forces us to consider the Amazonian region as an interface, a site of a significant divide from but also multiple degrees of continuity with the Peruvian Andes. I tried to explain this to a colleague unfamiliar with Peru, and he responded with a geographic metaphor, "You mean it's not like the Andes just stop, and then there's a big drop off down into Amazonia."[6] Indeed, the geography is telling in many ways. What counts as Amazonia in Peru makes up more than 60 percent of the national territory—an ironic fact given the degree of national forget-fulness about the region. It starts at the *ceja de selva* (brow of the jungle) at altitudes as high as four thousand meters and slowly descends to the *selva baja* (low jungle), a reference to the flatness of the Amazonian basin that extends toward the Brazilian border. Most of the nearly two hundred titled Aguaruna native communities are located in an interstitial zone known as the selva alta, where the Andean chain breaks up into valleys and foothills rich with tropical flora and fauna.

The diversity of peoples, places, and projects of customization in Peruvian Amazonia is impossible to summarize here. But estimates state that the region as a whole holds as many as three million inhabitants, approximately half a million of which claim indigenous status (Dean, 2002). Indigenous peoples in the region speak more than fifty different languages and are scattered through-out the region amid vast expanses of forest, small cities, rural agricultural settlements, and roads that range from a well-paved highway system to forgot-ten feeder roads that connect to major waterways. Added to this is an ever-expanding migrant population involved in legal (rice, coffee, ranching, etc.), semilegal (land trafficking, logging, etc.), and illegal (coca production) forms of economic activity.

Over the past half century greater and greater degrees of integration have emerged as prominent features of Peruvian Amazonia. In addition to substan-tial market expansion these include spatial incorporation via new road systems; political integration via land titling and access to state services; and interethnic exchange via education systems, increasing bilingualism, and social intercourse between native and nonnative segments of the population. Dedicated to managing this process of national integration, Peru's pan-Amazonian movement has roots in bilingual education efforts of the 1950s and native community land titling of the 1970s. It also has built transnational alliances with indigenous Amazonians in a number of other South American countries. Aguaruna activists have been at the forefront of this process to constitute a distinctly Amazonian profile of a politicized indigeneity in Peru. It is one that is both juxtaposed to but also in deep dialogue with the country's largely Andean self-image.

This brings me to the second layer that I explore in Aguaruna projects to customize indigeneity. For many Aguaruna activists a crucial intermediary step between being indigenous to Amazonia and being indigenous to Aguarunia is also belonging to Jivaria. Since the early twentieth century ethnological accounts have subdivided the Jivaro primarily into four ethnolinguistic groups dispersed along the Peru/Ecuador border: Aguaruna (or Awajún), Huambisa (or Wampis), Shuar, and Achuar (or Achual) (see Map 1).[7] More recent classifications include the Candoshi and Shiwiar as part of the broader Jivaroan group.

As far as anyone can tell the term *Jivaro* (or *Jibaro*; and originally *Xivaro*) is a colonial Spanish ethnonym dating to roughly the mid-sixteenth century. Given the context in which it originated, the term carries with it a lot of colonial baggage. Being identifiable as Jivaro, feared for their ostensible propensity to warfare, made legendary for sporadic resistance to Incaic and Spanish imperialism, and still infamous for the practice of shrinking enemy heads, is a decidedly dubious honor. From the point of view of early Spanish chronicles all the way up to contemporary tourist representations, Jivaro represents one of the most exotic of others in South American colonial imaginations (see Taylor, 1994; Rubenstein, 2007). Needless to say, Europeans constructed this colonial image through a complex mixing of truths and falsities. The male-gendered reputation as tried-and-true warriors is both the one that the colonial past attached to them and the one that notable male Aguaruna activists in many ways continue to embrace. They do so in part out of purposeful habit and in part out of ideological constraints entailed by their projects to customize indigeneity.

Although part of the same ethnolinguistic family, Shuar activists from Ecuador reject the Hispanicized term *Jivaro* outright. They simply see no value in trying to overcome its colonial baggage (Rubenstein, 2001). Yet both the Peruvian state and many Aguaruna and Huambisa activists recognize it as a

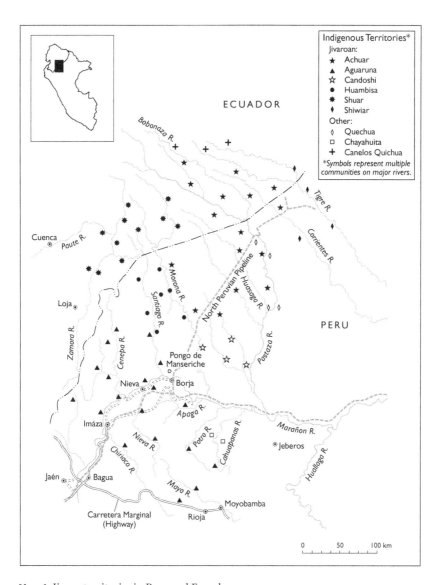

Map 1 Jivaro territories in Peru and Ecuador.

legitimate descriptor of the cultural and linguistic overlap between the Jivaroan groups. Peru's Ministry of Agriculture does so in administering native community land titles. And Aguaruna and Huambisa activists have appropriated the term to describe relations among the two groups as well as their occasional cross-border political projects with Shuar and Achuar in Ecuador. This has proven particularly common following the 1998 Peace Accord that finally put an end to the centuries-long border dispute between Peru and Ecuador (see Greene, 2008).[8]

The third and most experientially significant layer of indigeneity, that of being indigenous to Aguarunia, is the one I explore in the most ethnographic and historical depth throughout the book. In my interpretation Aguaruna activists speak about customizing indigeneity in their own terms as a problem of how to simultaneously "talk to paper" and "follow the path." I seek in the idea of customizing indigeneity an alternative vision to one that would see this problem as representing two different paths: one going forward toward modernity, the other going backward toward indigeneity. This alternative vision thus makes possible multiple paths that run in multiple directions, forward and backward, in and back out of different sites of analysis. At each of these sites of analysis I demonstrate how Aguaruna activists bring paper and paths, and all that these symbols condense, into a creative and critical dialogue about the importance of their projects to customize indigeneity. It is only then and there that the inherent foreignness of indigeneity becomes for them a bit more familiar.

On Aguaruna, Aguarunia, and the Problem of Partialities

I have tried to distinguish between the terms "Aguaruna" and "Aguarunia"—and with more or less the same logic, "Jivaro" and "Jivaria," "Amazonian" and "Amazonia." The distinction is meant to index the contradictions between acts and processes of identification as well as that between personal identification with a place and visiting a place with which identities other than one's own are associated.

I use "Aguaruna" in reference to persons or groups of persons who are identifiable as Aguaruna. By identifiable I refer to the dynamic of self-ascribed and socially imposed identification that explains virtually all forms of social identity, and particularly one as historically enmeshed in social hierarchies as being indigenous. In short, I recognize that being Aguaruna is both a matter of active choice and a product of a historical process of societal imposition. This does not mean that the indigenous actors I engage with here consider themselves exclusively Aguaruna, as the concentric layers of Jivaroan and Amazonian identification in which Aguaruna is enmeshed make clear. But I do argue that they identify most closely with the term "Aguaruna" because of its close attachment to a set of distinct lived experiences that sets them apart from other actors, including, importantly, other indigenous actors.

"Aguarunia" is used throughout to refer both to material and metaphorical spaces. It refers in part to the titled native communities, rural migrant settlements, and several provincial towns, scattered across four Peruvian departments (San Martín, Amazonas, Loreto, and Cajamarca) where the overwhelming majority of identifiable Aguaruna currently live. But the spatial dimensions of Aguarunia would also have to be stretched to include the small population living in urban Lima, mostly activists or university students and their families, and an even smaller handful of Aguaruna living internationally.

In other words I explicitly deploy the term "Aguarunia" in more than just a materially locatable sense. I also intend it to refer to any moment in which anyone—regardless of his or her identifiability as Aguaruna—engages seriously with the idea of being Aguaruna. Thus, Aguarunia refers as much to a mental space as it does to specific geographic places, as much to a particular frame of mind as it does to a precise territorial location. It is important to emphasize the use of the phrase "as much" in this last statement and clarify what it might imply for current attempts to theorize indigeneity globally. One example comes from James Clifford (1994, 2007), who has been developing the idea of "indigenous diasporas" for quite some time. The phrase is meant to call our attention to global processes of indigenous movement and contrast with assumptions about eternal indigenous rootedness in bounded territories. It is a provocative way of connecting indigeneity to discourses of the Africa diaspora and to what Paul Gilroy (1995) identifies as the problem of identity's roots versus routes. But Clifford also imagines his own limitations as part of a tendency to be "overly invested in the interactive, spliced, spatially dispersed aspects of tribal or native lives at the expense of continuities in place, kinship, language, and tradition" (2007: 215). This is an important caution we might heed. Rather than envision indigenous diasporas globally across vast expanses of time and space, as Clifford himself is wont to do, perhaps we might do so more contextually.

I do that here by acknowledging the inherent theoretical dilemma of indigenous identifiability—acts versus process; self versus societal ascription—in a term like "Aguaruna." But I acknowledge this without giving in to the slightly paranoid intellectual desire to see all identities as essentially unessentializable. Instead, I openly commit to describing the contextual essences of the material places and mental spaces of Aguarunia and sincerely hope to convince the reader such essences exist. This is a kind of emotional, social, and political commitment to Aguarunia that many an Aguaruna activist I have encountered shares.

The dilemma this contrast between the identity of Aguaruna and the material and mental space of Aguarunia is meant to resolve is twofold. Why is it exactly that one can be identifiably Aguaruna without necessarily always being inside Aguarunia? How is it that one can enter and leave Aguarunia without necessarily being identifiable as Aguaruna? Many of the Aguaruna activists and community members I engage with here find themselves in Aguarunia often but certainly not always. And although I, the gringo anthropologist, enter and leave Aguarunia frequently, I have yet to become identifiable as Aguaruna. This experience of being identified with a space without being in it and entering and leaving a space without being identified with it is in essence what the distinction between Aguaruna and Aguarunia hopes to convey.

It is also necessary to acknowledge from the outset the various forms of partiality internal to Aguarunia. These internal fractures are alternately concealed and revealed by those identified as Aguaruna in the text—and thus in my own representations of Aguarunia. The one form of partiality I underline throughout the book is the notable masculinity of the Aguaruna activists I describe—the way in which they simultaneously represent Aguarunia as a whole and leave it incomplete. But these forms of partial exclusion also include geographic divisions based on social allegiances to certain river regions as well as the impact of Aguaruna actors' incipient migratory patterns from forested community to provincial town to coastal metropolis. To this incipient geographic dispersal one must add emerging class and status divisions dictated by varying levels of inclusion in national and global markets and differential access to state services. In my time in Aguarunia I encountered every conceivable type of engagement to the external demands and internal desires that accompany an expanding monetary economy and Peru's particular forms of state governance. This ranged from grandmothers who depended on grandchildren to count their money, to Aguaruna landlords who earned considerably more income than did many people occupying Peru's highest professions. And it ranged from Aguaruna hunters who barter animal hides to get medicine from the nearest state clinic, to Aguaruna *sanmarquinos* (students in Peru's prestigious San Marcos National University in Lima).

The collective space and place of Aguarunia is also partial in an importantly paradoxical sense. It might disappoint indigenous movement advocates who seek solace in the ideals of a primordial indigenous communalism. But what these notable male activists practically embody via their paths to a visionary politics is an explicit form of collective emphasis on indigenous individualism. It is a coordinated form of individualism that in certain confrontational moments expresses itself in collective projects—these projects I call customizing indigeneity. But it is an emphatic individualism nonetheless. The entire point of following these paths through Aguarunia is to acquire a vision. And the point of acquiring a vision is to begin forging a path of one's own that others will someday follow. Indeed, as I understand it from my detours through Aguarunia, that is the inherent delight and dilemma, the essential promise and the problem, of customizing indigeneity.

Finally, I theorize this terminological distinction between being Aguaruna and being inside Aguarunia so that even though I am not Aguaruna myself, the book might be read as something more than just another exercise in scholarly self-representation. I also intend the text to represent a map of some of the physical paths and material sites found in Aguarunia; and something like a journey along the metaphorical paths and through the mental sites that I happened upon on these travels, during my time searching for my own path, through Aguarunia.

With that, we now follow the path that leads to Site II.

. . . A Path Between . . .

The following is a partial transcription of an MSN Messenger™ chat session between the author and Adolfo Juep, a longtime Aguaruna collaborator, from October 22, 2005 (original punctuation and grammar retained; translated from Spanish except where Aguaruna appears; bracketed remarks represent the author's clarification).

. . .

Start Time: 4:50:42 p.m.; End Time: 6:00:39 p.m.   *new path*

(5:07:27 P.M.) Adolfo: at last everyone is starting to participate in the jivaro's new path, they deny it, the unity, they deny the new way of thinking, but as you know when dealing with a science we can't escape from its technical and scientific basis, that's what in the end obliges them, i'm observing a lot of things which in the end take us all to the same destination

. . .

(5:10:44 P.M.) shane: yeah . . . well, it's also good to maintain the differences, different points of view, when the differences are workable and they lead to a common destiny instead of contradictory ones.

. . .

(5:11:59 P.M.) Adolfo: to me it seems that in the end the negatives become more important and it's not easy to follow the right path, which is uncertain

. . .

(5:12:18 P.M.) shane: yeah

. . .

(5:12:34 P.M.) Adolfo: or both things become important as if [dictated] by law, that's how the young people that come together to work toward these new paths are understanding it. well, i'll tell you that i lost my personal agenda, but i'll make another one

.   .   .

(5:13:59 P.M.) shane: what bad luck

.   .   .

(5:14:06 P.M.) Adolfo: have you read bikut's laws or not had time yet!

.   .   .

(5:15:13 P.M.) shane: well, the short version, the summary, i read it together with Mamais . . . very interesting, and relevant for something i plan to write in the future. one question with respect to that: Is Bikut a historical figure for the Aguaruna (in other words do they believe he existed like any other man) or do they see it as a legend about a man that never really existed?

.   .   .

(5:18:08 P.M.) Adolfo: generally, they see myths, legends, stories like a story part of a total package, something that really happened or that truly existed

.   .   .

(5:19:44 P.M.) shane: so, actually this is like saying Bikut is the most famous philosopher in Aguaruna history despite the fact that he didn't leave any writings, just words that circulate in the daily advice given by parents. . . .

.   .   .

(5:20:54 P.M.) Adolfo: yes, Etsa [the sun] and Bikut, they are the ones that implanted in him the jibaro's sense of discipline

.   .   .

(5:22:02 P.M.) shane: and if you had to compare Bikut with a figure from Western Culture, who would it be? or when the Aguaruna talk about it, who would they compare him with from european culture?

.   .   .

(5:23:48 P.M.) Adolfo: for example they say that socrates didn't write anything, but he left answers comparing things in relation to the dialectic, by contrast, what we jibaros call detse (a [visionary] phenomenon) they [Westerners] don't study instead they simply look at it as if it were an illusion or something that one sees while drugged.

in this case it's similar to western or eastern prophets, many reject them but they have fundamental principles about social discipline

. . .

(5:28:31 P.M.) shane: yeah. well, i asked because I'm interested in what kind of comparisons are possible in this respect . . . it's interesting that his [Bikut's] words still circulate because i've read two versions of the Bikut story, one published by Manolo [a Jesuit priest], the other by SIL [Summer Institute of Linguistics] . . . and so, it's not in the story where his [Bikut's] advice appears, instead it's just a story about what his life was like, so somehow his words circulate in the Aguaruna mind by another means, almost like "quotations" you know? words, or sentences, or counsel that are quoted separate from the story

history is also story

. . .

(5:31:22 P.M.) Adolfo: for us history is also story, we say augmatmau = augbatbau [lit., telling]

. . .

(5:32:14 P.M.) shane: what do you mean that history is also story?

. . .

(5:33:15 P.M.) Adolfo: for example, Hitler maaniamu [lit., war/killing], Hitler's war augmatbau [the telling of], history of Duik Muun [lit., Elders of Long Ago] or stories of Duik Muun. for example the fact that Tseatik [an Aguaruna man from long ago] ate his own body is story, but that my father made war recently, that too is story, but in western social scientific research things are more detailed: story, myth, history perhaps etc.

. . .

(5:36:45 P.M.) shane: in other words: they don't distinguish between "history" and "story": everything in history (meaning what happened yesterday, last year, or two thousand years ago) is known through stories?

. . .

(5:37:03 P.M.) Adolfo: exactly

Site II

Logics of Customization

2 Paths, Rivers, and Strong Men

Arrival at Site II: On Customization in Context

In the native community Bajo Naranjillo in the Mayo River region of San Martín Department lives a woman named Albertina Nanchijam whom I often consulted on matters of importance in Aguarunia. She once responded to my question about why she goes to the garden so early in the morning (about 5:30 A.M.) by referring me to an entire complex of daily labors. "That's just what we do. It is our custom," she said. She clarified a bit by adding that what she meant to say was that it is the "custom of Aguaruna women." She was alluding to the fact that women, not men, are the ones who habitually work household gardens and bring back manioc, plantains, and other subsistence items used in the daily menu.

I find this example particularly illustrative. Although her comments are explicitly about the gendered nature of what goes by the name "Aguaruna custom," the context of her comments reveals that there are multiple other ways in which Aguarunia is internally fragmented. Albertina's garden is about a twenty-minute walk well into the heart of the Bajo Naranjillo. To get there, she has to walk down a gravel road, past the communal office, and on a series of overgrown footpaths. Offset from the path are a few houses of her close relatives, surrounded by small patches of tropical hardwoods interspersed with concentrations of banana trees.

But my conversation about Albertina's garden practices took place not in her garden but in her cement block house, located right behind the municipal building of Awajún, the district capital, where she and several other Bajo

Naranjillo native community members actually live. It is a rapidly expanding migrant settlement of about a thousand residents with basic, if still poor, urban services: intermittent electricity, running water but no sewage works, a health post with a full-time doctor and nursing staff. Adjacent to Bajo Naranjillo's community border, Awajún is also right next to the asphalted rural highway that connects this settlement with provincial towns and, at much farther remove, Peru's coastal cities. The irony here is fairly obvious. The name of Albertina's Aguaruna community (meaning Lower Naranjillo), titled since 1976, is in Spanish and refers to its proximity to a river by the same name. Yet the migrant settlement where she lives carries the name Awajún. And Awajún is the indigenous pronunciation of the Hispanicized Quechua term *Aguaruna*. In fact, the community members of Bajo Naranjillo were primarily the ones who successfully petitioned the provincial government of Rioja to give the municipal district capital the name Awajún in the mid-1980s. But this was about a decade before the settlement of Awajún would become completely overrun with largely Spanish-speaking agricultural migrants from the northern Andean province of Cajamarca. Such are the cosmopolitan ironies of Aguarunia today.

Another example illustrates that Aguaruna actors' speaking about custom is inherently dependent on how they speak about the customs of these perceived ethnic others, particularly the migrants they routinely classify as mestizos. Most households in the native community Soritor, also in the Alto Mayo region, are heavily invested in coffee production for sale in San Martín's provincial markets. Although they typically self-identify as Aguaruna, I can't recall anyone ever referencing this activity as part of "Aguaruna custom." In fact, most of the Aguaruna agriculturalists I came to know routinely referred to cash-crop cultivation, like most other market activities, as "mestizo custom." Remarks like these usually denoted that it was an activity that did not properly correspond to them even though they were involved in it. Other activities that commonly fell into the category of mestizo custom included building a rectangular instead of an oval house, men wearing pants and shirts, women not making manioc beer because of religious beliefs, parents sending their children to school, anyone visiting the local health post. In reality, the list goes on and on.

Sometimes in the very same context in which someone would mention "mestizo custom"—a seemingly clear referent to something that exists outside Aguarunia—qualifying statements were offered. For example, one member of the native community Bajo Naranjillo remarked that almost all the Aguaruna living there have small rectangular houses, many with cement block founda-

[handwritten margin notes: "customization: large oval houses → sm rectangular houses w/ cement block foundations & tin roofs."]

[handwritten note: "~ accustomed → customization ~"]

tions and tin roofs. This, he said, was a clear sign of how Aguaruna routinely practice mestizo custom in Bajo Naranjillo, particularly if contrasted to the large oval houses found in a native community like Cachiyacu two days into the forest, a place he knew I had visited. But he then followed this up by saying, "Here the Aguaruna are getting accustomed to it."

For the anthropologist trying to make sense of all this, things got really tricky when particular objects or practices came under discussion. For example, every Aguaruna I've ever asked about it considers *ajeej* (the Aguaruna word for "ginger plant") to be a central part of Aguaruna custom, despite the fact that a few of the more linguistically inclined usually conceded my point that the term seems to be related to and likely derived from *jinjibre*, the Spanish term for ginger. On the other hand, an ethnobotanically oriented anthropologist views what is ostensibly the same object, representing it in the language of science as *Zingiber officinale*, as a plant of Asian origin (see Brown, 1978: 121). Referencing something called history, the anthropologist would no doubt clarify that Spanish speakers must have introduced the Asian species into the Aguaruna's pharmacopoeia at some previously undocumented point. So, what's the deal? Is ajeej Aguaruna custom, or is it not? Wouldn't it really be Spanish custom? Botanical custom? Or, more to the point, Asian custom?

I began to think that what Aguaruna speakers call "ajeej "changed from being something to get accustomed to and into something to be customized. And now it is something so thoroughly customized it reappears as simply Aguaruna custom. Something that once might have seemed dangerously foreign has gone past being semiforeign to become something deeply familiar. What was once "their custom" went through a phase of getting accustomed to. Getting accustomed to it was followed by a phase of customization in which social actors purposefully found a proper way to incorporate that foreignness into their social sense of self. As I elaborated in Site I, this is a process that undoubtedly entails encounters fraught with imposition and force but also circumstances ripe for creative forms of appropriation. And clearly it doesn't happen overnight.

This is what brings us to Site II, where we explore the logics of customization. My aim is to identify those meaningful practices rooted in current representations of Aguaruna custom. I am most interested in those specific representations of Aguaruna custom that have become both dominant and useful in Aguaruna activist projects to customize indigeneity. This is a temporary but necessary stopping point on the path toward Site III. There I describe how Aguaruna activists rework such meaningful practices into the politics of customization. In effect, they politicize Aguarunia itself as a site from which to customize indigeneity both within and beyond the boundaries of the Peruvian nation-state.

Divisions along the lines of gender, geography, ethnicity, class, and individual personalities will begin to emerge here. This is a reflection of the fact that they exist in the everyday dimensions of living in, identifying with or against, and traveling through Aguarunia. I do not claim to represent all those aspects that might fall under the broad rubric of Aguaruna custom nor assume that Aguaruna is a completely organic category of indigenous identification for the actors I describe. Less still do I claim to capture the entirety of being customarily Jivaro or Amazonian, the concentric layers of indigeneity to which the idea of being Aguaruna is attached.[1] However, I do believe Aguaruna to represent a category that is a bit more organic than others. It is somewhat less abstract than Jivaro or Amazonian and considerably more contextualized than the abstraction of indigeneity itself. I mean organic in the sense that despite being a partial and constructed representation, it is nonetheless one that resonates as a deeply meaningful way to talk about the lived experience of Aguarunia: both as a state of mind and series of tangible material sites.

Thus, although much of what follows is a detailed discussion of representations of Aguaruna custom used in a politics of indigenous customization, I pause at various points to make reference to those things thought to associate being Aguaruna with other customs found in the larger, slightly more abstracted ambits of Jivaria and Amazonia. I do this largely through the lens of anthropological literature that suggests points of partial overlap between being Aguaruna, being Jivaro, and being Amazonian. Arriving at Site III will make it clear that these various points of overlap contain deeply political dimensions.

Finally, in Peru, an Andean country as we're often told, being Amazonian (by virtue of being Jivaro and Aguaruna) also means being made and actively making oneself not Andean. It is a strange sort of thing to have to designate seemingly separate indigenous regions where the geographic continuity is so obvious to anyone who lives there. But Peruvian bureaucrats and politicians, like Peruvian ideologues and intellectuals, have created a virtual chasm between them for quite some time. In large part, historically Amazonian and Andean community activists followed suit by pursuing different paths of political mobilization. In my view this is due in no small part to the country's fascination with the Inca legacy. Historically, it has a way of exaggerating interregional differences and even making certain forms of indigeneity invisible. Thus, it overshadows the complicated points of connection through which the history of Peruvian Amazonia is intricately linked to the history of the Peruvian Andes and the Incaic history they symbolize (see Greene, 2006).

This complex dynamic between Amazonia and the Andes is one that also begins to surface here in the logics of customization. It is deeply revealing of the interwoven Spanish and Quechua histories that permeate Peru, even in those regions like Amazonia that are ostensibly set apart from that history. We might start by noting the hybrid Spanish-Quechua roots of the term Aguaruna. This ethnonym dates to as early as 1750 (Guallart, 1990: 108). Quechua speakers designated the people living on the Upper Marañon River and its tributaries in contemporary Peru the awajruna (people who weave). It was presumably a reference to the custom of male weaving common among all the Jivaro (Guallart, 1990: 13). Since then the term has passed through a series of transliterations to become Aguaruna in the minds and on the tongues of Quechua-influenced Spanish speakers and Awajún in the minds and on the tongues of the Awajún themselves.

But the mixture of lives and histories, sites and significances, doesn't stop there. The borrowing of Quechua place-names and terminology peppers much Aguaruna discourse, even though it is an entirely distinct language. This, too, will become more transparent as I navigate through Site II and move toward Site III, where the split between what is Andean and Amazonian transforms from a slightly fabricated geographic discontinuity into a real geopolitik of distinct indigeneities. →lacking physical form or shape. → invisible components

Family Matters: Kin without "Community"

According to anthropologists who have worked with other Jivaroan groups, and thus those most closely relatable to the realities of Aguarunia, there are some telling aspects of customary forms of social organization; probably the most telling is its amorphousness and concordant atomism. Descola (1994: 8) notes that the various Jivaroan groups exhibit little to none of the more durable structures of kinship that anthropologists customarily have searched for: no segmentary lineages, no moiety divisions, no clans, nor anything remotely resembling a "village" with the signs of an incipient "public sphere" (i.e., a central plaza, men's hut, etc.). Indeed, the anthropologists of yesteryear would all be terribly disappointed.

A consciousness of this customary social amorphousness became evident in my interview with the contemporary Aguaruna leader Evaristo Nugkuag. Asked to recall what life was like in Aguarunia when he was a child, he began,

"After I was born, I started to grow up, and I lived in a community. Actually, it wasn't really a community. It was a—like a group of families—with my uncle, my aunt, my family, kin that get together in a specific place to keep in communication with one another." Nugkuag's response is indicative of how loose the customary concept of corporate belonging is among the Aguaruna. He corrects himself when he calls it a community. It is only with the influence of Peru's missionary state logic that the Aguaruna came to articulate their residence and their localized notions of belonging in terms of an entity known as a *comunidad* (community). As I demonstrate in Chapter 4, this took root initially as a result of state-supported missionary schools that promoted nuclearization and a specific kind of "productive" indigenous citizen. Later, as Chapter 5 suggests, it became part of state land entitlements that confirmed the enclosure of the Aguaruna, like other Amazonians, in delimited units known as native communities.

Yet three important elements that explain customary corporate relations do in fact emerge in Nugkuag's statement: the family, the maintenance of communication, and the specificity of place. The first implies a kindred structure of genealogical lines. The second indexes a system of social relations based on the importance of collective alliances. The third refers to a recognition of the inherent connection between a group and its particular topographic location. These are indeed criteria that explain quite a bit about relations of kin and apparent amorphousness in Aguarunia.

The lack of any customary signs of "social complexity" (as anthropologists unfortunately call it) is in no small part attributable to the flexible way in which the Jivaro reckon genealogical connections. Aguaruna speakers translate *pataá* as *familia* (family), and it corresponds to no specific territorial limits, topography, or residential patterns. It is limited only by the capacity to decipher all the links that connect ego with another person. Being family is thus something that exists without regard to residence and without regard to other forms of group belonging, including prominently, ethnic differentiation. This means that pataá extends beyond the bounds of those who in an ethnic sense are identifiable (identified or self-identified) as Aguaruna. Pataá thus can and does include persons identified as *apach*, a frequent occurrence in certain areas of Aguarunia where intermarriage with migrants is on the rise. It even includes the occasional *irinku* who marries into an Aguaruna family, a considerably rarer but not unknown phenomenon. All that is needed are for lines of consanguinity or affinity to become known to an Aguaruna, and one is incorporated as part of a pataá in Aguarunia. The interesting detail, as I discuss later, is that becoming part of an Aguaruna family does not necessarily make one identifiable as Aguaruna. Indeed, other ethnic designations typically persist.

Despite a relatively shallow memory of lines of descent (usually only one or two generations deep), Aguaruna collaborators with whom I discussed kinship tended to stress the importance of being able to identify all the possible genealogical links one does know. The point of this obsessive attention to who is related to whom is to allow ego to recognize another as part of one's pataá and thus in theory put everyone at ease. I say in theory because in reality the amount of perceived familial distance between ego and alter inevitably determines whether or not anyone will be at ease. In Aguarunia, to be considered *takanchbau* ("distant" family, or a stranger), is essentially bad. As Brown (1984) and Taylor (1998) note, apparently all Jivaroans express this as the need to distinguish between true or close family and distant family. Distance, or worse still, complete disconnectedness (i.e., nonrelatedness), implies a potential, if not probable, hostility toward one's "close" family. The seemingly metaphorical association between genealogy and geography is quite literal in some respects. *Dekas pataá* (lit., true or close family) designates a member of the family who usually lives close by. By contrast, *iká pataá* utilizes the same word that connotes geographic distance and typically designates those who live at a greater physical remove from one's "close" family.

But geographic distance does not in the end define genealogical connectedness. As Taylor (1998: 189) and Brown (1984: 71) remark, the idea of familial closeness and distance is not fixed but highly variable and can at times fluctuate according to context. These markers of (dis)connectedness may be even more flexible than what these authors describe. At issue is not a simple categorical distinction but a series of movable and removable modifiers influenced by the speaker's perception of the best way to respond according to the circumstances. However, there are multiple ways to manipulate distance that neither author mentions. Aside from using the qualifiers *dekas* and *iká*, Aguaruna speakers also commonly modify the word *pataá* with *atushat* (lit., very far away) or *shiig* (lit., good/real/legitimate). Or sometimes they string several modifiers together to place extra emphasis. For example, I have heard on occasion someone referred to as *shiig iká pataayai* (very distant family) or *shiig, shiig pataayai* (really, really close family).

There are also more ambiguous forms. Probably the most ambiguous that exists in Aguarunia is someone declaring someone else as simply *mina patayai* (my family). In some contexts it appears to be an intentional way of leaving the question of distance/closeness ambiguous so as to leave the issue of one's "true" alliances and intentions in this or that matter a little unclear. Also, those kin that, genealogically speaking, should seemingly always be "close family" can be denied such status if the circumstances warrant. Closeness can simply be negated without the need to recategorize someone as distant family: *shiig pataagchauwai* (not close family).

I witnessed cases precisely like this where closeness was negated as a result of tense familial circumstances. For example, one Aguaruna community activist with whom I routinely discussed kinship played the role of categorically inclined social scientist. When asked about the notion of close family and who was included in it, he claimed that all half siblings from polygynous marriages were always considered close, the same as any full sibling. A few months later I met an Aguaruna man from the Marañon River area who insisted that his half brother was shiig pataagchauwai. When I asked why, he said his half brother failed to come to his aid when he became the subject of witchcraft accusations in his community. The implication seemed clear enough. Failure to act in alliance when it is expected can sometimes result in a denial of genealogical connection, probably not of familial ties altogether, but at least of familial closeness.

In a general sense genealogical distance does indeed map onto territorial space, just as generally speaking closeness is an implicit sign of trust in Aguarunia. But circumstances continually arise to contradict this pattern. Even "close" family can betray one's trust and be cast out of the inner familial circle. Even complete foreigners and ethnic others can become potential allies via their incorporation into an Aguaruna family.

Classifications of Person and Group

There are two key words, *aents* and *shiwag*, customarily used to reference social groups and persons in Aguarunia. Common translations I have heard of *aents* and *shiwag* include both "people" and "person." After hearing Aguaruna collaborators talk about it, my opinion is that *aents* means something like "human" or "human form"; *shiwag* connotes a range of terms, "person/people/enemy/group."

In Aguarunia, humans, certain animals, plants, and even meteorological phenomena are all considered aents, given the right circumstances. Such objects and events are also attributed a *wakan*, the word usually translated as "soul." Descola (1994: 93) incorporates these semantic conflations between persons, other natural, and supernatural entities into an argument about the absence of a rigid conceptual divide among the Jivaroan Achuar between nonhuman entities and humans. Descola, like Brown speaking about the Aguaruna (1984: 207), suggests that these other entities are personlike because they manifest in anthropomorphic form and possess many of the subjective qualities attributed to humans (they have their own social relations, speak, etc.). It should be noted, however, that these other beings typically only appear in human form and exhibit the capacity to communicate with humans within specific realms of practice. Primarily this takes place in the context of dreams, visions, and symbolic representations that are part of everyday life but do not encompass it entirely. As Descola himself notes, the Jivaroan Achuar make a specific distinction between nonhumans and humans. Similarly, in Aguarunia one can index a notion of humanity by using the phrase *shiig aents* (real/legitimate humans) specifically for human persons but usually not for nonhuman persons. In its more philosophical sense the word *aents* means something like "a being that takes on a human form or human capacities."

Aguaruna speakers typically translate *shiwag* as "people" and sometimes "enemy," according to context. One possible explanation for the Aguaruna word *shiwag* is found in Taylor's (1994: 9) account of the linguistic equivalent in other Jivaroan dialects, in particular the term *shiwiar* in the Shuar language. She argues that the best translation for *shiwiar* is "person of a different group" since the term is typically used to refer to a third party considered a part of a social grouping other than one's own. In Aguarunia *shiwag* is used to subjectively reference relations between one social group and the next. Its utterance indexes something like "that person" or "those people" from "over there." Customarily, there is a good degree of probability that the geographic distance implied in "over there" also implies a certain degree of genealogical distance. Thus, *shiwag* goes beyond simply indexing an opposition of self and other and includes the more specific implication of self versus enemy. Relational concepts of "self" and "enemy" are essential to how classifications of social groups including one's own are determined. If we take Viveiros de Castro's (1992) work as a guide, this possibly represents a kind of interchangeability of one's perspective with the enemy's that is common throughout Amazonia. It is thus from a certain perspective not only grounds for including Aguarunia in Jivaria but also in Amazonia writ large.

The definitions of enemy and self are constantly subject to changing circumstances and of such diverse scales that they range from just downriver to the other side of the planet. The appearance of a more distant actor, perhaps even from a completely different trajectory of customization, might be perceived as a common enemy. The appearance of such a distant enemy also sometimes necessitates a momentary large-scale alliance among groups that under other circumstances consider themselves enemies. But the alliance usually lasts only until the groups in question perceive that the battle or period of conflict is over. I can cite two examples at different scales. Within the realm of Peru's Amazonian politics, Aguaruna activists consider the Huambisa of the Santiago River their closest allies in large part because both are part of the Jivaro bloc. Yet some of these same activists occasionally boast that past Aguaruna warriors sought on more than one occasion to exterminate the Huambisa because they were customarily a common enemy. Agents of colonial capitalism are also caught up in this process. Indeed, as I go on to detail at Site III, those whom Aguaruna call "apach" and "irinku" have emerged as today's public enemy number one. One historic example is the 1904 rebellion of Aguaruna and Huambisa taking up arms together at a regionwide level to expel the rubber merchants flooding into their territory (Guallart, 1990: 189; *El Comercio*, 1991: 159). I revisit this case and much more recent ones at Site III.

This raises the question of what social classifications of non-Aguaruna actors exist in Aguarunia and what meanings are attributed to them. Both apach and irinku are acknowledged as aents or shiwag in Aguarunia. So they are certainly considered human. But their social status as friend or foe, ally or enemy, is constantly in question. As previously discussed, both mestizos and gringos can be considered family if and when they have the links necessary for genealogical inclusion. This does not so easily make them Aguaruna. It makes them mestizos and gringos who happen to be related to Aguaruna.

The reasoning has to do with how ideas about custom and its relation to groupness are constituted in Aguarunia. In fact, the way ethnicity is construed in Aguarunia is not easily encapsulated by some of the more influential models of indigeneity currently in circulation in Peru. For example, Marisol de la Cadena's (2000) brilliant illustration of the fluidity between indigeneity and mestizaje in Cuzco simply does not account for what exists in Aguarunia. In a political sense Aguaruna politicians, part of a broader circle of Amazonian activists, draw much sharper ethnic lines between being *indígena* (indigenous) and being mestizo. In a sociological sense Aguaruna actors at all levels frequently draw ethnic lines between being Aguaruna and non-Aguaruna even though multiple points of overlap, mixed marriages, and complex genealogies exist. There does exist a way of acknowledging the mixedness and messiness of social relations, but it operates without letting go of the implicit ideal of ethnic, and at times quasi-racial, purity.

The complex term *apach*, although routinely translated as "mestizo," has considerably different and contradictory connotations in Aguarunia. When translated as "mestizo," the word in Aguaruna refers to a very diverse sector of Peruvian nationals, ranging from Andean and coastal migrants to the Amazonian provinces to long-term residents of Amazonian towns and metropolitan Limeños. Although it might not be viewed as such from other parts of the country, from within Aguarunia, Peru is indeed seen as a predominantly mestizo nation, a nation that oppresses indigenous inhabitants with the threat of mestizaje. There are notable exceptions to who is labeled a mestizo. Aguaruna speakers typically call other indigenous Amazonians by their commonly known ethnonym (i.e., Ashaninka, Amuesha, Huambisa, Achuar, etc.) or its Aguaruna equivalent (Wampis = Huambisa). And the entire political discourse of the Amazonian movement in which the Aguaruna are centrally involved is dependent on the idea of a pan-Amazonian indigeneity as against a largely mestizo-controlled nation-state. Indigenous Amazonian politics depends in great part on not being seen as mestizo in the minds of Amazonian leaders.

People "indigenous" to Peru's Andean regions—who according to various experts are more likely to identify as campesino, as indigenous-mestizo, or by provincial origin—occupy a slightly more ambiguous status when they arrive in Aguarunia. I have consistently heard very different kinds of Andean migrants referred to as apach when Aguaruna were speaking in their own language and as mestizo when speaking in Spanish. Other terms are also occasionally used, such as the Spanish *campesino* or the Aguaruna *mujaya*, meaning something like "mountain person." This latter term is usually equated to the Spanish term *serrano*. So the Andean's ostensible mestizaje is qualified to a certain extent by association with a generic "mountain" landscape or with the well-known indigenous-peasant land institution of the Andes: the Comunidad Indígena from 1921 to 1968; the Comunidad Campesina from 1968 to present (see Chapter 5).

The majority of Andean migrants in Aguarunia hail from Cajamarca (specifically the provinces of Chota, Celendín, and the city of Cajamarca), and most are primarily Spanish speakers. There are also smaller influxes of Quechua-speaking migrants from the central Andean departments, including some from as far south as Ayacucho. Differences in dress, behavior, and language can easily determine who gets called what in what context. Yet there is a persistent perception that no matter how "indigenous" they might be somewhere else in Peru, they are not indigenous to Aguarunia or even broader Amazonia. This in essence is what the term *apach* is meant to convey in a sociological sense: not Aguaruna.

The last few decades of Andeans migrating into the upper Amazon is explicitly perceived as connected to the broader centuries-long dynamic of colonization of the Americas. Hence, Aguaruna activists in particular also routinely refer to Andeans, like all other migrants to the area, as *colonos* (colonists). This, in addition to an occasional reference to the Aguaruna having "resisted the Inca" before the Spanish arrived, results in Andeans being categorized as part of Peru's mestizo "elite." The politicized discourse often persists even in the face of poor, politically oppressed migrants whose lives are sometimes considerably worse off than those of many Aguaruna themselves (see Chapter 5).

The etymology of the word *apach* is also important. Seen through an anthropological lens, it means something like "classificatory grandfather," as it applies to all male elders. But it has much broader connotations that go beyond ethnic politics and internal kinship terminologies. The term is charged with the sacred, invoked when a speaker expresses a sense of reverence or awe. It can refer to dead ancestors, the earth itself, any sort of strange or never-before-seen phenomenon, and most important, the mysterious entity that grants visions to Aguaruna warriors (see Chapter 3). The handful of Aguaruna I have consulted about this term explain its use as a descriptor of mestizos and migrants as an artifact of the awe and reverence colonization was meant to inspire. It simultaneously connotes the awe they felt at the novelty of foreigners arriving in their area and the deferential attitude, indeed fatherly respect, that many such foreigners expected from them. The fact that in the Catholic tradition the priest is also the *padre* (father) no doubt served to reinforce this paternalistic first impression. But much like the postcolonial mind-set Frantz Fanon describes among the colonized, Aguaruna speakers both internalized that paternalism and seek to forcefully reject it. For this reason, when Aguaruna now use the word *apach*, it reverberates with perfectly contradictory connotations: adoration and admonition, consideration and contempt, love and hate.

In this sense an apach might indeed be a loathsome if also loved fatherly figure, perhaps even legitimately part of an Aguaruna family in cases of intermarriage. Being so does not readily make the person identifiable as Aguaruna. Certain apach figures might over time become *qwajunmagau* (Aguaruna-like; lit., transformed into Aguaruna). Likewise, Aguaruna speakers also talk about other Aguaruna as sometimes mestizo-like or _apachmagau_ (transformed into apach). But the local understanding is important because the transformation indexed in such phrases is rarely considered complete. Someone who is labeled awajunmagua in one context is simply termed an apach in another, and vice versa. So I prefer to translate this transformational aspect as a problem of likeness. It implies a context in which one actor, whose "real" ethnicity is implicitly known, is thought to be acting like another actor, whose "real" ethnicity is also implicitly known: a temporary and largely circumstantial transformation, not a permanent one. From within Aguarunia an apach being occasionally referred to as Aguaruna-like is something of a compliment, even if it doesn't really constitute full ethnic inclusion. By contrast, being mestizo-like is most often an insult and indexes a kind of ethnic inclusion in which someone known to be Aguaruna is told he or she is not acting as an Aguaruna should.

More is at stake than merely the occasional apach who marries into an Aguaruna kindred. This is a relatively frequent event in those Aguaruna communities in close contact with migrant settlements and among those living in provincial towns or urban Lima. It is not that frequent in communities farther afield. Clearly, marrying into an Aguaruna family creates circumstances in which an apach's becoming Aguaruna-like, and vice versa, are more likely to occur as the result of the intimate proximity of two differently perceived ethnic actors. The offspring of apach-Aguaruna marriages also force acknowledgment of the problem of ethnic mixedness. But here too there is an implicit drive to point toward an original ethnic separation. Such offspring are typically called _apachjai pachimdaejau_, literally, "mixed with mestizo" or "mixed with non-Aguaruna." The recognition of their mixedness depends on a constant sorting out of the mestizo, or non-Aguaruna, from the Aguaruna: the apach from the awajún. Implicit in being "mixed with mestizo," much like in being either mestizo-like or Aguaruna-like, is the belief in an original state of Aguaruna purity.

In my experience such social categorizations appear to have as much or more to do with custom and its logics, with how people act and think, than with biological bonds. Although mixedness does sometimes resort to a racialized language of blood and reproduction, ethnic designators of social behavior often predominate. Several years ago an Aguaruna community leader gave me some telling examples. He cited his own daughter as apachmagau, not because she happens to be married to a man from Cajamarca but because she speaks exclusively in Spanish to her own children. He then identified an unmarried man whom many Aguaruna simply refer to as apach but who has lived in the native community Bajo Naranjillo for many years: he has become awajunmagau because of his hunting know-how and functional fluency in the Aguaruna language.

In short, this is a theory of social relations rooted only in part in notions of kinship and racial purity. It is also a theory rooted in a notion of custom, its logics, and to whom these things properly belong. If someone identifiable as apach acts as an Aguaruna is thought to act, then the person becomes Aguaruna-like, but not really Aguaruna. If someone identifiable as Aguaruna thinks or speaks as a mestizo thinks and speaks, then the person becomes mestizo-like, but not really mestizo. Again the logic is one that acknowledges overlap, both biological and social points of connection, as well as the constant interchange of cultural experience. But it does so against an ideological backdrop of customary and biological purity.

This raises an obvious question. Am I, the irinku anthropologist from the global North, also apach? The answer is yes and no. Like the relatable but not fully conflatable nature of Aguaruna, Jivaro, and Amazonian, the relation of apach and irinku is also a concentric one. Irinku is a distinct subset within the more encompassing apach identity. This explains why I repeatedly heard different Aguaruna speakers in different contexts refer to me as both apach and irinku. Since the former in its broadest sense also means non-Aguaruna, it includes me. The latter is much more specifically a reference to white foreigners from the global North, be they tourists, development workers, petroleum company representatives, or anthropologists.

As far as I can tell, the logic of concentrically linking irinku to apach is also based in part on judgments about customs and to whom they properly belong. In addition to its other meanings, apach connotes a conscious familiarity, and simultaneously unconscious comfort, with a money-based economy and interactions with state agencies. For this reason, virtually all Aguaruna leaders whose familiarity with such things is widely known are constantly in danger of being insulted as being mestizo-like. Yet Aguaruna actors recognize a world that extends beyond the Peruvian nation-state, or, more to the point, a Three Worlds system created out of World War II development legacies. In doing so, they associate irinku with irinkunum, a place that is simultaneously connected to the place of the apach and symbolically and materially superior to it. Hence, as the irinku, I was subject to almost daily comments about how *mas avanzado* (more advanced) the United States was than Peru, how much better my education opportunities were, and, inevitably, how easy my access to money must be. The first two were usually a cause to treat me with habitual acts of respect, such as addressing me with the formal title of "Dr." in everyday settings (à la Peruvian custom) or giving me the largest share of the meal (à la Aguaruna custom). My association with money, or to be precise, an overabundance of it, linked me to profit motives of a much higher, more international, and definitely more greedy sort. This was always cause for treating the irinku with suspicion, which at times manifests in displays of envy, at others subtle forms of dependency, and at others still outright hostility. Like the love/hate implied in apach, irinku also resonates with a profound degree of ambivalence learned from the many colonial encounters that constitute the lived experience of Aguarunia.

Perhaps this explains why the condition of indigeneity in Aguarunia represents something a bit unique. It permits contact with the mestizo-gringo and the logics and practices such terms imply. It even permits Aguaruna to act *like* mestizo-gringos. But it doesn't easily permit them to become mestizo-gringos. The degree of fluidity between these identities is constantly kept in check by a sentiment of belonging that fixes a stronger ethnic border. Relatedly, like certain apach one finds there, I, too, have occasionally been called Aguaruna-like while traveling in Aguarunia. But from within Aguarunia no one can ever imagine me as simply being Aguaruna. In my experience even those Aguaruna who venture far beyond Aguarunia, and are insulted as mestizo-like, feel much the same way, only in the inverse. No matter where they are, no matter what they are doing, they somehow just feel Aguaruna.

A World of Rivers, a World of Strong Men, a World of Paths

Like the current division of the planet into Three Worlds (notwithstanding the virtual disappearance of the Second), Aguarunia entails a three-worlds theory of its own. These three worlds, or customary methods for determining group status, are made up of rivers, strong men, and paths. That there is no customary concept of a residential unit larger than the individual house does not mean that each house is an entirely self-contained social sphere. At times the emphasis on individual self-reliance and household autonomy within Aguarunia is overwhelming, as it is in other parts of Jivaria (see Descola, 1994: 109). However, the customary norm is a small grouping of semiautonomous households scattered at varying intervals along a small stretch of a river or stream. This informal river "neighborhood" consists of closely related households and is recognized as an important means of social grouping. In an interview, Adolfo Juep, originally from the Marañon River area, reflected on this pattern of residence that was part of his childhood:

> Shane: Did they [the Aguaruna] live in communities?
> Adolfo: We lived in separate houses but always communicating between families in one area. Where we lived in the Shimutas area it was called Putuim [a small tributary of the Shimutas River]. Putuim is a little stream where my father's neighbors were, but not that close by. Instead at a distance of at least fifteen minutes, twenty minutes, half an hour, one hour, two hours, three hours. Those were the neighbors of my father.

These amorphous residential groups are thus formed largely by endogamous-oriented kin. (Cross-cousin marriage was and still is the norm in some areas.) Above all, river neighborhoods reflect the geographic proximity of most of one's close family. Occasional exogamous unions do in fact take place. But before Aguaruna started marrying apach and the occasional irinku, these unions were customarily the result of interfamilial feuding or raids on an adjacent Jivaroan group. The term *bisaták* refers to women and children captured in such raids. Assuming they submit to resocialization with their new de facto husband/father, which happens often but not always, they are likely to be treated much like any other kin. However, judging from the personal testimony of an Achuar widow I met (the bisaták of a deceased Aguaruna war leader originally from the Potro River), the pain of becoming the new wife of your husband's killer is a difficult thing to forget.

Descola (1994: 9) coined the term "endogamous nexus" to describe the similarly atomistic and amorphous residential pattern among the Jivaroan Achuar. The whole idea is based on this loose pattern of close families who desire to maintain communication by settling down in a particular river location but without any sense or need to impose rigid residential boundaries. Although there is no local term with which to index the idea of an "endogamous nexus," the Aguaruna, like other Jivaroans, possess multiple ways of talking about it. Three methods in particular are important for talking about social groupness, and each constitutes a different way of thinking about the social structure of Aguarunia.

The first method is based on a very explicit association of topographically significant places (most often, but not always, rivers or other, smaller waterways) with these social groupings. A second is based on an elder or "strong" man's personification of the corporate group; in other words, his ability to stand in both politically and socially for the group. Such strong men authority figures are precisely what I have come to think of as those men deemed the most notable of their particular social group. This is a relative understanding, of course, since the group he seeks to stand in for might consist of anything from just a small number of households to the entirety of indigenous Amazonia, as Aguaruna leaders ascend through the ranks of the organized Amazonian movement. Strong notable men achieve their status by virtue of the fact that Aguaruna speakers constantly conflate an individual man's name with a group he is thought to represent. The third method requires more elaboration given how significant it becomes in the sphere of customary and contemporary Aguaruna imagination: the classification of paths as a means to mark social and territorial boundaries between individuals and groups.

These three superimposed logics—implicated in kin/river/path networks represented by strong men—reveal not a static social structure but a structure-in-motion. Talking about groupness in these ways reflects a concern to accommodate the shifts of periodic relocation, that is, resettlement from one river to the next. They also accommodate generational displacement of older leaders with younger ones and respond to the more contingent eventualities (i.e., sudden death or defeat) that determine the rise and fall of a given strong man leader. Thus, talking about groupness in these ways reflects a concern with ongoing reformulations of social groups in space and time. Significant places, significant (male) individuals, and significant corridors of movement represent the organizing principles of social and political group relations.

River Neighborhoods

Rivers are a particularly significant site for subsistence activities and a space of mythological proportions for all the Jivaro. They are inhabited by all manner of aquatic beings of natural, supernatural, and shamanic origin (see Descola, 1994: chap. 7; Brown, 1986: 51–52). Typically, but not exclusively, Aguaruna locate themselves and other groups by referencing rivers or other smaller waterways. At issue is not the specificity of rivers per se but the specificity of significant *places*—places that are made significant by the spatial and ecological characteristics of their sub-Andean Amazonian environment. Other features of the topography, including ecological niches of particular flora and fauna, also sometimes serve as distinguishing features of the socially defined landscape.

Using this logic, therefore, one routinely hears mention of other social groupings with reference to their river location: *shimutas aents* (people of the Shimutas
River), *numpatkaim aents* (people of the Numpatkaim River), and so on. These
river toponyms represent the kind of fractal logic described by Carneiro da
Cunha (1997); while the socio-territorial scale changes, the logic of waterway-kin
groupings stays the same. Smaller stream-kin groupings or tributary-kin groupings can be concentrically encompassed within larger river-kin groupings from
the perspective of a person external to that riverine network, a fact known since
at least Harner's (1972: 78) time working with the Shuar in Ecuador. Recalling
Adolfo Juep's interview: Putuim is a small tributary of the Shimutas, itself a small
tributary of the Upper Marañon, the large waterway that empties into the Amazon. From the perspective of an Aguaruna living on a completely different tributary of the Marañon, Shimutas aents would in fact encompass Putuim aents.

Migration within Aguarunia obviously changes this relationship. Resettling
on another river (or some other topographically significant place) will not au-
tomatically, but will no doubt eventually, result in a change of river address.
The people of river X become the people of river Y. Reflecting that complex dynamic between the Andes and Amazonia in Peru, Aguaruna commonly group
people by rivers but use river names that derive from mixtures of Spanish and
Quechua. This became apparent one day when I was talking to Adolfo Juep
from the community Bajo Naranjillo about the sociological importance of rivers in Aguarunia:

> Adolfo: Before they [the Aguaruna in the Alto Mayo] lived in locations
> referencing the rivers. Tributaries of the Mayo River, tributaries like, for
> example, Naranjillo, tributaries like, for example, the Shampuyacu stream
> . . . and another tributary also of the Mayo River, which is Cachiyacu.
> That's a stream where there is salt. *Cachi*, salt, *cachi* means "salt." But in
> Quechua one says "cachi." It has a Quechua name, you know, salt.
> Shane: And *yacu*?
> Adolfo: *Yacu* means "water, river," you know. . . . These people [the Aguaruna
> that first arrived in the Alto Mayo] lived, just referencing the streams and
> biggest tributaries. They just lived like that. Because of that it was said
> "people of Huascayacu," "people of Shimpiyacu," "people of Naranjillo." . . .
> That's what was said before. So "people" [*gente*] means "aents" in Agua-
> runa. Aents. Cachiyacu aents, Naranjillo aents, you know, Huascayacu
> aents. That's how they talked.

The names of the rivers don't have to be in Aguaruna to be included in Aguarunia. The logic of using river names as symbols of social groupings simply has to be customized.

Strong Man, Old Man, Visionary Man

Another customary form of identifying social groups is with reference to an experienced and respected elder, typically a visionary war leader thought to effectively represent his own kin grouping. This grouping includes not only women, adolescents, and children but also those men whose names are simply less well known and thus whose lives are, well, just less notable. Thus, it is common to hear someone reference another social group with statements such as *auk muun Tsamajainta aentsjiyai* (those are the elder Tsamajain's people). The point of reference for the social group is inevitably a male authority figure. The male elder who is considered *muun* (the most experienced), *waimaku* (the most visionary), and *kakajam* (strongest) war leader stands in for an entire kin network or river neighborhood. Needless to say, these qualities often cohere in the same individual. I discuss the nature of these two categories of male prestige and what they reveal about concepts of authority in greater detail in Chapter 3.

Changes in who is deemed significant within what social grouping are inevitable due to generational displacement. Elder X's people soon become elder Y's people when X dies. This logic also reflects the periodic political ups and downs of social conflict. One of the direct results of conflict is that those who were previously notable warriors sometimes lose such standing (if not even more precious things like life itself), and other notable men arise to take their place. Strong man X's people become strong man Y's people when X is defeated. Those who come to personify male power—and in the process stand in for the kin/river groupings of which they are members—are thus frequently shifting.

Throughout Aguarunia, as in other parts of Jivaria, narratives about the past are in large part made up of stories about noteworthy male leaders, those men deemed biography worthy (cf. Taylor, n.d.; Hendricks, 1993). There is also a tendency to collectively appropriate those most notable of notable men to stand in for virtually all of Aguarunia, regardless of its multiple internal divisions. One well-documented example is the reputable war leader Tsamajain of the Alto Marañón. Throughout the various parts of Aguarunia I have traveled his name has become synonymous with the fine art of mediation on behalf of the Aguaruna during the initial years of Nazarene mission schools and the

1920s era of Aguaruna pacification campaigns (see Chapter 4). His reputation and exploits—both in war and in negotiations with gringo missionaries—are so often noted that they have been memorialized. The postsecondary vocational institute in Chiriaco, a small town with both mestizo and Aguaruna inhabitants on the Upper Marañon River, now carries his name.

Another notable man whose deeds and discourse are completely unforgettable in Aguarunia is the legendary warrior Bikut. Indeed, Bikut's life serves as an inspiration to those Aguaruna eager to pursue the kind of passion for war visions, physical invincibility, and male authority he has come to symbolize. He is, in short, a kind of collective Aguaruna role model for all those men who attempt, but usually fail, to emulate him: strong, old, and noteworthy men. Such men are revered and admired as representatives of kin/river groups not only on the basis of their demonstrated strength but also in terms of the effectiveness of an inner visionary power they have acquired (see Chapter 3).

My Path versus His, Our Path versus Theirs

Judging from the inordinate amount of emphasis placed on them by my Aguaruna confidants, I believe paths constitute another method of dividing up the physical and social landscapes. Never is a path solely a corridor of bodily movement through space and time—although clearly it is that. Paths are a customary way to talk about the pursuit of male power. Paths are also a way to talk about the cosmos. And paths are a way to talk about the dynamic between social fluidity and social fixity, the connectedness and dividedness that characterize contact between different social groupings.

First, it is worth noting that within Aguarunia the earthly plane is connected to the cosmos via what Europeans came to think of as the Milky Way. In Aguaruna this dense constellation of stars is known as *iwanch jintamamu* (lit., the path made by the spirits of our dead ancestors). Iwanch jintamamu is the path used by the recently deceased. Aguaruna *iwanch* (spirits) must walk from this *nugka* (earth) to cross the *nayaim* (sky) in order to join their ancestors in *iwanchnum* (lit., where the spirits are), which lies just at the other end of this celestial path. On those nights when this astrological phenomenon shines brightly, it presages the death of some unlucky familiar whose spirit has already begun its long ascent: thus, the clarity of the path.

But let us descend from the cosmic space-time of the heavens and refocus our attention on the ordinariness of paths cut through the real space-time of the Amazonian forest. Imagined from a panoptic point of view, the territorial pattern of Aguarunia—at least those parts not yet covered by rice fields, migrant settlements, and provincial towns—appears as a complicated network of paths. Densely interconnected in river neighborhood areas, they are sparse, scattered, and sometimes practically invisible in the vast expanses of forest that connect one neighborhood with the next. Map 2 is a diagram I made of the native community Cachiyacu after my visit there.

Several elements (the school, rectangular structures, etc.) make it clear that these are not the idealized kin/river neighborhood groupings described as customary by contemporary Aguaruna. The significance of paths as part of the settlement's landscape is apparent nonetheless. Indeed, the reader might simply contrast this diagrammatic representation of Cachiyacu's path network (at least, those that I was made aware of) with any cartographic map issued by the Peruvian state that deals with native communities. What's inside a native community doesn't matter in the least to the state. All that matters are the precise geographic coordinates that establish political boundaries between one native community and the next or between a native community and lands with a different regime of public or private ownership. The difference is one of a space characterized by socially constructed infrastructure (houses, gardens, paths for hunting, paths toward destination X, etc.) versus an orientation toward representing propertied forms of legally territorialized boundedness.

Unlike amateur cartographers such as myself, however, Aguaruna living in native communities do not usually imagine themselves suspended in the air, looking down from a bird's-eye view upon their territory. Thus, my diagram itself misrepresents a space that in fact is better understood as materially grounded and inhabited by social actors practicing their daily labors. Invoking Bourdieu (1977), we might see them as participants in an embodied social space called a habitus, one held together in significant part by the connectedness of paths. To better approximate the Aguaruna habitus, therefore, we must consider the fact that any path in a kin/river group's area begins from and eventually terminates—after any number of possible routes through the forest, down to the river, to the garden, and so on—at someone's house. Paths are integral not only to the organization of cosmological space (connecting/dividing the earth and the heavens) but also to the lived realities of social organization. Paths are a material manifestation of the ties that bind and separate one social unit and the next. Only by moving on them do individuals create social commerce.

Paths are also what connect and divide one river neighborhood to and from the next. They thus serve as ambiguous "boundaries" that simultaneously tie

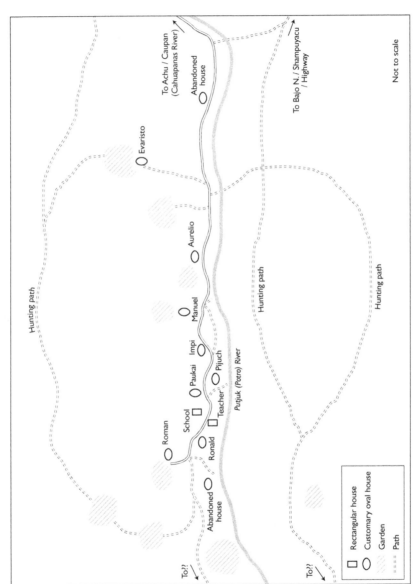

Map 2 Cachiyacu settlement in 1999.

together and clearly separate "close" kin and distant kin living, as is typical, at something of a geographic distance. Paths are the ordinary corridors of movement that both connect and divide people through space in extraordinary ways.

Within the network of a particular neighborhood, paths are the object of so much daily and routine movement that mention of them is scarcely necessary. As Bourdieu explains, the body has already memorized them. Utilizing this bodily memory, people move on them with a clear directional intention, oriented by a point of definite departure and a point of proximate destination. This is a form of everyday movement that occurs without need for conscious reflection. Paths and their directionality become the topic of conscious thought only when such is needed. For obvious reasons children sometimes require an orientation about where paths lead. As children grow up, the bodily repetition of walking on paths becomes habituated. And soon they exhibit similar patterns of intentional directionality but unconscious social movement that older folks' bodies have already mastered. A visitor to Aguarunia like myself, unfamiliar with the terrain, is placed in essentially the same position as the disoriented child. Thus, my frequent requests for directions while in Aguarunia also became a cause for bringing the directionality of paths consciously to mind. Typically, this conscious orientation to paths and their destinations occurs with a mixture of directional gestures and a brief referential comment like "that is the path to so-and-so's house."

Another cause for conscious reflection on the socially introverted paths that help one circulate within Aguarunia's river neighborhoods reveals the concern with extramarital relations. If a woman's garden wraps around her house (a common spatial arrangement), the garden effectively forms a kind of appendix to the domestic space. But not all women's gardens are annexed to their houses. Sometimes they lie at a distance of anywhere from five- to twenty-minutes' walk from the domestic confines of the house. Several personal stories—not to mention an Aguaruna joke or two—reveal that an Aguaruna husband discovering another man on the path to his wife's garden, or even just the sign of foreign footprints, raises great suspicion. In one case it even served as incontrovertible proof of an inappropriate relation and sparked conflict. Thus, the path to a particular woman's garden becomes itself a space as private and feminized as the subsistence garden itself should be in Aguarunia.

When found in the extended forest that connects one neighborhood to another, that space where Aguaruna hunt, collect forest resources, and travel to visit relatives, paths are again the main corridors of habitual movement.

Here, too, most anyone who ventures down a particular path has a reason to do so and knows exactly where he or she is going. Anyone who does not have a reason or doesn't know where he or she is headed is almost inevitably following someone who does. The young, the unhabituated, or the precocious anthropologist will occasionally ask about where certain paths through Aguarunia lead. General answers like "*juka Cachiyacu jintíí*" (that is Cachiyacu's path) actually reveal something deeper. Typically expressed with *ii* (a third-person-possessive suffix), such statements make explicit that from the speaker's point of view the destination invoked in such an utterance belongs to another social group.

While traveling, Aguaruna also sometimes find occasion to describe the route to others who might be following it for the first time. Particular rivers, streams, concentrations of palm trees, large fallen trees, large rocks, waterfalls, and other prominent and stationary aspects of the natural topography serve as reference points. *Aak* (human-made forest shelters), used to break up long journeys, also serve this function. Customarily, people also distinguish between the relative size or width of paths, a *muun jintá* (big/wide path) versus an *uchi jintá* (little/narrow path). Another phrase, *bashi jintá* (abandoned path), usually means a path with such infrequent foot traffic that the resulting overgrowth causes the path follower to have difficulty detecting the route.

Within the forest domain paths are also distinguished by the uses to which they are put and how they are made. Descola (1994: 65) notes, for example, the contrast the Jivaroan Achuar draw between the perceptible quality of paths that lead to a settlement or someone's house with the virtually undetectable paths used to mark private hunting grounds. A similar distinction is found in Aguarunia. A *jintá* is a path that despite its size or nature is at least easily recognizable and can often be followed by most anyone—whether Aguaruna or not. Paths in the forest are rarely wide enough for side-by-side travel so force single-file movement. They do, however, vary greatly in how visible they are to the untrained eye. Some are clearly marked by constant human movement, leaving a material groove in the forest floor that could be followed by even the most wilderness-challenged traveler imaginable. "Abandoned paths" require a much more discriminating eye, but most Aguaruna hunters can easily detect them despite the fading signs of human movement.

There is another kind of path that, strictly speaking, is not one, or at least, is not referred to as "jintá": Aguaruna speakers refer to a particular kind of intentional movement through the forest that nonetheless results in the construction of a private pathway. It results from the careful use of subtle markers that define a person's course through an otherwise undisturbed forest. These markers are sometimes so subtle that they are detectable only to the person who placed them there. In Aguaruna these markers are called *ápik*, a noun form derived from the verb *apiktasa* (lit., to bend/fold, or more generally, to leave a mark). This term refers to a customary method used to mark the path route in which one folds back leaves or small branches at short intervals. Other methods may in fact be substituted: for example, small machete cuts made to tree bark or piling up a few dead leaves or sticks on the forest floor. In contrast to the shared character of paths between houses and settlements—marked by constant human movement—these subtly marked paths are often used for creating private hunting territories. They are not restricted to that purpose, however. Aguaruna I've spoken to about this also associate such secret corridors with the stealth tactics deployed during periods of conflict.

Some paths also serve as physical-symbolic reminders that someone else's custom has come to impinge on the Aguaruna's own. The entrance of migrants into Aguarunia has also led to distinctions about the nature of paths according to who had constructed them, who widened them, who mostly moves on them and for what purpose. It is not at all uncommon to hear Aguaruna call one path an *awajun jintií* (Aguaruna's path) and another *apach jintií* (a mestizo path), signaling the difference in ethnic ownership that they attribute to different paths. Mestizo paths may be labeled as such because they lead to non-Aguaruna settlements. But they are also sometimes labeled as such due to the noticeably different material aspects of the path itself. Most any Aguaruna speaker will refer to a dirt road or a rural footpath on which livestock also travel as an *apach jintií*.

Having internalized the semantic difference between road and path, many bilingual Aguaruna will simply substitute the Spanish *carretera* (road), especially when referring to a road as distinguishable as the Carretera Marginal de la Selva. This rural highway—first envisioned by President Belaúnde Terry in the 1950s and finally paved by President Fujimori in the 1990s—runs throughout Aguarunia and connects it to the Peruvian coast. Those for whom Spanish remains something of a mystery call it the mestizo's path. I learned this one day on my way back from the remote community of Cachiyacu in the company of two men eager to visit their kin in the more urbane and bilingual Bajo Naranjillo. After emerging from our two-day trek from Cachiyacu and arriving at a rural settlement that borders the Marginal, I decided to splurge. Making a gesture about how tired I was, I invited my forest tour guides to a free ride on a pickup truck that would take us to Bajo Naranjillo via the Marginal. Mixing my Spanish and Aguaruna, I said, "*Carretera wemi*" (Let's go down the highway). "Okay, brother, let's take the mestizo's path." This was their customary way of taking me up on the offer.

3 A How-to Manual
for Visionary Warriors

In 2000, while I was living in Lima, José Lirio, founder and past president of the Organización Central de Comunidades Aguarunas del Alto Marañon (OCCAAM), came to see me during a visit to the capital city about an eco-tourist project he was peddling. I invited him into my not-so-posh apartment in the otherwise posh district of Miraflores. And somehow we got into a conversation about the changing nature of leadership in Aguarunia. He tried to sum up the relation between contemporary and customary authority by giving an example of a conflict between two Aguaruna leaders he knows well. One was a national-level leader based in Lima, and the other, more of a regional leader based in his home community Yamayakat on the Upper Marañon River. The conflict revolved around the latter's indiscreet use of a building that belongs to the regional Aguaruna organization OCCAAM. The national-level leader decided to politicize the issue and marshal support against the regional leader. The result was that the regional leader was marginalized on an ongoing development project in his area in which he had previously been centrally involved.

During our conversation about this episode José Lirio's young niece was present and decided to interject. Addressing Lirio as the voice of elderly male experience, she asked if Aguaruna leaders had always been so competitive with one another. "Are things always this ugly?" she asked. Lirio responded in his calm and contemplative voice as he often does: "Yes, mama, things are fierce. But it has always been that way in accordance with custom. He who is most prominent and he who makes himself heard is he who dominates. That's all there is to it."

So a crucial question arises as to how exactly one becomes "he who dominates" in Aguarunia. What paths must one forge to emerge as the most prominent? An even more important question is, What kinds of circumstances warrant this large-scale undertaking I call customizing indigeneity that necessitates those who were once in competition against each becoming allies against a common enemy? How is it exactly that Aguaruna strong men—these tried-and-true visionary warriors—take it upon themselves to take on the entire world to defend Aguarunia?

I am not the only one who sees this as an interesting dilemma. Longtime Aguaruna leader at the national level César Sarasara debated this problem in his work with a Ministry of Agriculture official quite some time ago (see Chang and Sarasara, 1987). Sarasara and Chang note that there is something paradoxical in how much customary importance Aguaruna actors attribute to figures of male visionary and military authority. It is paradoxical because although they are often considered the most obvious public spokespeople for the social groups they represent, their actions figure relatively little into the activities of everyday life in Aguarunia. The social authority they embody has little direct connection with the hunting, planting, harvesting, cooking, selling and buying of commodities, socializing children, going to school, spreading gossip, and so on that make up daily life in Aguarunia. Only in times of conflict and crisis—and in moments when a common enemy has been identified—do these notable men and their recourse to the insights of visionary knowledge become so collectively useful.

From my point of view, therein lies the answer to the dilemma. What others might call the history of modernity Aguaruna activists articulate as a prolonged moment of confrontation with a common enemy. They view this continuing encounter as, in effect, a war of a different kind and with an enemy that is simultaneously local, national, and international in scope. Thus, since this encounter is seen through the lens of a conflict, it demands a response from Aguarunia's most notable men, these strong individuals, these visionary warriors. Customarily, the wars that visionary warriors engaged in took place only sporadically and on a small scale. The violence was indeed visceral and the casualties real. But the weapons were by modernity's military standards weapons of minimal, not mass destruction—mostly just spears and shotguns. Today's visionary warriors, Aguaruna activists, see conflict as something that is constant, existing at multiple scales from the community micro to the international macro. And the weapons they wield are less and less spears and shotguns and more and more pens and paper. In short, the visionary warriors of yesterday make excellent indigenous politicians of today. They engage in this task not by configuring their own alternative space within modernity but by customizing the only alternative modernity lays out for them: their abstracted condition of indigeneity.

As noted in the Path Between Site I and II, this dynamic is implicit in Adolfo Juep's cybernetic identification of a Socratic philosopher indigenous to Aguarunia who went by the name Bikut. Indeed, this chapter is a kind of tribute to Bikut and all that he symbolizes about the notability of Aguaruna strong men and the central role they play in envisioning a politics of customization. Yet Bikut's metaphorical placement as a Path Between Sites I and II serves as more than a mere sign of how visionary warriors pursue social principles of customary authority—of how to speak, how to act, how to succeed, and thus how to follow the right path. He also embodies the enduring sentiments of indigenous cosmopolitanism found in Aguarunia. Bikut represents more than a path toward success in the practical politics of visionary warfare. He—along with the logics of customization he embodies—also represents a path toward Aguaruna activists' own Socratic dialogue with Peru's concentrically layered orders of indigeneity. He espouses a specific philosophy of indigeneity found and heartfelt in Aguarunia that explains how to find a path through the worlds that impose themselves on Aguarunia.

Anne Christine Taylor (2007) in her work with the Jivaro describes a societal emphasis on visionary war leaders and strong man types as those individuals deemed most biographically remarkable. Those visionary warriors who emerge as the most visible are those who become known both inside and, perhaps more important, outside their particular kin networks and river neighborhoods. One of the things they become notable for is their extraordinary ability to mobilize others. This ability to mobilize is, in turn, dependent on a kind of visionary "capital" they possess and put to use as much as it is on the generational and gendered status they occupy in Jivaria. Their prestige is socially recognized and respected. But it is also challengeable by other visionary warriors eager to prove their own capacity for effectiveness in the arena of visionary warfare. In other words, competing visionary warriors are in constant pursuit of a form of social authority that is constantly up for grabs.

Typically, the scope of any one visionary warrior's mobilizational capacity is constrained by the genealogical relations that are overlaid on the Amazonian geography. The primordial alliance to "close family" within a particular river neighborhood—combined with the everyday distrust of "distant family" in others—makes large-scale mobilizations infrequent phenomena. But the readiness for collective self-defense and the social value derived from triumph in conflict always include, potentially at least, the possibility for a larger-scale mobilization of distant allies should the right circumstances arise. This is the kind of large-scale confrontation Aguaruna activists currently imagine themselves taking part in. And the terrain of mobilization is truly complex. It consists of both allies and enemies operating in various contexts that range from Aguaruna communities and mestizo migrant settlements to state offices and international NGO branches.

Placing such a high value on visionary warfare becomes a means to demand respect and demonstrate their individual sense of political self-importance. Examining this phenomenon of seeking to become a visionary warrior in order to become a good indigenous politician is how we arrive back at the importance of paths. As elaborated in the rest of this chapter, much of this issue of visionary male leadership can easily be summed up with the simple Aguaruna phrase *jintá weamu*, "going down the path."

Paths of Thought, Hearts of Action

Obviously, notable men do not emerge from nowhere. They are born, socialized, and progress through adulthood like everyone else. To figure out how they become visionaries, we must first take a look at how they proceed through the normative life-course that living in Aguarunia prescribes. We might start by looking at the body. Biomedical practitioners conceive of the heart as a blood pump enclosed in the chest cavity and protected by the rib cage. Western poets and songwriters aesthetically represent it as the symbolic site of romantic love. In Aguarunia *anentai* (heart) is the center of individual self-hood, where one's intelligence, capacity for self-reflection, ability to act appropriately, and deepest emotions reside.

Many Aguaruna elders draw on this notion of the heart's centrality when they advise younger generations (and usually boys more so than girls) that in order to "*shiig anentaimjati tusa*" (think right; lit., to have a good heart) they must "*jintá weta*" (go down the path). In the first instance this is a reference to the pursuit of a life-affirming visionary experience employing probably the three most significant plants in all of Aguarunia: *tsaag* (tobacco, *Nicotiana tabacam*); *datem* (ayahuasca, *Banisteriopsis caapi*); and *baikua/tsuak* (two varieties of jimsonweed, *Datura arborea*).

Although the catchphrase "go down the path" is often taken to refer primarily to young men's quest for a war vision (discussed in more detail later), the variety of contexts in which these plants are used is extraordinarily broad. We can customize the Anglo phrase to a certain Aguaruna mentality: there are many circumstances in which you must get "your heart on straight." People use the same plants to obtain vision and insight into things other than war. These uses include employing the plants as a way to see one's future well-being or sometimes lack thereof; as a means of corrective punishment for inappropriate behavior; as a source of counsel in times of personal or social crisis; as a medium for the transmission of *anen* (songs of seduction) from instructor to learner; and as a curative remedy for sickness and wounds.

It should be no surprise that the constant counsel to "go down the path" is now creatively customized as a reference to the need for more and better institutional education. In fact, many people within Aguarunia compare "going down the path" to what Westerners mean when they say "get an education." Another good example of this comes from Gerardo Wipio Deicat, the first native director of the Summer Institute of Linguistics Pedagogical Institute at Lake Yarinacocha. He begins an essay on his experiences in Aguarunia by stating, "The Aguaruna lived for centuries without knowing about schools. They received the wisdom of their ancestors from their fathers by means of a system called jinta ainbau, meaning 'follow the trail made by our forebears'" (1981: 67). Much like institutional education, going down the path is about being socialized in what are deemed appropriate ways. And much as occurs in institutional education, some individuals emerge as more exemplary students than others.

Ethnographic data I collected with the assistance of an Aguaruna collaborator and several elderly Aguaruna (four men and one woman) from the community of Bajo Naranjillo helped me paint a picture of the ideal life-path imagined for men and women in Aguarunia. This presentation is unquestionably overly schematic. In Aguarunia the life-course is a rather fluid thing. Their descriptions did not reflect rigid social stages or ceremonial age-sets with perhaps the exception of a notably intense emphasis on the period of male adolescent vision questing that many consider to mark a distinctive stage in each man's social development. Interestingly, as my collaborators and I constructed this idealized and seemingly timeless outline of customary understandings of Aguaruna life-paths, distinct temporalities entered into the mix. References to men wearing a customary skirt handmade from *itipák* (cotton), which one rarely sees these days, mixed with references to women who desire the *jaánchnaskam pegáwai* (nice clothes) found in local mestizo markets. Hence, there was no easy way to smoothly separate a custom "then" from a custom "now" in our attempt to outline the idealized life-course of people in Aguarunia.

In the broadest terms, the developmental vision we constructed might be divided into stages known as *uchi* (childhood), *datsameu* (for adolescent boys/ young men) or *múntsugtameu* (for adolescent girls/young women), and *muun* (adulthood/elderly status). My collaborators broke down each one of these broad categories further and associated them with specific social or natural characteristics considered normative for that stage of development. Children progress through a series of natural steps before becoming distinguishable as gendered and socialized individuals. Newborns are thus called *kapantuch* (from *kapantu*, "red") because of the redness of their skin after birth. As they develop, they pass through a series of stages characterized by biological states or be- haviors (becoming more robust/plump, sitting up, crawling, standing, walking, etc.). As they develop the capacity for verbal communication, young boys and girls are immediately cast into a gender track through the usage of terms of address that invoke sexual differentiation. Pretty much uniformly throughout Aguarunia people address little boys once they reach the toddler stage as *suki* (lit., testicles) and little girls as *muntsu* (lit., breast). These gendered terms of endearment persist well into adolescence.

Primary caretakers provide younger generations with certain forms of eso- teric knowledge thought to be vital to one's long-term well-being and forma- tion into a distinguished and authoritative self. Particularly important in this regard is the intergenerational teaching of powerful anen, thought to be useful for influencing other humans and other beings (plants, animals, etc.). Such songs are useful in the positive pursuits of love, affection, hunting, and crop cultivation but also in the dark arts of deception, betrayal, and manipulation (see Brown, 1986).

Adolescence represents a real divergence between young men and women in Aguarunia. Customarily, learning how to make and beginning to use gender- specific adornments from Amazonian flora and fauna represent a significant aspect of this divergence. In my experiences in Aguarunia, aesthetic styles are rife with different fashions, from those defined as customary to those more reflective of the consumerist desires peddled in local mestizo markets. Interest in male head adornments and female bead necklaces is down. Interest in ironed dress shirts and multicolored dresses is up. Ways and modes of verbal commu- nication also change significantly during adolescence. Customarily young boys and adolescents begin to practice and try to perfect *enemamu*, a highly ritualized form of forceful dialogic speech. This kind of dialogue, rarely witnessed anymore, is performed with rhythmic gestures of the spear (or more recently a shotgun) and short lunges forward and backward. Such dialogues are referenced with the expression "*ya, ya,*" a reference to the call-and-response-type interjections verbalized by the listener during his counterpart's oratory. Such dialogic competitions tend to occur when a host is greeting arriving visitors, when kinsmen reunite, when an organizer of a war mission addresses his invitees, or on much less frequent occasions when a pair of unknowns meet for the first time. Most often these performative dialogues entail a public expression that reinforces shared familial ties, establishes alliance, or serves as a declaration of one's intentions in visiting a host's household (see Figure 1). Despite the rare occurrence of such ritualized formal dialogues these days, the display of confidence in one's verbal ability is still highly valued in Aguarunia. Any creditable Aguaruna activist knows how to speak aggressively when engaged in face-to-face dialogue. It is in significant part his capacity to compete verbally in dialogue with others that makes him an effective politician.

Without any comparable form of public oratory performance many women are nonetheless noted for developing a loud, shrill, and unmistakably female form of laughter. It often punctuates public social occasions, particularly manioc beer parties. The sound is expressed onomatopoeically as "*jajajai*"; the elders I spoke with about it say that such expressive laughter only fully blossoms when a young woman becomes less inhibited and the shyness associated with young girls really starts to recede.

The gendering of household subsistence behaviors is also currently fluctuating depending on where one is in Aguarunia. In largely self-subsistent communities the paradigm of man-the-hunter versus woman-the-caretaker is still dominant. In those areas with intermediate or high volumes of market commerce another paradigm has been added: man-the-money-manager versus woman-the-guardian-of-subsistence. In those communities with agricultural surplus production this behavior usually manifests in terms of male heads of households managing cash crops for sale in provincial markets and women taking care of small gardens for the household's daily needs.

In Aguarunia both men and women are encouraged to seek visions and to learn the songs of seduction that allow one to do everything from awaken the power of sacred plants to make someone fall in love. Vision quests involve learning to use the three powerful plants mentioned earlier: tsaag, datem, and baikua. But kinds of visions differ, ranging from insights into one's domestic

Figure 1 Enemamu (top) and seated variation (bottom). Drawings reproduced with permission of Linder Gomez Juep.

future to visions specifically useful for times of conflict. One who possesses the more domestic vision is *niimaju*; one who possesses a vision for war is *waimaku*.

Adulthood is most often marked in Aguarunia through use of the word *muun* to refer to anyone, man or woman, who is fully mature. As an adjective it means "big" and is associated with the same relative sense of size as in English. However, when the term is deployed as a noun, it refers typically to a specific adult male head of household or a visionary warrior authority figure who stands in for an entire social group, as in *muun Salomon aentsijai* (those are the elder Salomon's people).

Aguaruna senior citizens—those persons identifiable as having reached the last stages of life—are called *muuntuch*, a diminutive form of *muun*. These are typically people whose bodies have been consumed by their life-path and are left without the strength to labor or act independently. In such a state they typically morph into a kind of temporary appendage to one of their children's households. In Aguarunia the presence of the elderly conjures up images of a series of mysterious phenomena and unpredictable powers associated with the afterlife. The elderly come to symbolize one power in particular, *ajutap*, the ethereal essence of all the dead ancestors and the grantor of war visions. It is after all the ajutap that has the power to breathe new life, via new visionary experiences, into the ancestors' living descendants still on earth. The ajutap gives men the chance to become notable in the first place.

Exemplary Paths Linked to Exemplary Male Selves

Women also occasionally seek and are granted war visions that make them waimaku. Others familiar with Aguarunia have also remarked on the various roles women have played in military endeavors (see Guallart, 1990: 213). Rebecca Detén, a past director of the Consejo Aguaruna Huambisa's health program, reminded me of this during a follow-up visit in 2003 to present my research to Aguaruna interlocuters (see the Epilogue). She intervened in the conversation to make this unambiguous remark about the ambiguously hidden nature of Aguaruna women in a discussion about visions for war:

> Women also entered in that process to become waimaku that they say is for men. There are also some women that practiced the custom of taking ayahuasca, of taking toé, of taking tobacco. It wasn't all of them, but there were women that made that decision, and those women were also the ones that participated

in war. . . . The point is that up to the present we aren't so public like that . . . we don't stand out. This is a cultural thing that persists even up to now. . . . It's as if men are our intermediaries or spokespersons. Since they have been in leadership roles, they just say what they think. They never say that this is a woman's idea, or this is my wife's idea, or the idea of so-and-so woman leader. Even now they never express that. That makes us women out as if we're always hidden.

This statement is important because it simultaneously contests and confirms the normative idea that becoming waimaku is an explicitly masculine pursuit. The way she contests it and carves out a space for "some women" is clear enough. Yet she also implicitly confirms it. She was responding to my comments about men pursuing war visions. She begins by saying "they say is for men." This implies not that I say it (although I do) but that "they" say it, a reference to essentially all Aguaruna men. This effectively demonstrates that some women demand inclusion in the category of visionary warriors, but the price of inclusion is to find oneself deploying an already thoroughly masculine discourse.

In her work with the Achuar Taylor (2007) makes a compelling case that what distinguishes Jivaroan societies is the constant search for a unique and individual selfhood, a kind of maximal individuation of the person through search for a unique life-path. Jivaroans are, in other words, truly a society of self-maximizing individuals, at least in terms of the logics of customization that have become dominant. Adam Smith would be proud! Women do this in multiple ways within the gendered realms of house and garden.[1] Men do it primarily by seeking self-realization via the search for life-altering war visions, or, as the saying goes, the constant need to *jintin wainkame* (find one's own path). Men seek not an ordinary life-path but an exemplary one. Not all men find one, but many men try. And according to a certain understanding of things, without such a vision a man is just a man, doomed to a fate of lifelong mediocrity and obscurity that many men secretly fear.

Finding one's own path is dependent primarily on two things. The first is to successfully, and if at all possible repeatedly, acquire visionary experience. This requires that one seek out the self-revelatory powers of the ajutap. Also sometimes referred to as apach in song (the same word as for mestizo), the ajutap evokes the same kind of awe of an unexplainable phenomenon and foreign power that mestizo custom does in Aguarunia. The second important dimension of pursuing self-realization is to prove that one's visionary capacity is actually effective in practice. As Taylor (2007) notes, the pursuit of an exemplary and unique selfhood is not something one is born with or something that is simply granted. It is something one constantly struggles for and claims to have achieved. When others start to believe it as a result of one's deeds, then a visionary warrior status has become recognized. Becoming waimaku, a possessor of vision, then, is the first step toward becoming kakajam, a strong man who has repeatedly succeeded in proving his vision's effectiveness. The question left to answer is what precise procedures one must follow to find a path like this one.

The Power of Visionary Warriors, Not the Secrets of Shamans

Before proceeding, I will clarify any doubts as to what other kinds of customary practice might represent an alternative path toward male political authority. Given recent literature in Amazonian studies, one might logically wonder if there is not a role for a shamanic healer. Recent debates point to shamanic figures in the Amazon as political go-betweens, interethnic mediators, as well as symbols of contemporary environmental-indigenous alliances in international negotiations over the fate of "traditional knowledge" (see Taussig, 1987; Gow, 1996; Carneiro da Cunha, 1997; Conklin, 2002). Yet here, too, things in Aguarunia are a little different than in other parts of Amazonia.

In Aguarunia the forms of mediation in which practicing shamans engage are often more imaginary than real, more inspired by voyages into the occult than by actual physical mobility. During my travels in Aguarunia the contrast has always been striking. Visionary warriors of today, the many Aguaruna activists and politicians I have met, travel constantly—from community to community, from community to provincial town, from provincial town to Lima. The two Aguaruna shamans I have met pretty much stay put.

When the occasional shamanic practitioner aspires to such a position of political ascension and social mobility, the consequences are often dire.[2] As Michael Brown (1989) notes in his own work with the Aguaruna, instead of inspiring reverence and respect, many shamans in Aguarunia represent something considerably less attractive: a vortex of deep and pervasive distrust about the ambivalent nature of human intentions as manifested through witchcraft. Shamans' vocational specialty in detecting witchcraft is certainly considered necessary at times. But in Aguarunia, generally speaking, these are not the kinds of individuals in whom one places much of the public trust.[3]

The public trust is placed in those visionary warriors who emerge as successful in negotiating war missions. Most any war mission begins as an *ipaamamu* (from the verb *ipaamat*, "to invite"), in effect, "by invitation," a meeting of those who are asked to participate in military action convened by one or more strong men authority figures. The convocation of an ipaamamu to invite one's fellows to war is one of the few occasions where one is expected to reveal the private content of an ajutap vision. Those eager to participate must display what it is they have to offer the mission through something called the *kaja atiamu* (revelation of the vision). Such an encounter is presided over by the most experienced of strong men or whoever organized the event.

Here, too, a man must exhibit a capacity for forceful speech. The kaja atiamu is another instance of an aggressive dialogic encounter with one's verbal opponent. Each man faces a dialogic other, weapon raised, and launches into a short, animated verbal display that reveals the specific nature of his vision, to which his opponent responds in kind (see Figure 2). Those presiding over the dialogues serve as interpreters of visions and begin to think tactically in terms

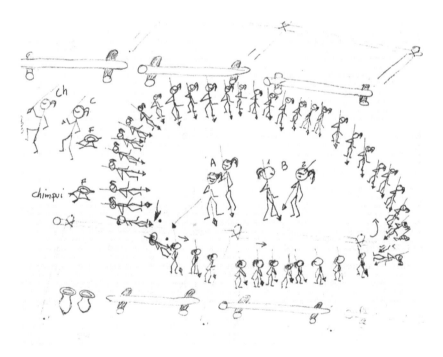

Figure 2 Representation of the ipaamamu and kaja atiamu. Evaluators of visions (A) look on as two men (B) face off in a dialogue to reveal their visions. Drawing reproduced with permission of Adolfo Juep Nampin.

of what vision is appropriate for which role during the mission. One longtime collaborator with whom I discussed the kaja atiamu compared the event to a "thesis defense" undertaken by those with less war experience that is judged by a "thesis committee" consisting of those with more experience. Again, this is another site where the pursuit of customary paths is fused with the contemporary knowledge of paper in the mental state of Aguarunia.

The particular manifestation of an ajutap vision becomes an inextricable addition to the seeker's sense of self. It defines his self-worth and is the basis for his ability to prevail in moments of crisis and conflict. When this eternal ancestral essence finally reveals itself to a vision seeker, it can take any number of physical forms. These include forest animals, insects, spirits, body parts, inanimate objects such as a stone, astronomical phenomena like stars, and sometimes even a recognizable human form. These visionary apparitions are not equally valued. Some visions are conventionally considered superior (like the jaguar, anaconda, or iwanch, a lost soul that wanders the forest). Others are routinely associated with negative, rather than positive, visionary messages (like the fox). During an ajutap vision the seeker is confronted with a seemingly contradictory image. According to those I questioned, the verbal message that the ajutap brings typically resonates with the seeker's own internal voice, more evidence for the fact that the ajutap encounter is profoundly self-revelatory at the same time that it is, technically speaking, dependent on the apparition of an unpredictable and external ancestral presence. When it hits, however, its external presence is almost immediately internalized.

One Aguaruna collaborator was generous enough to relate an account his father passed on to him of an ajutap experience, an example that will help make this experience more concrete. Given the secrecy that surrounds such experiences, I will refer to this man as Samik. During one of his ajutap experiences Samik was confronted with the apparition of an unknown warrior. It spoke in Samik's internal voice and metaphorically compared him to a lightning bug at the same time. It brought the following message:

AJUTAP:

Witjai! Samikwaitjai!	It's me! It's Samik!
Isha-ishamjukaipa! Ishamjukaipa!	[Stuttering rhythmically] D-Don't be afraid of me!
[repeats]	
Dis-diisia!	[Stuttering rhythmically] L-Look!

Wii ikanmash asana!	I, as the lightning bug does!
Anentain ikatajai!	Shut off his heart! ["his" refers to the enemy]
Bashi jintan!	I quickly disappear from the path!
Akintakun tajai!	I make it so! [lit., I say so]
Tuwigki iikamu ataja!	Vengeance will never find me!

SAMIK ANSWERS:

Aan chichachumush!	That's enough of your nonsense!

There are several important aspects to note. The ajutap bestows upon the seeker a set of traits that characterize the particular phenomenological form that the ajutap takes. These traits are then internalized as a core part of the seeker's own sense of self. In Samik's case, the ajutap compares him to a lightning bug. It thus transfers the capacity to "shut off" the heart of the enemy. According to the explanation of Samik's son, the most characteristic trait of a lightning bug is its ability to turn on and off its taillight. To use his word, it is an *apagador* (a shut-offer). That quality was thus passed on to Samik, who henceforth was able to "shut off" his enemy's heart, where the Aguaruna source of intelligence, alertness, and emotion lies. Similarly, the ajutap transfers to Samik the lightning bug–like skill of "disappearing from the path," in essence an ability to appear and disappear in a flash.

Curiously, despite the repeated cycles of ritual privation, personal suffering, and moments of desperation one can undergo before finding the ajutap's life-giving, self-affirming force, the actual encounter should be very short. An overly long or complicated message provokes confusion instead of the clarity of mind that ajutap seekers are looking for. Worse still, any ajutap that repeats its message or appears to deliver multiple contradictory messages is taken as a bad sign. Only by highlighting this desire for a short burst and a clear message can one make sense of Samik's curious answer to the ajutap: "Aan chichachumush" (That's enough of your nonsense). Vision seekers come prepared with this standard response in order to cut the ajutap off to avoid any possible confusion.

The fact that Samik's verbal response is also a bit insulting points to the fact that the encounter is supposed to be confrontational. Enduring the privations associated with seeking the ajutap involves appealing to it with a great degree of reverence. But once the ajutap finally descends to reveal itself, the seeker must approach it without fear and demand immediate, unambiguous self-empowerment. Here, I must offer apologies to generations of Christian missionaries whose religious inclinations have led them to translate the ajutap as an indigenous manifestation of God in Aguarunia. In my opinion, unlike the Christian God, master of the meek and fatherly forgiver of all shameful sinners, the ajutap rewards those who confront it aggressively, not those who bow down before it submissively. Not only are you supposed to tell the ajutap to shut up but the encounter is supposed to end when the seeker violently punctures the ajutap's earthly apparition with the *payag* (short staff) he carries. With that the ajutap returns to the mists of incorporeal time and space beyond the visible realms of Aguarunia.

Seductively Singing to the Grandfather While Molding the Enemy's Head

Now that we know what an ajutap vision looks like once it manifests, what procedures exactly does one follow to call the elusive spirit? Generally, one must rely on a mixture of personal dedication, intergenerational training, songs that work to seduce the spirit, and an endurance for the effects of the three plants used to pursue such visions: tsaag, datem, and baikua.

For the ingestion of any of these plants, or any combination of them, certain basic ritual precautions are standardized. The seeker must avoid sexual contact and certain foods (particularly meat) for several weeks before and after the vision quest. The only food consistently allowed the seeker during this extended fast is *tuum* (a thick manioc soup) or boiled plantains, a diet bland enough to make even the most dedicated question their level of commitment. For those adolescent boys or young men taking these plants in search of a first visionary experience, the lengthy repetitions of these same ritual privations month after month can seem particularly overwhelming. But only through dedicated repetition is one likely to achieve the desired result. Thus, Noé Cahuaza, a confidant from the community Bajo Naranjillo, says that his father taught him he would have to drink datem at least ten to fifteen times before having the slightest chance of success. Only when the accumulated vapors of datem—boiling time and again on the fire—had finally risen to the sky to capture the ajutap's attention would he find what he was looking for.

In Aguarunia the leaves of tsaag are employed as a means of acquiring the musical knowledge necessary for seeking visions. Tsaag is the key ingredient in the transmission of anen, those songs of seduction that circulate as a kind of inheritable private property from mother to daughter and from father to son. Etymologically speaking, anen are songs of the heart, considered to be deeply expressive of emotion and imaginatively poetic. As a result they often contain extremely esoteric language that is not at all easy to interpret for the average Aguaruna young person these days—much less to translate for the eager anthropologist.[4] Armed with these mysterious melodies, one can impact the real world directly. When sung properly, they affect the behavior and attitudinal changes of one's closest fellows, affect future outcomes, and can awake or deaden the various powers that animals and plants contain.

Most anen are transmitted between same-gendered persons within the "close family." However, if solicited from someone other than an immediate caretaker or some other close familial contact, the request can imply some sort of valued exchange. The learner desiring to acquire the anen offers some sort of valuable object (an adornment, for example) or, nowadays, money as compensation for the song(s) requested.[5] The method of transmission of anen requires specific ritual prescriptions that involve the ingestion of tsaag and require a private space away from the ears, eyes, and polluting influence of others. The instructor first purges his or her mouth and stomach with saltwater and then masticates the leaves of tsaag. Chimpa, an elder of the native community Alto Naranjillo, explained to me that the instructor's own saliva is the other essential ingredient in the transmission. The reddish black liquid is deposited into a small container from which the learner must drink each time upon hearing and repeating the instructor's song.

Whatever the specific purpose of the anen learned, the goal of acquiring them is always the same: to affect the world in ways that favor whoever possesses the seductive song. As such, anen are also crucial in empowering the very plants used to seek out the elusive ajutap spirit and acquire its powers of self-enhancement. On any occasion in which one takes datem or baikua, the more powerful plants used to seek a vision, tsaag is often ingested first as part of a ritual warm-up exercise to put the seeker's mind on alert. Sipping the juice of masticated tobacco leaves from a small clay container, one sings some version of a musical lament that tells tsaag to assist the seeker in finding the ajutap:

1   Oh tobacco! Tobacco! Tobacco! [asewa = poetic term, refers to tsaag]
2   My grandfather [apach = refers to the ajutap spirit], what did he convert into?

3 Maybe he converted into an owl. Is that what he would have converted into?

4 You [the ajutap] would be saying, "I'm going to find my child."

5 That's what you would say because it is in your nature to love us.

6 Oh tobacco! Tobacco! I'm really suffering because of my fast. Listen!

7 Other young people follow the path of blood [i.e., imminent death].

8 But I follow the path of the wild dove [*shimpa* = a bird associated with purity, cleanliness, and quickness].

9 I follow the path of the wild dove. I follow the lucky path.

10 I follow the lucky path.

11 Oh tobacco! Tobacco! Tobacco!

12 Other adolescents follow the path of blood.

13 They follow the path of blood.

14 But I follow the path of the wild dove.

15 I follow the lucky path. I follow the lucky path.

Sung by Zacarias Wajush, native community Yankun

Here, the singer considers himself the grandson of the ajutap's ancestral essence. He consistently refers to it as apach, meaning customarily a grandfatherly spirit or contemporarily a mestizo migrant living in Aguarunia. The singer deploys the term to convey that generalized sense of awe that one finds in Aguarunia. It is expressed at different times and in different ways toward elder generations, the dead, and those foreign social actors perceived as politically and economically powerful.

In other versions of the tsaag anen just presented, the interdependency between the three central plants used to seek visions is explicitly expressed, as in the final two stanzas of this version:

1 Oh tobacco! Tobacco! [repeats]

2 I, I, [repeats 3 times]

3 I become well known with datem.

4 I become well known with the essence of tsaag.

5 That's how I carry on.

6 Tobacco don't bring me bad luck. [repeats]

7 Transform yourself in that spirit [i.e., ajutap] that we wait for.

8 You, tobacco reveal it to me. [repeats]

9 I, I, [repeats]

10 I become well known with the essence of tobacco.

11   I become well known with baikua.

12   That's how I carry on.

13   become well known on the path of learning [*ayamtainum*, lit., in the shelter of vision seeking].

14   That's how I carry on.

Sung by Santiago Pijuch, native community Shimpiyacu

This version also makes the seeker's desire for becoming "well known" (i.e., biography worthy) quite clear. It also refers us to the *ayamtai*, a carefully designed shelter of branches and palm leaves constructed in the forest where individual seekers pursue their vision away from the contaminating sphere of domestic social space. Ayamtai indexes less the physical structure than it does the fact that it is a ritual space used to house, protect, and isolate the individual vision seeker during the vision quest. Indeed, other essentially similar shelters used while hunting or traveling are marked with the entirely different term *aak*. One philosophically inclined collaborator I know consistently translates the word *ayamtai* as "house of self-reflection," thus making clear its symbolism as a ritualized space for visionary pursuits.

The translation of this second version of the tsaag anen directly links the ayamtai to the "path of learning." The reference to paths again is not merely metaphorical. The actual physical shelter does indeed lie at the end of a path cut through the forest; thus, the mental associations between paths and questing for vision are much more than the products of poetic imaginations. They are reflected in the actual material movements of people through the landscape of Aguarunia that I have already described as a complex network of paths. The point is that paths are invested not only with social, genealogical, and territorial meaning but also with a deeply sacred significance. When I have asked young Aguaruna artists to illustrate the vision seeker in the ayamtai, the appearance of the path that leads one there is a prominent part of the depiction (see Figure 3).

The ritual consumption of baikua, the most powerful hallucinogen used, requires the oversight of a caretaker, usually a father or other male relative with the necessary combination of know-how and responsibility. While continuing his fast, the seeker builds an ayamtai and prepares mentally to endure the plant's effects. The caretaker's presence may be necessary in order to instruct a younger vision seeker in the appropriate procedures. But the guardian's most important duty is to watch over the seeker and protect him from harm. This might mean protect against potential animals. Or it might mean protect the vision seeker from himself as the radical state of altered consciousness that results from in-

Figure 3 Vision seeker in an ayamtai. Drawing reproduced with permission of
Linder Gomez Juep.

gesting baikua can sometimes lead to self-destructive behavior. The plant is so
powerful that it can render a person unconscious in a matter of minutes. Later
the person begins talking, gesturing, and walking around, seemingly unaware
of his own actions or those of others around him.[6]

To give baikua its full effectiveness and call the ajutap's attention to one's
intention to ingest it require reciting the appropriate anen. To prepare baikua
for consumption, one must cut several pieces of the stalk, each about five or six
inches long. While he scrapes the stalk and watches the pieces fall onto a banana
leaf, the seeker will sing:

1 I'm not drinking baikua. [repeats]
2 I, I, I, I,
3 It's the enemy's bone
4 That I am scraping, that I am scraping. [repeats]

Conjuring up an image of the femur, the singer imagines he is shaving off the bone fragments of the enemy he plans to confront and defeat (see Figure 4).

After scraping the stalk of baikua, he mixes the shavings with a bit of water in a small clay bowl and then begins to shape the shavings together into a small round mass, molding it into a ball and squeezing out the juice over the bowl. The anen continues:

1 It's the enemy's head
2 That I am molding, that I am molding. [repeats]
3 I, I, I, I,
4 It's the head of the murderers who killed my kin
5 That I am breaking
6 And dropping into the little round bowl. [repeats]

Here, a metaphor relates the wet mass of baikua shavings to the enemy's head that the singer symbolically massages into a shape of his own choosing (see Figure 5).

Figure 4 Scraping the enemy's bones. Drawing reproduced with permission of Linder Gomez Juep.

Figure 5 Molding the enemy's head. Drawing reproduced with permission of Vossler Juep Cahuaza.

The reference to murdered kin provides the seeker with his motive for pursuing effectiveness in future conflicts and campaigns of revenge he imagines.

The remainder of the song seeks to gain the attention of the capricious grandfatherly spirit, grantor of the warrior's vision.

1   I, I, I, I,
2   Toward the inevitable destiny of finding my grandfather [i.e., ajutap]
3   I am shouting. [repeats]
4   It's the enemy's bone
5   That I am scraping. [repeats]

Obviously, this particular song also reveals the occasionally morbid imagination found in Aguarunia. He who consumes baikua also consumes the bones of his enemy. The intersubjective relation between self and enemy is held together by metaphors of cannibalistic consumption. After all, hunting game is not unlike hunting down one's rival. And the aggressive act of eating is not unlike consuming the enemy's bones, an effort to devour the source of his strength and diminish his chances of resistance.

The logic of cannibalism, implicit in warfare and the vision quest, goes much deeper with the plant baikua since this plant in particular is in fact synonymous with the legendary warrior, giver of social norms, and Socratic philosopher known as Bikut (see Brown, 1978; Chumap Lucia and Garcia-Rendueles, 1979). In fact, Bikut's name is often used as a synonym for baikua, sometimes in reference to specific varieties of the plant and occasionally for the entire species. Fully appreciating the importance of baikua to becoming a visionary warrior thus necessitates an understanding of Bikut.

Bikut was born a relatively normal boy. Still innocent from sexual impurities and at his father's insistence he began to "follow the path" and pursue his own ajutap vision with the plant baikua. The father's original guidance soon became the adolescent Bikut's obsession. Emerging into young adulthood, he demonstrated an unmatched dedication to the ingestion of baikua in search of more and more powerful visions. History has it that he took baikua so many times that he one day simply stood up and in a moment of profound self-realization declared to his family, "Chii! [an expression of realization] I converted into Bikut!" (Chumap Lucia and Garcia-Rendueles, 1979: 297).

From that point on Bikut became half crazed. He was consumed by aggression, so much that his family was forced to restrain him in the house by tying him to his stool. Bikut's baikua-induced dementia was, however, also the source of a unique and unbeatable warrior spirit. And it was this that transformed him into an incontrovertible and unforgettable historical figure known throughout Aguarunia. His visionary capacities allowed him to detect even the slightest violation of social norms. For example, he was able to simply sense when someone had committed adultery. And to most who saw him in military action, he appeared absolutely invincible in battle.

Bikut's rage symbolizes not merely the purity of vision notable men seek but embodies the material character notable men aspire to possess. This is clear from the fact that Bikut's bones are what most remember about him. In life his bones became so hardened from ingesting baikua repeatedly that they began to click and grind when he walked. In his death—which was brought about after a large enemy army was amassed for the express purpose of killing him—his bones fruit two varieties of baikua. They shot up through the earth from his grave. And it is precisely those two varieties of baikua that his Aguaruna descendants now ingest for themselves.

Baikua is thus considered the purest medium for gaining access to the authoritative self-empowerment offered by the ajutap and other visionary experience. It is the purest because it is the one Bikut himself so religiously consumed and by consuming eventually became. The idea that baikua hardens the bones and strengthens the physical person is commonly understood as one of its primary properties. To have strong bones these days, one must consume the strong bones of Bikut.

But Bikut was more than just a warrior and expert in the art of becoming one with baikua. As a visionary, he was also a lawgiver. While tied down in his house, he began to dictate a body of social norms and prescriptions that he told all those whom he encountered to follow. In everyday discourse his name is frequently uttered as part of a preface to giving someone advice about proper behavior. Thus, any sentence that begins "*Bikut tawai*..." (Bikut says...) often continues with some sort of counsel intended to make sense out of a difficult situation, offer a warning about bad behavior, or comment on the proper social etiquette. Working through an assistant and translator, I collected a long list of more than sixty kinds of advice, stated moral norms, and predictions about the future attributed to Bikut. We consulted with four older men and one elderly woman. See Table 1 for a small selection of each from the different categories established by my collaborators.

Some versions of Bikut's life, including those documented in the 1970s by bilingual Aguaruna teachers, say that the army that killed Bikut was not a rival Aguaruna faction but a group of apach (see Summer Institute of Linguistics, 1978: 94). As some of Bikut's warnings make clear, he is often cited as having predicted the generalized state of conflict and confusion Aguaruna activists attribute to their experience with neocolonial assimilation into the Peruvian nation-state and the broader world. Salomon Katip, an elder, once remarked to me that this prediction shows Bikut's extraordinary ability to see into the future of Aguarunia, into their contemporary condition of indigeneity. Bikut knew, Salomon insisted, that the path they are on would lead them to what he, quoting Bikut, called "a stage of impurity."

This is what is most intriguing about his life and teachings. Bikut spoke not only to and of Aguarunia but also of and to mestizo society. Here we must take the meaning of mestizo in the broad Aguaruna sense of apach and a world that is in constant contact with but also beyond the metaphorical bounds and material boundaries of Aguarunia. This is, in fact, what the extraordinarily multivalent term *apach*—ancestral spirit, things that invoke awe, things that

Table 1 Bikut's laws and advice

Bikut tawai	Bikut says
Nuwa	Women (according to men):
1. Nuwa ajanúm wéu dijigmájuk maénun inajúk ayúgtamjume.	1. Don't marry a woman who doesn't know how to manage a garden.
2. Nuwa wájej datsátaijum jukiígpa.	2. Don't marry a widow if you are a young man.
3. Nuwaj kugkugtií bayáiji kujájaigpa wáimakchaijum.	3. Never inhale the scent of a woman because you won't become a visionary warrior (waimaku).
4. Nuwem senchi suwimaáwaigpa.	4. Don't brutally beat your wife.
5. Nuwa pataím nuwatkámu dijijaígpa.	5. Don't have sex with a woman if she is married to one of your relatives.
Yawaa	Dogs
1. Yawáa suwimaáwaigpa.	1. Don't beat your dog.
2. Yawáa ijápakmaunum ayaúmkam yuwáwaigpa.	2. Don't eat near dog shit.
Yuwamu	Eating
1. Yúwa yúwakjuamesh áyaj wéegpa.	1. Don't be a glutton.
2. Shiíg inajuam yuwátajum (atash, kúchi, tíkich néje aidaushkam).	2. Cook things well-done (chicken, pork, and all other meat).
3. Nijamanch akakáj ampigmáu uwájaigpajum.	3. Never drink leftover manioc beer (i.e., that's left over in a serving bowl).
Magkagtin	Killers/killing
1. Mántamuk maátajum.	1. Kill the one who killed you.
2. Magkágtin kakajam yuwamunum uchi pachiínak yuwáwaigka.	2. Don't let children eat near where a killer is eating.
3. Magkágtuamek intashím tsupíkam.	3. Cut your hair after killing someone.
Tsuwamat	Curing/health/well-being
1. Jéen agaágmeskam siig japimkájum pujustaájum.	1. Live well by sweeping both your garden and your house.
2. Jíi ikapaájam daweam kanágtajum.	2. Sleep with your feet next to the fire.
3. Datem tsaag nampíchin kajeawai, baikua ukunchin ikatsuawai.	3. Datem and tsaag kill worms; baikua strengthens bones.
4. Waís yukumpitajum.	4. Drink wais (a purgative).
Intimat	Overstepping your bounds
1. Muun chichaamu tsujigkaipa.	1. Don't interrupt when an elder speaks.
Etsegkamu	Warnings
1. Apach waigtin ainagme nua nui shupaajúktin ainagme nuanuiyai átum tajiaja batsámsashtin tujash nuunu pújusum yantsaptin waigtin ainagme.	1. Someday [the Aguaruna] will convert into mestizos and arrive to a state of putrefaction [or "all go to shit"; shupa = shit], but later they will come to know purity.

NOTE: Translations by Mamais Juep Cahuaza.

are old, things that are new, power that we aspire to, power that oppresses us, mestizo migrants in our midst, foreign anthropologists that come to visit—implies. It is no accident that contemporary Aguaruna who recite Bikut's life story or recall his words of counsel compare him with the best prophets that the world imposing itself on Aguarunia has to offer. Comparisons of Bikut to Jesus, Buddha, and Socrates abound among those who seek to understand how it is he could be Aguaruna and yet still know so much about the present state of Aguarunia's critical encounter with apach society.

Bikut represents substantially more than the model of masculine authority to which every visionary warrior aspires within Aguarunia. He also provides a vision of clarity for how to imagine that which is beyond the material places and mental spaces of Aguarunia. He is both a conduit to a customary indigenous past and a vision of how to customize indigeneity in the future. He presages the conflicts, the confusion, and the confrontations that contact with a mestizo world in contact with Aguarunia entails. He also offers clarity about a path that leads past such circumstances. His ability to articulate this simultaneity of backward and forward vision is what makes Bikut perhaps the best symbol for Aguaruna activists' expressly political projects for customizing indigeneity. And it is toward that site of analysis—where the logics become a politics of customization—that the next path leads.

. . . Another Path Between . . .

The following is a transcription of a *nampet*, a genre of Aguaruna song sung during manioc beer parties and always accompanied by a dance. This song is said to have originated somewhere in the Nieva River region, but the original author is unknown. Adolfo Juep sang this version.

1	Janu yama yajanu (3 times)	1	(standard melodic prelude/ interlude to any men's song)
2	Policía minawai,	2	A policeman is coming,
3	Policia minawai,	3	A policeman is coming,
4	Policia minawai.	4	A policeman is coming.
5	Policia asaikaj,	5	When you are a policeman,
6	Yajamach umuchtai ayi,	6	Since you never drink manioc beer,
7	Yajamach umuchtai ayi,	7	Since you never drink manioc beer,
8	Tsabau namugsatajum.	8	Have them make you banana juice.
9	Tsabau namugsatajum.	9	Have them make you banana juice.
10	Tsabau namugsatajum.	10	Have them make you banana juice.
11	Wii chichachastajai.	11	I am going to speak.
12	Wii chichachastajai.	12	I am going to speak.
13	Wii chichachastajai.	13	I am going to speak.
14	Tutit chicham awaitkuish,	14	Even if there are problems to resolve here,
15	Chicha pujatsapita.	15	I'm not causing problems.
16	Chicha pujatsapita.	16	I'm not causing problems.
17	Kutag aputustajum.	17	Give him [the visiting policeman] a bench to sit on.

18	Kutag aputustajum.	18	Give him a bench to sit on.
19	Kutag aputustajum.	19	Give him a bench to sit on.
20	Tusa wajainak,	20	In this way,
21	Pegkejan igku igkunmamas,	21	Elegantly grouped together,
22	Zapatin wegamaju ijunas,	22	With their nice shoes,
23	Takeg takeg, takeg takeg wajainakui.	23	They [the policeman's hosts] make the sound "takeg takeg" [onomatopoeia for drum sound accompanying song/dance].
24	Wii policia tabaun niimakman,	24	Looking at myself as a policeman,
25	Wantauchin nugkuasa wainmakan,	25	And seeing myself dressed with ragged clothes,
26	Datsajan dujiuchik kutugkaja	26	Ashamed with my nose all loosened [a phrase indicating embarrassment, perhaps akin to "with my tail between my legs"]
27	Ukuiniajan ekeemsabiajai.	27	That's how I felt sitting there

Site III   Politics of Customization

From Schools of War to Schools at War
Bilingual Education and Becoming Indigenous

> *Words on paper have revolutionized Aguaruna life.*
> Summer Institute of Linguistics, *Twenty Years*, 1966

Arrival at Site III: On the Politics of Customization

What could be the significance of the path between Sites II and III? There we find an Aguaruna man musically imagining himself as a policeman who has come to visit his kinfolk downriver. Even as he sings the masculine refrain "yama yajanu," he swears off manioc beer. Even as he envisions himself with this incipient sense of governmental authority, his policeman's vision is cut short by recognizing the inadequacies of his own apparel. Perhaps one might interpret it as a reference to Aguarunia's entrance into its modern condition of indigeneity. This then begs the question of when that condition began. From the point of view of a contemporary Aguaruna listening to the policeman's song, the answer is fairly clear: sometime during the twentieth century. His preference for banana juice over manioc beer immediately conjures up images of missionary education that began in the early decades of the past century. Faced with a crowd of kinfolk wearing nice shoes references a set of consumerist desires that followed from that missionary education.

Surely the unspecifiable global time of indigeneity didn't start in the early decades of the twentieth century. This is particularly true if, as established in Chapter 1, the idea of indigeneity is predicated on an abstract contrast to the equally abstracted notion of modernity. Any purported theorist of modernity would depict it as having roots that go much deeper than the early 1900s. And those academics who work on the history of the Jivaro and their interactions with Spanish colonialism no doubt would be forced to push these dates back several centuries. Anne Christine Taylor (1994) in particular has done an admirable job of reconstructing the Jivaro past and its various engagements with and disengagements from colonial operations. Perhaps even more important, she has demonstrated that the purported rootedness of the Jivaro in the Amazonia of today is in part a product of a largely forgotten era. Jivaroans in what is now Ecuador lived in those regions now known as the Andean highlands. But they were either pushed out or decided to retreat to less accessible jungle terrain as the colonial frontier expanded.

Despite these academic versions of how they got involved in these concentric layers of indigeneity to become Aguaruna, Jivaroan, and Amazonian, the Aguaruna activists I work with operate with a different periodization scheme. From their point of view their experience with today's indigeneity really begins at the outset of the twentieth century. The early decades of the century mark an entrance into indigeneity in its contemporary form and thus the beginnings of their contemporary projects to customize it. In other words, they remember and recount their history from then until now as part of an ongoing indigenous present that they are in many ways still experiencing. It is made up of an extended confrontational encounter with an apach world that simultaneously surrounds and intrudes into Aguarunia.

The crucial point is that Aguaruna activists tend to portray the period before the twentieth century as a period of successful rejection of their entrance into apach society. Indeed, they often conceptualize it as a period of absolute resistance to the modern condition of indigeneity now imposed on them. Thus, academics trained in the methods of reconstructing history from the archives are bound to construct a version of Aguaruna, Jivaroan, and Amazonian history differently. But my purpose here is to listen attentively to the version of history told by Aguaruna activists themselves. And from their point of view people living in Aguarunia before the twentieth century were not yet really in the position of having to get accustomed to the conditions of contemporary indigeneity and thus not yet in need of purposefully customizing it in the way they do today.

Consider, for example, a statement made by Evaristo Nugkuag, a longtime Aguaruna leader who was present at one of the follow-up meetings to discuss my research with local representatives in 2003 (see the Epilogue). He began his commentary by distinguishing the Aguaruna's role in Peru and, by extension, the broader postcolonial world: "The Aguaruna and Huambisa people have had a different kind of strength than other indigenous peoples in Peru. Because of that neither the Inca nor the Spanish conquered them. That is the pride that all of the Aguaruna have, men and women, children, from every generation." Or consider this rendition of the Spanish colonial encounter written into a recent thesis coauthored by Alfonso Chavez Kuja and Cesar Sanchium Kuja (n.d.: 17), two young Aguaruna finishing their bilingual pedagogical training:

> The most serious danger appears with the Spanish conquest in 1549 with the foundation of Jaén de Bracamoros and then with Santa Maria de Nieva in which reducciones are established. The Aguaruna together with the Huambisa and the extinct Bracamoros offer serious resistance to the Spanish penetration.

There are two remarkable things about these general kinds of commentary from Aguaruna activists and intellectuals about the distant past. The first is that they tend to represent the Aguaruna as stalwart allies of other Jivaroan peoples, most prominently the Huambisa. In short, they tend to rely on a narrative of not only Aguaruna resistance to colonialism but Jivaroan resistance more broadly. As such, they operate on the idea that the Aguaruna are intimately connected to or indeed simply are also Jivaro at heart.

The other intriguing aspect of such accounts is that, except for Taylor's (1994) more recent and better-documented history, Aguaruna activists' and intellectuals' rendition actually corresponds quite well to several older anthropological accounts. Earlier accounts of Jivaroan history also depict them as successful resistors to the imperial projects of both the Inca and the Spanish (Brown, 1984; Harner, 1972). Thus, there is not nearly as much distance between Northern academic versions of Jivaroan history and those of my Aguaruna activist colleagues as one might think, and in fact, they are likely closely related.[1] In any case, the widespread understanding is that since they were part Jivaroan, Aguaruna from prior centuries lived in a time that is so remote as to constitute an entirely different era. Living in a different era means living in different conditions, ones that are unmistakably different from the condition of indigeneity today. These days what matters is not what happened before the onset of indigeneity but what has happened since.

Unlike this recollection of a bygone era of Incaic and Iberian imperialism, Aguaruna activists represent more recent campaigns of resistance with considerably more detail. They do so in ways that recognize the kinds of ambivalent confrontations entailed in getting accustomed to and beginning to customize indigeneity. Consider, for example, Adolfo Juep's recollection of a rebellion of Aguaruna (and possibly Huambisa) from the Upper Marañón River area against the rubber traders who established outposts there at the end of the nineteenth century:

> Before [my father] was born, there was a conflict in Marañon with the mestizos, with the mestizo merchants that bought rubber latex, that bought animal skins, that bought gold. . . . Anyway, according to the story, it is said they [the mestizos] abused the [Aguaruna] married women, the girls, and they brought diseases. . . . The Aguaruna could not take it anymore, and they rebelled. . . . In that era the region was managed by valiant war leaders [kuraka]. An Aguaruna war leader commanded the Nieva River; there was another war leader closer, near Imacita close to the Marañon; over there on the Santiago River there was another war leader. . . . Everyone respected what the war leaders said. . . . So, the war leaders rose up, organized, and coordinated. They organized and began to attack the mestizos. They began to destroy. Some Aguaruna defended them [the mestizos], and they took them on rafts, sending them to Iquitos, and others defended them, getting them out to go toward Bagua. But they weren't able to defend all of them because it was an uprising of the Aguaruna army and they destroyed everything.

Juep's memory of this event is corroborated by the archive. The Peruvian newspaper *El Comercio* (1991: 159) reported on a large-scale attack carried out by Aguaruna on various rubber merchant posts on the Marañon in 1904. Two things are important to note about Juep's account. One is that he does not present the Aguaruna as if they were all united, all equally involved in building a single front of resistance against mestizo society. Instead, he forthrightly recognizes the role that internal fractures and ambivalent alliances played. Some Aguaruna attacked the mestizo merchants. Others defended them. In short, in this recollection the history of Aguaruna indigeneity is more reflective of what Aguaruna currently experience. And it is fundamentally different from the idealized representations of a unified Jivaroan past of full-on, effective resistance against Spanish and Incaic outsiders. It recognizes that contemporary life in Aguarunia is internally complex and involves a constant dialogue with the outside apach world. But it does not give up on the idea that Aguaruna still have something of their own worth defending.

Second, it is important to note his use of the Quechua term *kuraka*. During the Spanish colonial period kurakas were part of an Andean noble Indian class and served as imperial intermediaries for the more directly exploited Andean commoner class. Juep's use of the word in the context of our conversation— which was in Spanish—is significant for two reasons. People all over Peru, including in many parts of Amazonia, use Quechua terminology. As in the Andes or even the urbanized coast, they interweave it into Spanish conversations. Particular phrases and terms in Quechua thus serve as a kind of national lingo (if not language) in a way that no other indigenous terminology, and least of all indigenous Amazonian terminologies, can. The implication for the concentric layers of indigeneity in which Aguaruna actors find themselves is once again clear. Becoming Amazonian is in many ways inseparable from not being Andean even while the Aguaruna are frequently subjected to Peru's predominantly Andean-centric view of its indigenous history (see Greene, 2006, 2007).

Yet in this context Juep employs the term *kuraka* to refer to what in Aguaruna is known as a visionary or strong man warrior. This, too, is deeply significant. It implies that in Aguarunia visionary warriors are in some sense equatable to Andean kurakas. Although contextual historical differences abound, a certain logical similarity exists. Like kurakas, Aguaruna visionary warriors claim the entitlement to act as designated spokespersons for the groups they represent. And like kurakas, they stake claims on the position of interethnic intermediary, whose job is to critically engage the world of the apach, be they mestizo merchants, Andean migrants, gringo anthropologists, or whoever else comes down the paths that lead into Aguarunia.

Since I have now arrived at Site III, my objective is to narrate how Aguaruna activists describe their historical entrance into these concentric layers of Amazonian, Jivaroan, and Aguaruna indigeneity in Peru. More specifically, I seek to document the way in which they actively politicize that history and work purposefully to customize the experiences of indigeneity it imposes on them. I divide this history into three distinct, if still overlapping, periods in which an Aguaruna politics of customization becomes vital to their contemporary projects to customize indigeneity. I periodize the history in this way following my impression that many Aguaruna activists periodize it in much the same way.

I also seek to self-consciously reflect on how I have chosen to narrate each of these historical periods. In this and the following two chapters I devote the first half to detailing a customary modernization narrative of how the Aguaruna emerged within these concentric layers of Aguaruna, Jivaroan, and Amazonian indigeneity. Toward the end of each chapter I seek to disrupt that historical narrative by infusing it with examples of how Aguaruna actors customize this condition of indigeneity. In other words, I seek to juxtapose a dominant mode of historical reasoning with the subversive mode of historical action in which Aguaruna activists and community members are engaged. The first part of each chapter tells history as it is most often told—based on a combination of primary, secondary, and oral historical sources. The later part tells tales of how history is customized: through names and songs; native community boundary conflicts and indigenous consumerism; weapons that can kill and others that critique. Through it all Aguaruna activists search for new paths that lead toward a visionary indigenous politics.

The first of these periods I explore in the remainder of this chapter. It entails detailing how state-supported missionary education and its gradual transformation into a state-run pan-Amazonian bilingual education system became part of Aguarunia. This transition to an institution-based education also marks a transition away from debt-peonage laborers for rubber merchants. It marks a movement from being laboring indigenous subjects to becoming schooled ethnic agents under the tutelage originally of missionary educators and eventually indigenous intellectuals. Also implied is a confrontation of state-supported missionary educators seeking to capture Aguaruna souls and citizenship, and Aguaruna intellectuals looking to customize precisely that process.

The second period, discussed in Chapter 5, is best symbolized by the confluence of paths, roads, and borders that constitute the territorial realities and spatial imaginaries of Aguarunia. I document the political-economic effects of road expansion, territorial fragmentation, and the state's institutionalization of native communities' land titling in Aguarunia since the 1960s. Together these processes of spatial rearrangement gave rise to forms of state-authorized indigenous governance that Aguaruna actors at diverse levels also eagerly customize.

Finally, Chapter 6 explores how the Aguaruna entrance into indigeneity has come to entail a great deal of explicit organizational politicking and involvement in indigenous movements at regional, national, and international scales. Without question Aguaruna activists have emerged as some of the most vocal proponents of Peru's Amazonian movement. I trace this process back to the movement's roots in the late 1970s in order to demonstrate the different events and actions through which Aguaruna activists customize the self-organized indigenous authority they now wield.

El Pastor Gringo

In the early twentieth century Aguarunia was in the middle of a gradual military buildup in Peru's Ecuadorian border region, largely a result of increasing state attention to the centuries-old conflict with Ecuador. The border tension eventually sparked a brief conflict in 1941 that resulted in the failed Rio Protocol. After another long stalemate, and then another conflict in 1994/1995, Peru and Ecuador signed a Peace Accord in 1998 and finally demarcated the border. Essentially what this long history of border tension has meant for Aguarunia is a slow and steady militarization of the region and thus an arrival of the Peruvian state's monopoly on the legitimate use of force. It is yet one more thing to which Aguaruna communities, like their Jivaroan counterparts in southern Ecuador, have been forced to grow accustomed.[2]

The early part of the twentieth century also marked the expansion of a debt-peonage economy based on the extraction of rubber latex—a phenomenon that is familiar throughout much of Amazonia. It was in this context that a foreign visitor arrived in Aguarunia to leave an indelible mark on the forms of indigenous consciousness that inhabit it. Indeed, the arrival of this man, "the gringo pastor" as he is sometimes known, marks for many Aguaruna activists their first sign of a full entrance into the condition of indigeneity. Most remember him as the first of many incursions made by foreign missionaries who were hell-bent on pacifying what they viewed as some of South America's most savage Indians. The new visitor's name was Roger Winans, a missionary from the Church of Nazarene. He dedicated more than half his life to, in his own words, "a vision and a call from God to an unknown Indian community in the Peruvian jungles" (Winans, 1989: 7).

Roger Winans was born in 1886 to a poor family in Osawkie, Kansas. A devout evangelical, he traveled to Peru in 1914 to spread the Protestant faith to Catholic Latin America. After several years on the coast, during which he married Esther Carsons, his second wife, he turned his attention to Jaén in the Department of Cajamarca. At the time Jaén was a little provincial town about four days' trek from the closest Aguaruna settlement. There Winans made the appropriate contacts to visit Simon Cossio, a river merchant and labor boss said to be from the Andean town of Chachapoyas. Cossio migrated to the Marañon River to settle at Pomará in search of rubber latex, as did most of the other apach compatriots found in Aguarunia in those days. Winans first visited Pomará in 1923. He discovered that Cossio had an Aguaruna wife and, as a result of his incorporation into local kin networks, maintained an alliance with an Aguaruna strong man named Tsamajain (or Samaren). Cossio also actively exploited subordinate Aguaruna laborers, who traded rubber latex and animal hides for newly desired commodities.

In 1924 Roger and Esther Winans opened the first Nazarene school in Pomará with just a handful of young Aguaruna boys as students. After experimenting with the school and setting up a house in the area, they returned to the coast to gather supplies. They were truly surprised to return to Pomará and find a Jesuit priest living in the unoccupied house they had left behind. The misunderstanding was resolved promptly.[3] Tsamajain's brother-in-law, Shavit, complained of not having enough access to the goods that foreign visitors brought with them and thought the Jesuit looked like the better candidate for relocation (Winans, 1989: 38–43; Guallart, 1990: chap. 24). The encounter between the Jesuit and evangelicals was a sign of things to come. It signaled the early stages of an imposition of new "civilized" customs and their corresponding logics: profit margins, state citizenship, literacy, and the deliverance promised by Christian spirituality.

In 1925 Winans and his wife moved from Pomará to a creek just a kilometer away, where a few years later Esther "slipped away to be with the Lord" (Winans, 1989: 55). Her remains still lie buried in the contemporary native community Tsuntsuntsa, a world away from the midwestern prairie where she was born. Winans took a long furlough following her death; his Aguaruna recruits quickly abandoned the settlement built around the school he had started. But a few years later Winans returned with a third wife, as well as a married couple who were Peruvian converts from the coast. By 1938 Winans had relocated to a flat strip of land farther down the Marañon River and constructed a new school. The Aguaruna who followed him there called it Yamayakat, or "new town" (see Winans, 1989; Personel de la Iglesia del Nazareno en esa Tribu, 1946). And in the 1940s Winans solicited a title for Yamayakat from the Compañía Industrial del Marañon, a rubber company that held large concessions on the Marañon River during World War II. The title was in the name of the Nazarene mission, not his loyal Aguaruna subjects. But Winans's intention was to make it a reserve for his Aguaruna converts at Yamayakat. In fact, the Aguaruna who now live there still retain a tattered copy of Winans's original deed and map (dated September 22, 1947). I had the chance to see it in 2000 when I visited. José Lirio, chief at the time, remarked that Winans's map and deed served as the template that was later used to determine Yamayakat's territorial boundaries under Peru's 1974 Ley de Comunidades Nativas y de Promoción Agropecuaria de las Regiones de Selva y Cejas de Selva (hereafter referred to as the Native Communities Law).

Yamayakat was the site of the Aguaruna's first encounter with ideas of civic duty. A group of Winans's students were the first to solicit national-identity documents from provincial governmental officials—Chachapoyas in the northern highland Department of Cajamarca was the closest site for state paperwork at the time (Guallart, 1997: 125). By the 1940s, the Nazarene school at Yamayakat had produced a select group of Aguaruna who spoke Spanish well enough to become bilingual teachers. Daniel Dánduchu, Moises Inuash, Francisco Kaikat, and Silas Cuñachi are some of the best remembered of Winans's early protégés. At approximately age seventy-five, Inuash still kept active in Yamayakat when I was there. As Winans's former student and occasional laborer, Inuash remembers well what relations with Winans were like. In an interview, he remarked to me, "Since he was a missionary and evangelical, he bought this land for us out of pity." Yet that effervescent missionary "pity" established the conditions of possibility for later organized indigenous action. By no coincidence I think it was the Aguaruna at Yamayakat who launched the first effort to organize Aguarunia and with the direct guidance of Winans's disciples (principally Inuash and Dánduchu).

Winans's activities in the jungle did not merely expose Aguarunia to the teachings of the Bible, to their civic duties, and to the importance of reading, writing, and arithmetic. His everyday economic transactions and activities wove new values of materialism and utility into the idea of a "civilized" education. Winans (1989) never mentions it in his autobiography. But other experts recall that the gringo pastor was in fact a sales rep, involved in selling rubber collected by Aguaruna laborers to the Compañía Industrial del Marañon (Serrano Calderón de Ayala, 1995: 248–251; Guallart, 1997: 101). The Amazonian rubber economy had suffered an almost total drop-off in the second decade of the century when the British smuggled rubber seeds out of Brazil and used them to found vast rubber plantations in the Far East (Wolf, 1982: 329). But World War II made access to plantations in the Pacific an increasingly risky endeavor. Thus, an international political economy of raw-material extraction, wartime production, and hemispheric alliances connected Aguarunia with market commodities as mundane as raincoats and as significant as the parts for B-52 bombers used to defend the Allied Forces in Europe.

In this encounter the Aguaruna at Yamayakat learned an important lesson that their previous rubber patrons had deliberately failed to teach them. Winans taught them that through schooling they might gain a more advantageous position in the rubber economy and presumably market relations writ large. Hence, this revealing excerpt from Winans's autobiography:

> The Aguarunas were slow to see any advantage to education. They did not understand its nature. They turned away from books as "useless paper." One day I took an Indian boy with me to Jaén. We went to a store to cash a check and purchase dry goods for trade. . . . When I returned home, a group of Indians

wanted to see my book. I asked what book they meant. They explained it was the little book, a single page of which was sufficient to buy a mule-load of dry goods and a pile of silver. I showed them my checkbook. They asked the value of each page. I told them they had no value until I wrote on them. Then why didn't I write more? I tried to explain the need to have funds in the bank, but they could not understand this. *With this incident a new interest was created in learning.* (Winans, 1989: 52–53; emphasis added)

Money made paper not so useless after all. One might even say, invoking Weber, that Winans's Protestant ethic became the Aguaruna spirit of capitalism. Aguaruna educated in the ways of the apach quickly interpreted the skills of reading, writing, and arithmetic as a means to gain more control over and more direct access to money. Indeed, it was the means to grasping the very notion of market value implied in a commodity-based economy. Winans's lesson was clear: mastering the mystery of market value meant first solving the secrets of paper.

For the Nazarene missionaries the appropriate trade-off for providing Aguaruna actors with the skills and scriptures of Western civilization was giving up precisely those customs that create visionary warriors. The missionaries believed that all of Aguarunia was "plagued" by "beliefs and customs that . . . are infuriating because of an unreasonableness that sometimes borders on bestiality" (Personel de la Iglesia del Nazareno en esa Tribu, 1946: 51). Paramount was the missionaries' desire to repress what they believed was the most obvious sin: the masculinized will to visionary warfare and its accompanying practices. Stamping out the use of hallucinogenic plants was thus also at the top of the missionaries' list.

Winans left others in charge of the Aguaruna mission in the late 1940s and retired to the United States. His departure was virtually simultaneous with the entrance of two other proselytizing educational enterprises. These two competing powers, one devoutly Catholic, the other devoutly Protestant, proved to be immeasurably more successful in extending the reach of "civilizing" campaigns in Aguarunia. Both missions pushed their Aguaruna subjects even farther along the path Winans had first forged.

Los Internados: Enter the Catholic Boarding Schools

The Jesuits were the first of the two missionary powers to arrive in Aguarunia land as Winans was leaving. Following the 1941 border conflict with Ecuador, President Manuel Prado began to strategize to ensure that the territories in the disputed border zone north of the Marañon River, granted officially to Peru under the 1942 Rio de Janeiro Protocol, would remain under Peruvian control. The state began designs on a *carretera de penetración* (penetration road); this road, revealing as it was of the state's neocolonial plans, would start on the northern coast at Olmos, cross a low pass in the Andes at Porculla, and end at a westerly point on the Marañon River.

The plan also contained a social component. President Prado's studying at a Jesuit school in Lima led to his decision to grant the border area in northern Peru to the Jesuits as a new ecclesiastical territory (Guallart, 1997: 32). After centuries of political persecution the Jesuits were delighted to accept this offer. It amounted to a presidential pardon after the Jesuits' expulsion from colonial South America. Prado's government also offered the generous monthly budget of twenty-seven hundred Peruvian *soles*. Straddling the largely Spanish-speaking population around the city of Jaén and the Upper Marañon River region, the Prefecture was formally established as La Misión de San Francisco Javier del Marañon in the mid-1940s.

Crusading missions into Aguarunia in search of *los infieles* (nonbelievers) followed. Father José Martín Cuesta was the initial pioneer to venture down the Marañon and set up mission camps among the native population. During his first expedition in late 1945, Father Cuesta baptized and gave Spanish names to sixty children. He saved the adult Aguaruna he encountered for December 3, *el día de San Francisco Javier* (St. Francis Xavier Day). On that same day he marked the occasion by saying mass, planting the cross, and declaring his small post just the "beginning" of a Christian town that he decided to name San Javier de Chingusal (Cuesta, 1992: 98–99). Father Cuesta offered these Aguaruna men, women, and children at Chingusal more than their new Christian names and the promise of purer souls. He also gave them registered birth certificates: magical pieces of paper on which their new Christian names corresponded to civic identities.

In a report to his superior dated February 25, 1947, Father Cuesta recalled his first round of duties carried out at the mission post at Chingusal:

> The entire first day is spent getting comfortable. The Aguaruna quickly make me an altar from chingús [a species of palm] in the middle of the school to say the daily mass and to hang the images and pictures that I have brought. I sent them to cut three long tree trunks and in front of the school we raised three Peruvian flags. The Indians look at them with respect and admiration. The first

thing I do is show them all the things I bring them: images, pictures, clothes of various kinds, machetes, axes, salt, matches, needles, thread, buttons, safety pins, soap, mirrors, combs, rindónes [small musical instruments], medicinal pills, and knickknacks of all sorts. (quoted in Guallart, 1997: 85)

Much as Winans did with his Nazarene efforts, the Jesuit priest took it as his responsibility to familiarize his Aguaruna subjects with desirable commodities and the demands of a "civilized" nation on its citizen subjects.

After these preliminary explorations Father Cuesta decided to found a better-equipped missionary post on a major river. Under his direction, the Jesuits resurrected the colonial town of Santa Maria de Nieva in 1949, abandoned since the late eighteenth century (Cuesta, 1992: 162). The mission, located where the Nieva River empties into the Marañon, soon included separate internados for Aguaruna boys and girls. It also was an ideal location for a medical post to combat the recurring measles epidemics that contact with transient river merchants provoked among the native population (Guallart, 1997: 135–139). The small settlement quickly became a trading post. It was a home for labor bosses and a temporary resting place for the military assigned to the border region. The Jesuits were really just getting started when word arrived in Nieva in 1950 that a new gringo had appeared in Aguarunia and had started up his work at one of the fledgling Nazarene missions upriver (139).

A Surrogate Nation-State and the Birth of Bilingual Education

The gringo that the Jesuits heard tell of in 1950 was a member of the Summer Institute of Linguistics (SIL). This North American organization initiated contact with the Aguaruna around Nazaret on the Upper Marañon following two invitations: one from Roger Winans and another from his successor, Elvin Douglass (Larson and Dodds, 1985: 15). In 1950 Douglass wrote the SIL, essentially pleading for assistance:

We've had work among the Aguarunas for nearly thirty years, and we cannot see any results of a permanently desirable nature. . . . Our greatest handicap is our inadequacy as trained linguists. Without the aid of competent translators we cannot see how the work is going to be done. . . . We request translators be sent as quickly as possible to complete the work. Whatever our mission has in resources is at their disposal. We want them. We need them. (quoted in Hefley and Hefley, 1972: 171)

Douglass's plea for the help of translators would soon be answered. But for its part the SIL had much more in mind than to play the role of translators, much as it did throughout Peruvian Amazonia and many other Latin American countries. SIL was a new and more powerful missionary contender, an organization that from its inception operated with a dual identity. To politicians throughout Latin America where it got its start, representatives of the organization consistently introduced themselves as the Summer Institute of Linguistics. In Catholic Latin America, SIL's official profile was as a group of well-trained linguists interested in working with indigenous populations on bilingual education, translation, and community development. In the United States, SIL was directly linked to the organization Wycliffe Bible Translators, Inc. (WBT). The latter organization's name reflects the original motto: "To Translate the Bible in Every Language upon the Earth." Members of SIL diligently learned it at Camp Wycliffe in Arkansas as they prepared to spread the evangelical word to Catholic Latin America.

SIL was initially formed in 1936 when Cameron Townsend charmed one of Mexico's most famous postrevolutionary presidents, Lázaro Cárdenas (Stoll, 1982; Hefley and Hefley, 1981). With this clever Janus-faced strategy Townsend founded one organization with two profiles, an ideologically secular one for its foreign beneficiaries and a transparently evangelical one for his largely faith-based supporters in the United States. SIL raked in financial donations from all walks of life, ranging from good midwestern Christian families and universities (in particular, the University of Oklahoma in Norman) to major corporations like Standard Oil, Quaker Oats, and Belk (see Stoll, 1982; Colby and Dennett, 1995).

SIL expanded into South America (initially Peru, then Ecuador, Bolivia, Brazil, and Colombia) following World War II. And it was in the Peruvian Amazon they built their most extensive missionary transport-communication system. SIL's Jungle Aviation and Radio Service (JAARS) consisted of a fleet of amphibious propeller planes and a junglewide radio service. It quickly became one of their principal assets in negotiation with Peruvian state and private interests. JAARS was founded with support from the Reverend Billy Graham and supplied by the U.S. Defense Department. SIL offered its communication and air services to the Peruvian state as well as resource extraction corporations interested in quick transport to Amazonian provinces where there were still few roads (Colby and Dennett, 1995: 202–203). During the 1950s and 1960s it was not uncommon to see an SIL plane boarded simultaneously by a government prisoner in transport to a jungle penal colony, a native Amazonian teacher returning from bilingual education courses, a Peruvian soldier en route to a remote military outpost, and an oil company surveyor on his way to an exploratory petroleum site.[4]

SIL's rapid expansion throughout Latin America eventually culminated in a period of political crisis in the 1970s, revolving around accusations of conspiracy and, of course, *yanqui* imperialism. The crisis resulted in SIL's expulsion from Brazil, Panama, Ecuador, and Mexico (see Stoll, 1982: chap. 7). Despite similar moments of confrontation, particularly during the Velasco military regime in the early 1970s, SIL weathered the storm in Peru. As a result it still maintains an administrative facility in Lima despite constant talk of its having entered a "phasing-out" stage for more than a decade.

Its long-standing friendship with the Peruvian state began when SIL launched a bilingual education program in the 1950s specifically for indigenous Amazonians. In fact, their bilingual education efforts would eventually encompass virtually every minority linguistic group in Peru's Amazon. This was another crucial feature in making the Aguaruna, along with many other indigenous populations in the lowlands, specifically Amazonian—and thus *not* Andean.

Indigenous education in most parts of the Andes has a decidedly different history from what one finds in Peruvian Amazonia (see de la Cadena, 2000; García, 2005). Peru's early twentieth-century indigenista writers—from the Marxist José Carlos Mariátegui to the more folkloric José María Arguedas—were completely uninterested in Amazonia. They were so uninterested as to be more or less unaware it existed. This is in fact a form of systemic ignorance common among Peru's intellectual class and has much to do with the dominant role the Andes and, of course, the Inca play in Peru's national imagination. As a result, it also has a lot to do with why indigenous Andeans, and not indigenous Amazonians, have played such a central role in most Peruvianist social science (Greene, 2006).

Arguedas once proposed a bilingual education model for indigenous Andeans, but it was never widely implemented. In the 1960s SIL launched a few pilot projects with Quechua speakers, mostly in northern Andean provinces. But those, too, were short-lived experiments. Much more recently, following the trend of multicultural citizenship models found everywhere in Latin America, the Peruvian state has begun bilingual education efforts anew, at least in the southern Andean areas where Quechua is widely spoken. Yet, as García (2005) documents, Quechua villagers express a serious lack of interest and even actively reject bilingual education models. They associate the state's ostensible attempt to revalorize their language with a covert operation to continue excluding them from Spanish, which is the dominant language of Peruvian citizenship and thus social mobility.

The long history of bilingual education efforts by the SIL—acting *on behalf of* the Peruvian state—has produced something different in most parts of Amazonia. The result is that native Amazonians perceive bilingual education as the only kind of nationally institutionalized education that has ever existed, at least in the rural indigenous areas outside provincial Amazonian towns. This is unlike what occurred in the Andean region, where the history of Spanish-language education and state-sanctioned Quechua-suppression strategies stretches back centuries. By contrast, in most parts of Amazonia the education "system," implying a nationwide coordination and curriculum, has effectively been bilingual at least as long as a regionwide effort to establish a national educational infrastructure has been in place. This is true even though SIL, as the state's North American evangelical surrogate, rather than the Peruvian state originally implemented this Amazonia-wide education program. Thus, it was also SIL's bilingual education campaigns that instilled in many indigenous Amazonians the ideals of citizen participation at a regional level using a bilingual education model.

This long history of making Amazonians into educated bilingual Peruvian citizens began in November 1952 during General Odría's military government. The Peruvian minister of education released an official resolution to authorize SIL to begin a bilingual training course for selected Amazonian natives at Yarinacocha:

> That the purpose of the Government is to extend the benefits of the Rural Campaign to the jungle, where the tribes are isolated due to special geographic conditions of the terrain and to the varied linguistic characteristics of the ethnic groups;
>
> That in order to accomplish this objective it is necessary to prepare teachers, using natives who are literate and establishing a special type of school in which, besides teaching the essential elements of basic education, the students will be trained for productive work and taught the basic [cultural] norms of [Western] civilization [necessary for participating in national life], the concept of citizenship, and principles of hygiene; and
>
> That it is advantageous to make use of the experience acquired by the members of the Summer Institute of Linguistics of the University of Oklahoma

during recent years among the jungle tribes. (Larson and Davis, 1981: 393; bracketed remarks inserted by Larson and Davis in the original text reflect their intent to contextualize the original language of the document)

This select group of natives already spoke Spanish, and most had received some elementary school training. At Yarinacocha the SIL exposed them to an expanded academic curriculum that encompassed civic affairs, bodily hygiene, and vocational training in mechanics and carpentry. The short-term project was to train these selected natives to become bilingual educators and provide them with the necessary resources to set up bilingual schools in their home communities. With the bilingual teachers' help, the long-term goal was to convert as many Amazonians as possible into clean, committed, and Christian citizens of the emerging nation-state system. Drawing on linguistic expertise, SIL also entered into production of indigenous language primers, textbooks, grammar guides, and dictionaries in order to convert many of Peru's Amazonian languages into written ones for the first time.

The Catholic hierarchy recognized this threat to their smaller-scale missionary campaigns almost immediately and launched a campaign of criticism. The objective was to expose SIL's other side, its inherently evangelical premise. In fact, it was none other than Father Martín Cuesta, who founded the Jesuit mission at Nieva in the heart of Aguarunia, who registered the first public complaint. Following the announcement of SIL's initial training course for bilingual natives at Yarinacocha, Father Cuesta wrote an editorial in the major Lima newspaper, *El Comercio*, in which he openly accused the organization of being a machine for Protestant propaganda (see Cuesta, 1953). SIL's connections to North American investors also perturbed the Catholics, particularly the relation of mutual support maintained between Cameron Townsend, SIL's founder, and Robert LeTourneau, a U.S. investor (Stoll, 1982: 108). A self-made millionaire from Texas, LeTourneau made his fortune in the sale of bulldozers, jungle crushers, tree stingers, and other tangible instruments of capitalist, technological progress. He worked by the motto "there are no big jobs, only small machines" (LeTourneau, 1960: 259). When he was not selling heavy machinery or investing in development projects in Peruvian Amazonia, LeTourneau was giving talks in churches across the United States. His message was a familiar brand of corporate gospel guided by the idea that "God needs businessmen as partners as well as preachers" (1). It's no wonder that he felt compelled to respond when he received Townsend's call for help in simultaneously carrying Christ and capitalism to the Peruvian jungle:

> We still have to carry Christ to the jungle Indians . . . but we have another job, too. The eastern foothills of the Andes Mountains are being colonized by several hundred Peruvians. They have brought with them small schools and churches, and law and order, but they need help. They need your machines and your program. Mr. LeTourneau it will take them 50 years with hoes and axes to do what you can do for them in a year. (Townsend, quoted in LeTourneau, 1960: 258)

General Odría essentially ignored the Catholic complaints. Instead, he signed on to several development ventures with LeTourneau, including a colonization and oil concession scheme in the central jungle (see Stoll, 1982). Townsend served as liaison and translator.

SIL's first courses began in 1953 with just a handful of native students from the Piro, Amuesha, Cashibo, Aguaruna, Huitoto, and Bora peoples. But the program soon underwent a rapid expansion throughout the remaining years of the Odría government, the second term of President Manual Prado (1956–1962), and the first term of President Fernando Belaúnde Terry (1963–1968). In fact, SIL's state-sponsored bilingual schools in the Amazonian region grew by a factor of 10.8 between the years 1953 (11 schools) and 1966 (118 schools) (see Summer Institute of Linguistics, 1966: 50).

By 1974 SIL had carried out linguistic work on forty different languages and dialects in Peru. Peruvians in the Ministry of Education certainly played a role in approving the curriculum and providing funds for bilingual teacher salaries. But by the 1970s it was also increasingly clear that SIL was in control of all key decisions, effectively acting as a surrogate state in Peru's Amazonian area. SIL completely monopolized the role of intermediary with Peru's various Amazonian native communities (see Varese, 1972a: 136–137). Because of the long-standing lack of interest in the Amazon among Peruvian intellectuals, SIL also became the major, and in some cases the only, source of basic statistical, geographic, and cultural knowledge about the region and its inhabitants. There was a long domestic tradition of commentary about and study of the Andean and coastal regions, but Peruvians knew next to nothing about Amazonians at mid-twentieth century (Varese, 1972b; Greene, 2006). SIL was in a unique position to gather information and perform most of the standardizing functions associated with contemporary statecraft—acting as a North American surrogate.

SIL produced the first ethnolinguistic maps of the Peruvian Amazon, which were later used to construct the state's ethnic categorization of Amazonians following the passage of the Native Communities Law in 1974 (see Chapter 5). Equally monumental was SIL's Amazonia-wide project to convert oral languages into standardized written ones, a process that further reified the ethnolinguistic groupings with which the state and contemporary indigenous activists still operate. In addition to translating the Bible, they sought to produce comprehensive dictionaries and grammar guides for indigenous languages that are still in use in Amazonia's bilingual schools.[5]

The early primary school texts that SIL distributed in the bilingual schools provide an interesting picture of the future SIL envisioned for their school subjects. The symbols of nation and market and other representational artifacts of "civilization" are prominent. For example, in 1963 Mildred Larson (1985) published the first widely used textbook intended to teach Spanish to Aguaruna primary students (see Figure 6). It is replete with many drawings showing all the classic symbols of Peruvian nationalism (flags), civic education (the

Figure 6 Mildred Larson of the Summer Institute of Linguistics and Aguaruna boy. Photograph by Don Hesse. Used by permission, © SIL International.

schoolhouse), "productive" labor (hammers, saws), Western dress and hygienic standards (shirts, pants, shoes, soap, mirrors), and, of course, the fetishized tokens of the magical marketplace (money and myriad commodity items, some depicted in the form of mysterious, inviting packages).

SIL's economic projects with Amazonian natives intended to instill a sense of *desarrollo comunal* (communal development) and release the natives from the bonds of debt-peonage labor in order to remake them into petty entrepreneurs. The bilingual teachers inevitably occupied the vanguard position of this economic transformation since they possessed a new kind of knowledge based on numbers, papers, and market values that many of their elder kinfolk did not fully understand (Stoll, 1982: 122–123). The SIL's civic agenda began by helping the bilingual teachers become documented citizens and eligible voters. And bilingual teachers began teaching the students to sing the national anthem, salute the flag, and read a map of Peru, injecting Peruvian nationalism into a daily routine in a way most Amazonians had never before experienced.

Despite all its apparently secular social work and surrogate statecraft, SIL never lost sight of the vision that originated at Camp Wycliffe. By 1966 they were translating scripture into sixteen indigenous languages (Summer Institute of Linguistics, 1966: 48), and SIL fieldworkers assured that the bilingual school curriculum included daily Bible studies, which continued to anger the various Catholic missions (Stoll, 1982: chaps. 4, 5). Yet evangelization clearly was only one aspect of a much more ambitious project. The grand vision was to turn diverse and dispersed groups of indigenous Amazonians into God-loving, market-oriented, well-dressed, well-groomed, and documented Peruvian citizens. The plan was to fix their place in God's divine plan for an international system of capitalist nation-states.

Missionaries on the Warpath

There is no better way to illustrate the influence of SIL's program in Peru than to detail their deeds in Aguarunia. This indigenous population became subject to SIL's most extensive social experiment. The exponential expansion of Aguaruna trained as bilingual teachers, communities formed around bilingual schools, and native students served by SIL is astonishing in terms of the sheer statistical increase over a relatively short period of time (see Figures 7 and 8). In 1953 they started with one Aguaruna teacher in one bilingual school. By 1975 there were 133 Aguaruna teachers teaching in sixty-seven different nucleated "communities," most of which formed spontaneously upon the arrival of a teacher

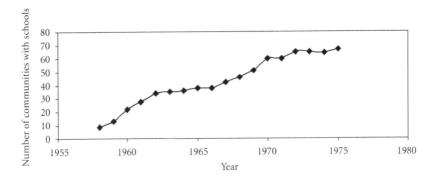

Figure 7 Aguaruna communities with SIL schools, 1958–1975. From Larson (1981a).

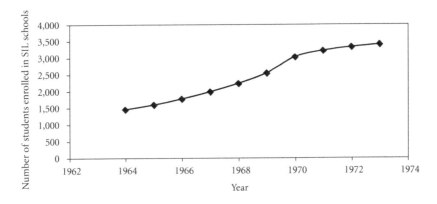

Figure 8 Aguaruna students served by SIL schools, 1964–1973. From Larson (1981a).

and construction of a school (see Larson, 1981a: 338). Together the Aguaruna schools represented more than a third of the SIL's entire jungle school system (Stoll, 1982: 159).

By the late 1960s several experienced Aguaruna teachers occupied supervisory roles in the bilingual education system, essentially replacing SIL personnel in some of their vital functions. Although this exponential expansion tells the tale of SIL's impact in Aguarunia in broad quantitative terms, the finer details allow us a glimpse into the complex nature of the transformation that was taking place.[6] Aguaruna activists commonly cite one of Roger Winans's young protégés, Daniel Dánduchu, as the father of their bilingual education experience. Dánduchu was among the first group of Amazonian recruits to graduate from the SIL training program launched at Yarinacocha in 1953. After completing his studies, he returned to the Marañon River and founded the first bilingual primary school in Nazaret. The following year he founded another farther downriver in Chicáis (Wipio Deicat, 1981: 73).

Winans's protégé was a natural choice for the educational revolution that was about to take place in Aguarunia. Mildred Larson and Jeanne Grover, the two SIL personnel in charge of the Aguaruna district, quickly realized that as a bilingual teacher Dándachu represented an entirely new kind of authority figure. "Dantuchu had not just become a teacher. He was also the proverbial 'doctor, lawyer, merchant, chief'" (Larson and Dodds, 1985: 55).[7] Chicáis, located on the southern bank of the Marañon River about midway between Yamayakat and Nieva, did not even exist as an Aguaruna settlement before Dánduchu's school was established (Morote Best, 1961: 308). A few years after the school opened, Chicáis was settled by dozens of Aguaruna families and had 140 students, enough to warrant five bilingual teachers and five dormitories to shelter those students who traveled from remote Aguaruna settlements (54). Aguaruna came from near and far merely to watch Dánduchu teach his Aguaruna students. He demonstrated to them how schooling would allow them to "talk to paper" (the more literal translation of *papi ausata*, "study"). It would also thus afford them a better handle on the custom of writing down numbers, weights, prices, and so on that seemed so essential to learning the customs practiced by the various commercial actors traversing Aguarunia.

In 1957 the Ministry of Education named a Peruvian, Efraín Morote Best, as the first coordinator of the Jungle Bilingual Education Program. Morote Best's leftist tendencies made him a strange bedfellow for SIL in some respects.[8] But his interest in folklore and his background as an indigenista intellectual made up for the difference. Morote Best became a public critic of the system of *habilitación* (debt-peonage) through which the *patrones* (labor bosses) exploited nonliterate peoples by forwarding merchandise and perpetually manipulating their labor debts. In 1957, under the guidance of Morote Best and SIL field personnel, Dánduchu organized an all-Aguaruna cooperative. The aim was to provide a fairer economic alternative to natives who collected rubber and animal hides and to help extricate them from their relation of perpetual indebtedness to labor bosses (Morote Best, 1961: 304; Larson and Dodds, 1985).

SIL and Morote Best also initiated a civic awareness campaign to expand native participation in civil government. Morote Best convoked assemblies in the new school-based settlements and taught Aguaruna community members how to elect mayors, sometimes also called community *promotores* (organizers). They held no official status with the state since there were still no formal land titles in Aguarunia. But the impetus to create civic leadership structures was clear. Mildred Larson of SIL witnessed one of these first electoral assemblies in Chicáis and marveled at the novelty it represented when contrasted to customary logics of authority:

> The idea of democratic leadership was totally new to the Aguaruna; they were used to a system based on power, fear, and supernatural forces. Thus, the idea of voting as a means of determining leadership was scarcely fathomable to them. When it was time to vote, the first name was read, and everyone's hand shot up. The second name was read—and every hand shot up again. The third name was read; again everyone voted. It took much more talking to get the principles of election across. (Larson and Dodds, 1985: 57)

The idea of a sole representative elected to each office, whose centralized authority is made possible by summing the wills of all the individual voters, was totally foreign. What we learned at Site I is that in Aguarunia a strong man's power is not the sum of the people's collectively articulated will. It is the result of his demonstration of being a notable and militarily successful leader. His success is dependent on his acquisition and practical implementation of a life-changing experience of visionary self-enhancement. In other words, a kakajam is not elected to lead. He searches for and acquires a vision. And then he just leads by practical example.

SIL's attempts to organize Aguaruna communities produced an immediate backlash from the other interested actors on the scene: namely, the river merchants, military personnel, and civil officials operating out of the burgeoning river port of Nieva. In 1958 these competing forces sparked a war spectacular enough to inspire *La Casa Verde*, the first major novel of the famous Peruvian author Mario Vargas Llosa (see Larson and Dodds, 1985: 59; Morote Best, 1961: 303). The incident started with a botched robbery of the Aguaruna settlement Urakusa on the Marañon. Suspecting military personnel to be the robbers, some of the affected Aguaruna from Urakusa captured and beat a Peruvian soldier. Unable to locate those directly responsible for the beating, a group of Peruvian soldiers, merchants, and a few rival Aguaruna from the town of Nieva retaliated. Upon arrival in Urakusa, they took prisoner a man named Jum, SIL's recently elected "mayor" of Urakusa. In Nieva's public plaza they tied Jum to a pole, cut his hair in an attempt to humiliate him, and tortured him by applying freshly boiled eggs to his armpits. All this while reportedly declaring that SIL's schools and Dánduchu's rubber cooperative were destined to fail.

Morote Best used the incident in Nieva to publicly reprimand the civilian officials who allowed it to happen and to humiliate the Jesuit mission for doing nothing to stop it. Father Cuesta was in charge of the Nieva mission at the time. And although he is liberal with his criticisms of SIL in his memoirs, he says nothing to address the scandal that Morote Best used to shame his mission (Cuesta, 1992: 266–271). Padre José Guallart (1997: 146), who later took over the mission in Nieva, accuses Morote Best and SIL personnel of wild exaggerations. He also clarifies that it was precisely that ordeal that led the Jesuits out of their complacent "distance" down the river from the North American evangelicals and directly into a full-scale competition. In Padre Guallart's own words: "In 1958 the missionaries of Nieva, seriously worried, decided they had to do battle with the SIL on their own turf" (147).

The ensuing battle between the Jesuits and SIL consisted of an epic struggle of one-upmanship all in an effort to become the more respectable Aguaruna patron. The Peruvian state supported the struggle on both sides. Following the scandalous accusations about Jesuit involvement in the public torture of Jum, Father Cuesta traveled to Lima and presented reports to officials in the Ministry of Education that compared the educational activities of SIL and the Jesuits. Ironically, he left with funding to create eight Jesuit-run bilingual schools from a different department within the very same ministry that employed his SIL-affiliated rival, Morote Best (Cuesta, 1992: 272).

At this point, the battle tactics of the SIL and the Jesuits began to mimic one another almost tit for tat. SIL solicited small plots of land for some Aguaruna settlements through the Ministry of Agriculture. The Jesuits soon followed by requesting land titles for Aguaruna living around Nieva (Guallart, 1997: 147–149). The Jesuits organized a rubber cooperative to compete with the one set up by Dánduchu (149). They also became more and more convinced that they had to refashion their entirely Spanish-language curriculum into a bilingual one so that they could more directly coopt Aguaruna intermediaries by employing them in teaching positions. By the time Fernando Belaúnde Terry reached the Peruvian presidency in 1963, the competition between the two bilingual school systems was at its peak. Before the war really began, there were only nine SIL and two Jesuit schools. By 1967 SIL was operating with forty-six, and the Jesuits, forty-two (see Guallart, 1997: 151).

New Leaders and New Paths

Despite their ongoing ideological warfare, the Jesuits and SIL shared one fundamental aim. They both clearly intended to expand the missionary pacification
campaign that Roger Winans had begun. As one Aguaruna author remarks, all
the missionaries actively discouraged the customary practices related to the use
of sacred hallucinogenic plants and vision quests (see Tii Ikam, 2000: 82).

Most contemporary Aguaruna activists I have met gloss over the biblical
"truths" they were being taught during this period. Instead, they frequently
emphasize the power of discovering what was hidden inside the written word,
in gaining an ability to "talk to paper." This is the skill that they believe released
them from the exploitation of labor-debt merchants and complicit military officials. And indeed, the Aguaruna becoming literate, and thus school oriented,
did irreversible damage to the system of debt-peonage. Gerardo Wipio Deicat,
career bilingual teacher and political organizer, reflected on the significance of
this transformation:

> It began when the Spanish-speaking outsiders told the Aguaruna that the land
> where they lived did not belong to them but to the "State." They used this as
> the justification for coming to work the land. They brought many things with
> them—guns, shells, cloth, mirrors, etc.—things which really impressed the
> Aguaruna. . . . Now at this time the Aguaruna were illiterate and did not know
> how to keep accounts. Thus, little by little the whole Aguaruna society fell under
> the power of the Spanish-speaking bosses because the Aguaruna went into debt
> to them. . . . The Aguaruna lamented, "If I could only read and write I'd know
> what my accounts really are! The boss is robbing me of my rubber and keeps
> asking for more." . . . Because of all these problems, some Aguaruna began
> thinking about studying. They realized that if they learned to read and write
> and speak Spanish, they could claim their rights and sell their products without
> anyone deceiving them. (1981: 70–73)

At the time, uprisings such as the 1904 expulsion of rubber traders were still
vivid in the social memory. But violent struggle and riotous rebellion became
increasingly less attractive and less realistic alternatives.[9] Finding themselves
in new circumstances, many Aguaruna were forced to face their desire for and
dependence on foreign goods. They were also confronted by a greater presence
of military power and civil governmental officials trickling into the region with
better firepower to impose the state's monopoly on the use of force. Learning
to read, write, and speak Spanish offered them a new kind of battle tactic and

one that didn't necessarily require violent confrontation or a simple retreat into the forest. The new plan was to take control of the very skills with which they were being civilized and convert them into weapons that would serve their own projects of customization.

Going down this new path, the path of talking to paper, produced a class of bilingual Aguaruna agents: not docile Christian subjects but politicized, inter-ethnically conscious agents of Amazonian indigeneity. The bilingual teacher emerged as a new kind of indigenous authority figure previously unknown. He acted as the principal intermediary between his kinsmen and the dominant society.[10] His powers of mediation rested on a linguistic capacity to speak both the native and Spanish languages. And he possessed skills that allowed him to manage the world of books, documents, maps, numbers, and financial accounts. Furthermore, his extended exposure to using money, buying and selling commodities, and earning and accumulating foreign goods was made possible by a teacher's salary (Morote Best, 1957).[11]

Striving toward ethnic consolidation among Aguaruna and interethnic alliance building with other Jivaro and other Amazonians meant appropriating the assimilationist project of the missionaries' pacification campaign and customizing it for their own political ends. The endogamous character of customary social and political relations in Aguarunia had to change. This forced many Aguaruna to rethink the complex interplay between the customary logic of corporate groupings (based on river location, allegiance to particular strong men, and close kin networks) and that group's relation to its distant enemies. Reducing hostilities among different Aguaruna factions and neighboring Jivaroan groups became one of the bilingual teachers' main tasks. Adolfo Juep, a second-generation bilingual educator trained by SIL in the 1960s, reflected on this change in an interview:

In about '48 or '50 SIL came to work [with the Aguaruna]. . . . In the Marañon SIL recruited the young people or the Aguaruna that had studied in the Nazarene school, in the school of the gringos. They were the first teachers because they had first, second, third grade, you know. The first teachers were the ones that spoke out about stopping the killing [among Aguaruna] because it isn't good, you know. A new doctrine. A new teaching. . . . From there the Aguaruna organization, the organized struggle [i.e., warfare] between Aguaruna declines and an organized [i.e., armed] struggle against mestizos declines too. . . . So, once this was lost, with the massive entrance of colonists in the Marañon there was only one idea left: No longer rise up with arms, but instead rise up with another type of strategy, you know. Because we couldn't confront the army or the mestizos because they are the majority, you know. . . . We could only defend ourselves by having a new structured organization, but based on education, you know, having a lot of people [i.e., Aguaruna] with postsecondary education that could direct the organization better.

Bilingual teachers' internalization of the need for a "civilized" form of politics made possible an entirely new kind of social and geographic mobility that broke with customary social relations and residence patterns in fundamental ways. Adolfo Juep's own biography is exemplary in this regard. He is the second-eldest son of a respected strong man originally from the Shimutas River, a small tributary of the Upper Marañon. After receiving his SIL training, Daniel Dánduchu sent Juep and his close cousin, Israel Katip, off to establish bilingual schools for the first time on the Upper Mayo River in the Department of San Martín in 1970. This small group of Aguaruna, genealogically unrelated to Juep and Katip, migrated to the Mayo River from the more remote Potro and Apaga Rivers (tributaries of the Lower Marañon), probably sometime in the 1930s or 1940s. When Juep and Katip arrived, these Aguaruna still lived in small river settlements amid ongoing feuds and occasional contact with a labor boss from the provincial town of Rioja.

Upon their arrival Juep and Katip set up schools, reorganized settlements, and in effect permanently relocated to the area upon marrying the daughters of the two most respected visionary warriors in the area (Pancho Cahuaza and Uwek). In the long run their arrival amounted to a kind of long-distance and peaceful—as opposed to war-related—mobility within Aguarunia that was virtually unheard of before bilingual education, a time when genealogical-cum-geographic distance was equated with entering enemy territory. In short, greater mobility and new forms of long-distance, pacific social commerce developed as a result of the emergence of a class of "career-motivated" Aguaruna. Originally this meant primarily bilingual educators. But it quickly expanded to include Aguaruna health promoters, community officials, indigenous organization leaders, provincial mayors, and many other Aguaruna actors who offered to Aguarunia their mestizo-like expertise.

This consciousness raising was simultaneously intraethnic and interethnic. Bilingual teachers from distant regions within Aguarunia routinely came together at teachers' conferences or in their classes at SIL's Yarinacocha base camp in the central Amazonian town of Pucallpa. Such encounters gave rise to discussions about the need to end hostilities among competing Aguaruna families and factions and create a pan-Aguaruna consciousness. It also gave rise to a much more ambitious political discourse about the need to create alliances with indigenous Amazonians near and far: those as close by as the Huambisa on the Santiago River, their Jivaroan cousins, and those as far away as the Ashaninka in Peru's central jungle provinces. Bilingual school units, around which sedentary and nucleated settlements formed, thus became the basis for what we know today as the pan-Amazonian movement.

SIL played a more significant role than the more isolated Jesuit operation in this construction of the Aguaruna's Amazonian indigeneity. SIL's entire program was founded on the idea of extracting those young, bilingual Aguaruna from their home environment for training ex situ. SIL relocated teachers in training to Yarinacocha, where many of them learned for the first time of other Amazonian ethnic groups. There they also learned to relate to these other groups as Amazónicos. As Gerardo Wipio Deicat (1981: 74) recalls, "With all this help from the government and from members of SIL, the indigenous communities are blooming in the midst of the immense green jungle. They are learning to know their brothers [hermanos]—other indigenous people who for centuries have lived in the same region without knowing each other." His choice of the Spanish word hermano makes the point clear enough. Yarinacocha was the place where bilingual teachers really began to think of themselves in terms of a grand pan-Amazonian indigenous fraternity. Indeed, hermano and, less frequently, hermana [sister] continue to be the primary terms with which indigenous representatives address each other in the context of Peru's pan-Amazonian movement.

Customizing an Aguaruna *Kritik*

The Aguaruna began to customize their own *kritik* to the more monolithic accounts of European empires, world systems, and geopolitical nation-states—and to the equally monolithic and monological alternatives to them. To the state-supported missionary project to civilize the indigeneity it imposed on them, Aguaruna actors responded with a project to customize a form of indigeneity that mocked the state's civilizing mission.

The process of customizing bilingual education began with seemingly ordinary aspects of life. Before the appearance of missionary schools there was no need for documentation to show individual Aguaruna students enrolled in a state education system. There were no individual rights and responsibilities expressed in terms of being nation-state citizens. The students had no birth dates and no surnames. These are both features of personal identification that have become so customized in apach society that we've lost sight of the way the state uses them to track a national citizenry and normalize things like property holdings, inheritance rights, and tax records (see Scott, 1998: 67–69). In the Aguarunia of the 1950s, these seemed like rather bizarre customs. Faced with ageless children, newly enrolled in bilingual schools, SIL personnel instructed Aguaruna teachers to estimate the student's year of birth based on height and arm length (Larson and Dodds, 1985: 65). Teachers then asked children's parents to specify the season (rainy or dry) in which the child was born in order to assign a birth date, typically either January 1 (New Year's Day) or July 28 (Peru's Independence Day).

Naming was also a problem in need of a missionary solution. Aside from a few whose prior contact with the Catholic mission or labor bosses resulted in taking on Christian surnames, the majority of Aguaruna individuals had only a given name or nicknames attributed by kinfolk. With the SIL's guidance the bilingual teachers invented an entirely new system for establishing family names. It was based on paternal and maternal lines of descent. Depending on how far back the person could remember, the person usually took the mother's or grandmother's proper name as a maternal surname and the father's or grandfather's name as a paternal surname, following the Spanish tradition (Larson and Dodds, 1985: 65). The result is that most contemporary Aguaruna now give their children Spanish or sometimes English first names but continue to pass on inherited surnames—which were originally Aguaruna first names.

SIL's naming method produced dilemmas that Aguaruna teachers often resolved by resorting to the Aguaruna sense of humor. The persistent use of kin terms as the primary terms of address in social contexts means that an individual's name is seldom used in the person's presence. Furthermore, a recently deceased relative's name becomes virtually unmentionable in the presence of the person's living kin, a coping mechanism to avoid the intense grief that follows a familiar's death (see Taylor, 1993). When asked to do so by SIL-trained bilingual teachers, some Aguaruna undoubtedly revealed their paternal and maternal names despite customary practices. But a significant number of these first names converted to surnames were in fact either humorous nicknames or meta-commentary on the peculiarity of SIL's effort to rename all the Aguaruna they encountered.

As an example, a common Aguaruna surname these days is Entsakua. It derives from the verb *entsát*, meaning "to carry on one's back." According to several accounts, the original man from whom this surname derives was given this label as a nickname. He earned it because of his habit of carrying his lover on his back for their secret rendezvous in the forest. This was his clever strategy to leave just one set of footprints on the forest path and hence to avoid detection by her jealous husband. The surnames Atsatsua and Dánduchu are two more humorous examples. Atsatsua derives from *atsau*, which means literally "there isn't one." This, too, is commonly supposed to be the result of an inside Aguaruna joke. According to the story the man who originally inspired this surname was asked by a bilingual teacher to identify his most distant paternal ancestor. Exhibiting the genealogical forgetfulness common in Aguarunia, he is said to have replied simply "atsau," implying that he didn't recall any distant ancestors. In need of an answer and eager to move down the line, the bilingual teacher laughed and simply recorded the man as "Sr. Atsatsua," or "Mr. There Isn't One." The last name of the famous bilingual teacher Daniel Dánduchu has a similarly ironic story attached to it. Dánduchu derives from a negated form of the word *da* (name). Translated literally, it thus means something like "Mr. No Name."

Several generations have passed, and inheriting surnames is no longer a problem for the Aguaruna. It's just one more "mestizo custom" to which they have become accustomed. After generations of inherited usage, these comical-sounding names—Mr. There Isn't One or the even more humorous Mr. Carries His Lover on His Back—sometimes provoke great laughter. This is particularly true in mixed linguistic contexts where Aguaruna speakers make inside jokes in front of unsuspecting Spanish-speakers. The Aguaruna laugh partly at themselves and the absurdities of apach customs they must now grow accustomed to. But they also laugh among themselves, which is the real point.

SIL's initiative to elect Aguaruna mayors or community promoters resulted in a similarly complex reconfiguration of customary authority. The first generation of bilingual teachers were also considered bearers of a strong man–type of authority. Such was the case, for example, with Alias Dánduchu (the brother of the more famous Daniel). He worked closely with Mildred Larson as an informant and teacher. Yet he was also a feared and respected kakajam in the Nazaret area, constantly struggling between competing ideals of visionary warfare and the war of pen and paper he imagined by more "educated" means (see Larson and Dodds, 1985).

The original generations of Aguaruna bilingual educators, something akin to Gramsci's organic intellectuals, were also known for their ability to approach the encounter with Amazonian indigeneity critically. And to find ways to customize it. What emerged from bilingual education was not complete assimilation but rather a complex process of negotiating a compromise. That again is what customization is about—the active attempt to negotiate a proper relation with a foreign set of customs and logics that imposes its own set and system of politically driven constraints. What emerged was an Aguaruna kritik forged through this conscious recognition that the encounter of competing customs entailed inherent asymmetries. Recognizing those asymmetries was the first and crucial step toward subverting the web of missionary-state power that was taking hold in Aguarunia. Getting accustomed to the demands of state and capital—via their neocolonial missionary surrogates—during the era of bilingual education led to the first widespread efforts to engage in the project to customize them.

This reminds me of a bit of humorous musical custom commonly heard throughout Aguarunia. The little ditty is (or was, until now) a nontextual but nonetheless tangible artifact of the ways in which the Aguaruna marvelously mold custom to meet new circumstances. This particular artifact is representative of a genre known in Aguarunia as nampet, a revealing word that simultaneously connotes singing, dancing, and the festive drinking that goes along with them at manioc beer parties that often cap off a collective work effort. In saying "nampekmi," one is saying "let's dance/sing/drink" all at the same time. Nampet do not share the secretive aspect and ritualized method of transmission that enshroud the more seductive songs known as anen (see Chapter 3). Instead, Aguaruna men—as this is largely a male genre—spontaneously invent them in the very act of public performance. Typically they consist of celebratory tales of personal exploits in war, love, betrayal, and adventure: a kind of exaggerated musical autobiography performed in front of an eagerly awaiting kinfolk public. A particular drinking song/dance that really catches people's attention might then become part of one's personal repertoire. On occasion it might even be passed down as a kind of family property to others who think it worth remembering or even reinterpreting into a performance of their own.

According to his contemporary relatives, the late Silas Cuñachi—Kuyach to those who know him by his Aguaruna name—first sang the following short nampet. Kuyach was a contemporary of Daniel Dánduchu and another of the Aguaruna's oft-mentioned pioneers in SIL's bilingual education program. But like many of his colleagues he was also more than an SIL-trained teacher. He was renowned for his visionary exploits in the fine art of war and an admirable defender of his family in the area around Nazaret. He is best-known for this song, passed on to me by his contemporary distant relatives:

1	Jaanu, jaanu, jaanu, jaanu	1	Jaanu, jaanu, jaanu, jaanu[12]
2	Jaanu, jaanu, jaanu, jaanu	2	Jaanu, jaanu, jaanu, jaanu
3	irigku wagachawash	3	I thought gringos don't get lost
4	timaijai, timaijai.	4	That's what I thought, that's what I thought.
5	irigkush wagamapiyi.	5	But gringos get lost too.
6	irigkush wagamapiyi.	6	But gringos get lost too.
7	agkamusa iyagmaijai	7	That's how I landed in Angamos [Ecuadorian military airfield]
8	agkamusa iyagmaijai.	8	That's how I landed in Angamos.
9	Ecuadora iyagmaijai.	9	I landed in Ecuador.
10	Kuturiano iyagmaijai.	10	I landed in Ecuador.
11	kuyachi, kuyachi, kuyachi	11	Hey, Kuyach, Kuyach, Kuyach
12	Ame jinkime chichasta tujutmayi	12	He [the SIL pilot] told me to get out and talk [to the military official]
13	Wii tsakagmauna juu takmayajai	13	So, I grabbed my identity document
14	Tseken jinkimiajai, tseken jinkimiajai.	14	And got right out, got right out.
15	Tuwiyampaitpa aya tujutkuwiya.	15	Then they asked me where I was from.
16	Awajuni apujitjai	16	I am the Chief of the Aguaruna
17	Timaijai, timaijai.	17	That's what I told him, that's what I told him.
18	Awajunish imauk aina?	18	What! The Aguaruna are that powerful?
19	Tujutmayi tujutmayi.	19	That's what he told me, that's what he told me.
20	Waamak weta tujutmayi.	20	Leave right away, he said.
21	Waamak weta tujutmayi.	21	Leave right away, he said.
22	Au apu pujanu, au antukagka	22	If that ranking officer over there hears about you landing
23	Aya aminaka juwi emetjamattam.	23	He will hold you and take you prisoner.
24	Aya tujutkuwiya.	24	That's what he begged me to do.

25	Ayu timaijai timaijai.	25	I told him ok, that's what I told him.
26	Yacha ishinu wajakmaijai.	26	As if I was an expert I started the plane.
27	Yacha ishinu wajakmaijai.	27	As if I was an expert I started the plane.
28	Chia, chia awagmamiag	28	And the engine sounded "chia, chia"
29	Chia, chia awagmamiag	29	And the engine sounded "chia, chia"
30	Irigkush sapigmamapi.	30	That's how I found out gringos get scared too.
31	Irigkush sapigmamapi.	31	That's how I found out gringos get scared too.
32	Irigku sapigmachawash.	32	Before I thought gringos didn't get scared.
33	Timaijai, timaijai.	33	That's what I thought, that's what I thought.
34	Jaanu yamayajanu	34	Jaanu yamayajanu
35	Jaanu yamayajanu	35	Jaanu yamayajanu
36	Bisagti, Bisagti, Bisagti, Bisagti	36	Bisagti, Bisagti, Bisagti, Bisagti [Kuyach's wife]
37	Bisagti umayi jakui, jakui, jakui,	37	When her brother died,
38	Saig shimpu jakui,	38	When my brother-in-law Shimpu died,
39	Wishigka mamiajai.	39	I killed Wishig [the suspected witch].
40	Yatsug kagkap jakui,	40	And when my brother Kagkap died,
41	Yatsug kagkap jakui,	41	And when my brother Kagkap died,
42	Wampuchana mamiajai.	42	I killed Wampuch [the suspected witch].
43	Wampuchana mamiajai.	43	I killed Wampuch.
44	Jaanu jaanu, Kuyachi, Kuyachi	44	Jaanu jaanu, hey, Kuyach, Kuyach
45	Kuyach imanapame.	45	That's how Kuyach proves his valor.
46	Kuyach imanapame.	46	That's how Kuyach proves his valor.

Contemporary Aguaruna audiences are extremely receptive to the humorous criticism that SIL personnel (referred to as gringos in the song) along with gullible military officials receive here. More important, it helps them remember Kuyach as a man of vision and valor rather than simply a "mestizo-like" native teacher working at the beck and call of his gringo bosses. The Aguaruna accounts I have heard about the context surrounding this nampet suggest Kuyach authored it after a trip to SIL's base camp at Yarinacocha. Shuttling Kuyach back home in one of SIL's amphibious propeller planes, the SIL pilot apparently got disoriented by cloud cover. He accidentally crossed over into Ecuadorian territory, which following the 1941 border dispute was essentially enemy territory. To get his bearings, the pilot was forced to land at an Ecuadorian military base he spotted in the southern jungle (lines 3–10). The ongoing border tension between Ecuador and Peru made the SIL pilot profoundly nervous. In a panic, he handed the keys to the plane to Kuyach and pleaded with him to act as negotiator with the Ecuadorian military officials in the hopes they would take pity on and pardon an Indian. Kuyach agreed to play the role of spokesperson but not necessarily to the job of self-effacement. Instead, he exited the plane and summarily declared to an approaching Ecuadorian soldier that he was the pilot of the plane and the chief of the Aguaruna (lines 12–16). The soldier was a bit taken aback at the arrival of a plane piloted by an indigenous Amazonian from the other side of the border. He instructed Kuyach to turn the plane around as quickly as possible and exit Ecuador before his superior officer found out what was going on (lines 20–24). Thus, Kuyach returned to the plane and started it "as if he was an expert" (lines 26–27). Imagining himself as master of the plane, much like Aguaruna hunters imagine themselves as seductive masters of game while out on a hunt, he described the sound of the engine as "chia, chia" (lines 28–29). This is the same onomatopoeic noise attributed to jungle birds that shriek when they perceive a predator in their midst.

Just as impressive in Kuyach's masterful musical composition is the apparently seamless transition he makes in his autobiographical details. He goes immediately from remembering his exploits with an SIL pilot to recounting a series of war adventures he led to defend his close kin (lines 36–43). The adventure with an errant SIL pilot is just one among others in his life story, just one along the personalized path of visionary authority he was customizing for himself. Together, all these autobiographical tidbits—full of North American missionary pilots, Ecuadorian military personnel, jungle bird-planes, and family enemies— allow him to pronounce his claim to a visionary kind of valor (lines 45–46).

A master of an emerging indigenous consciousness, Kuyach implies some-thing extraordinary to his Aguaruna audience. Despite all their expert mastery of sophisticated foreign technology, "gringos get lost too" (lines 5–6). Not only do we gringos get lost, we "get scared" (lines 31–32), a jab at our inner fragil-ity, our apparent ineptitude, our sophisticated stupidity. In reality, Kuyach—an extraordinary example of the complexity entailed in Aguaruna projects of customization—is only one of many instigators of this arduous task: to cre-ate a space for Aguarunia within the space of indigeneity that was created for them. The revolution in words—this original conjuncture of paths and paper—unwittingly unleashed by Winans and then expanded by the SIL (and to a lesser degree by the Jesuits) was in fact only the beginning. Next on the agenda was the careful customization of Amazonian rights to native commu-nity land and the bureaucratized forms of communal governance that came with it, handed down as if from above by a revolutionary Peruvian state.

5   Paths, Roads, and Borders

The Fragmentary Logic of the Native Community

In 1999 the Dirección de Comunidades Campesinas y Nativas, the division of the Peruvian Ministry of Agriculture that oversees Andean and Amazonian communal land titling, released the *Directorio de Comunidades Nativas del Perú.* The *Directorio* is a compendium of information, including date of inscription, geographic location, and territorial extension, on the more than forty distinct ethnolinguistic groups that the state recognizes as holding communal territories known as native communities. The Peruvian state first created the native communities institution in 1974 with the ratification of the Native Communities Law, which was articulated as part of a broader "farm promotion" legislation.[1] Yet the native community tenure system was based on the preexisting model of Andean communal land rights legislation, which dated to the 1920s indigenista era of President Leguia.[2] In the Andean region (and certain areas on the coast) communal titles were granted to *comunidades indígenas* (indigenous communities) until 1968, when General Juan Velasco changed the name to *comunidades campesinas* (peasant communities). At the time when native community titling began in Amazonia, most indigenous groups were still oriented toward hunting and slash-and-burn agriculture. Thus, the fact that the state originally granted Amazonians native community land rights as part of a farming-oriented legislation makes the influence of the Andean template all the more clear. The state's granting native community titles to these hunter societies more or less mandated that the Andeans' agrarian past should become the Amazonians' near-term future.

As of 1999 the Peruvian state had registered titles for 1,175 native communities that together represent 10,503,889 hectares, roughly 13 percent of the selva, the only geographic region of the country where the native communities are found. It also accounts for 8 percent of the entire national territory for indigenous populations, which are estimated at around 500,000. By any measure this is an impressive turnabout from the almost total legal invisibility and complete lack of territorial recognition that indigenous Amazonians experienced just over thirty years ago.

After the Ashaninka, the Aguaruna population represents the second-largest ethnic constituency in the Peruvian Amazon. As of 1999 they held titles to 187 native communities, scattered across four geographic departments in the northern part of the country. Their territorial holdings amounted to 1,763,192 hectares. This area is larger than the state of Connecticut for a population that was calculated in the 1993 census at 45,137 people (an official figure that is by now very out of date). Unlike the state of Connecticut, however, the Aguaruna native communities do not form a completely contiguous geographic territory, nor is there a single governance institution that oversees them. Instead, as in all other native and peasant areas in Peru, the Aguaruna are divided into a series of individually titled and autonomously administered "communities." Some of these do share boundaries with other native communities to create small de facto blocks of contiguous native territory. However, a significant portion of native communities throughout the Peruvian Amazon are surrounded by nonnative settlements populated by poor agricultural migrants, small towns, national parks, or areas of open forest considered "free lands of the state." The result for the Aguaruna, as for most native Amazonians, is a series of decidedly fragmented territorial holdings and a de jure legal regime that considers each native community a self-contained, individual administrative unit.

As discussed in Chapter 4, the comprehensive scope of the Summer Institute of Linguistics' bilingual education operation, built in the two decades prior to the Native Communities Law, had already begun to radically change settlement and social patterns. The result was a trend toward nuclearization of dispersed indigenous households around bilingual schools and the appointment of community "promoters." Both of these antecedents played centrally into the way state-mandated native community norms became institutionalized. To examine this three-decades-old legislation and how it became a part of Aguarunia requires that we place it in its full historical context.

From Belaúndismo to Velasquismo:
State Architecture and Military Populism

In October 1968, in what seemingly became a regional Latin American trend, a military coup ousted Fernando Belaúnde Terry from power and sent him into exile before he could finish his first term as president. Unlike leaders of the highly repressive military governments elsewhere in the region, General Juan Velasco Alvarado proclaimed himself the leader of the "Revolutionary Government of the Armed Forces," and the military state soon initiated the most sweeping series of economic, agrarian, and social reforms Peru has ever witnessed—although via tried-and-true top-down state politics. To understand the impact of such reforms, we must first become familiar with the atmosphere of Belaúndismo against which the Velasco regime acted so forcefully.

Fernando Belaúnde Terry, commonly called "el Arquitecto," first assumed the presidency in 1963 during the heyday of Cold War politics and Truman's post–World War II development triumphalism: the era of decolonization that would redefine nation-states within an emerging "new world order" of Firsts, Seconds, and Thirds (see Escobar, 1995). By the time Belaúnde held the reins to Peru's government, the logic of development had infiltrated every aspect of international relations. And Peru's internalization of its Third World "underdeveloped" status was well under way. Belaúnde's presidency is most often remembered in terms of his technocratic plans for a final "conquest" of Peru's ostensibly "empty" Amazonian regions (Smith, 1982). He planned to conquer the forgotten Amazon through the construction of a network of rural highways that would integrate Peru's tropical territories into the national space. His Carretera Marginal de la Selva project thus became the key factor in a plan to increase exploitation of the selva's natural resources. It was also proposed as an answer to the increasingly rebellious nature of land claims by the Andean poor. Highways down the slopes of the Andes and into the jungle would push poor Andean migrants east toward the Amazon, expanding the commercial agricultural frontier, and simultaneously ease Andean migration toward coastal Lima.

Belaúnde's role as nationalist ideologue and technocratic visionary was apparent by the late 1950s with the founding of his political party, Acción Popular, and the publication of his now classic book, *La Conquista del Perú por los Peruanos* (*The Conquest of Peru by Peruvians*). The title alone points to an undisguised cooptation of the language of conquest, reflective of a latent criollo

desire to finish the project of civilization by finally extending it to Peruvian
Amazonia, where it had never been fully realized:

> It is worth asking now, in the height of the republican era and the middle of
> a national and racial unity achieved by the common denominator known as
> mestizaje, a fusion of two cultures, if we as Peruvians have fully conquered our
> own territory. And the answer comes back negative. . . . The incorporation of
> the high jungle into the national economy—not just at one or another point but
> throughout its entire extension, from north to south—is the great battle that
> has still not set us free in the conquest of Peru. (Belaúnde Terry, 1994: 141)

Belaúnde's administration was not the first to "penetrate" the jungle with
roads funded by foreign capital and fueled by the dreams of an integrated
national territory ripe for international development. President Prado's projected carretera de penetración via the pass at Olmos and into the heart of
Aguarunia was the direct result of the 1941 Peru/Ecuador border dispute. The
real novelty of Belaúnde's idea was not in planning roads here and there but
rather in planning roads here, there, and everywhere. The plan laid out in
his book and later translated into policy during his presidency projected the
Carretera Marginal as a road network that would be simultaneously interpro-
vincial, interregional, and international. It would connect the low jungle with
the high jungle by means of strategic road-river junctures. It would connect
coastal cities with the Amazonian frontier via the Andean highlands. And it
would connect Peru with the rest of South America (see Belaúnde, 1994: 129).
And unsurprisingly in a country where the political elite has long been ob-
sessed with the Incaic past, the ancient and expansive Inca road system served
as Belaúnde's principal source of inspiration. It was as if the Inca—through
reincarnation in Belaúnde's criollo state—were trying to reconsolidate the ancient imperial corner once known as Antisuyu. This situation set Aguarunia
and many other Amazonian areas marginal to the Andes on a crash course
with poor Andean migrants in search of a plot of land. It also facilitated the
entrance of more and more extractivist corporations.

   However, Belaúnde's neo-Incaic-highway solution to Peru's development
problems was soon interrupted by a military coup. The military junta spoke,
or so it said, in the name of the people. Belaúnde's liberal economic policies in
the foreign oil–concessions arena and the regionwide popularity of anti-yanqui
rhetoric became the main factors in the military decision to oust him from
power. Thus, General Velasco began his very own "October Revolution" on

October 3, 1968. He ordered the armed forces to occupy oil fields on the coast and sent Belaúnde packing along with his foreign oil executive cronies. In reality what followed from the military takeover was a series of populist-oriented reforms that were not so much socialist in nature as corporatist, clientalistic, and state capitalist. The Velasco government sought to renegotiate the national terms for foreign capital investment, not to reject the premise of international capitalism altogether (see Hunt, 1975).

In the economic sector the Velasco regime nationalized significant parts of all the main industries, including oil, electricity, mining, fishing, and steel. The creation of the state's petroleum company, PetroPerú, became part of a larger push to further assert national interests over Amazonian territories that promised future oil revenues. Indeed, PetroPerú's discovery of petroleum deposits in 1972 on tributaries of the Lower Marañon River led to investment in the northeastern pipeline. Constructed in the mid-1970s before the consolidation of Amazonian land titling, the pipeline runs all the way to the coast, traversing Aguarunia and many neighboring ethnic groups' territory.

Although the spirit of "revolution" led to significant social reforms, most were implemented in a decidedly hierarchical form. The Velasco administration initiated at least three key programs for social transformation that had lasting impacts on Amazonians as well as Andeans and other marginalized populations. The first was a widespread land reform initiative that demolished oligarchic control over Peru's cultivable land in the Andean highlands and on the coast. One of the most significant impacts of the land redistribution efforts for highland and coastal communities was the official redefinition of "indigeneity." Citing the term's pejorative colonial origins, the Velasco state officially changed the name "comunidades indígenas" to "comunidades campesinas." This marked the culminating moment in the long, complex transformation of Peru's Andean peoples from officially "indigenous" people to officially "peasants" according to the state's purview (see de la Cadena, 2000). As de la Cadena and others have noted, this act of renaming is not exactly what it seems. In large part it reflected a logic that was already present in Peru in which the terms *campesino* and *indígena* both imply being an indio in precisely the pejorative colonial sense Velasco sought to overcome. In short, the ethnic dimensions of indigeneity and the class dimensions of peasant are so inseparable that, at least when used to refer to the Peruvian Andes, to become officially a peasant in no way allows one to escape the prejudices that come with being indigenous.

Since the Velasco era, Andeans have in fact represented themselves publicly and politically primarily as campesinos through the country's various peasant and agrarian unions—at least until quite recently. Alejandro Toledo's attempt to symbolically embody the returning Inca in 2000 to oust the corrupt President Fujimori has changed things a bit. So, too, have the state-led "multicultural" efforts the Toledo government initiated that have helped provide a political context in which the overt ethnic language of indigeneity is being revalorized. Certain emergent Andean social movements, particularly those rooted in environmental concerns, have begun to explicitly reindigenize their political image and even to forge initial alliances with indigenous Amazonians. This effectively challenges the norm that has been dominant for the last several decades (Greene, 2006). Up until this recent multicultural turn most community organizing was characterized by a distinct lack of alliance between Andeans, mostly self-representing as peasants, and Amazonians, mostly self-representing as indigenous. One is thus forced to reflect on the fact that the Velasco period was a critical moment. The state took a major step toward consolidating the peasantization of indigenous Andeans and a major step toward explicitly indigenizing Amazonians via the Native Communities Law. All this, ironically, while using the Andean peasant community as the legislative template for the Amazonian native community.

Land reforms were matched by a comprehensive educational reform policy, commissioned in 1969 and finally decreed in 1972 (Drysdale and Myers, 1975). One of the most significant results of the 1972 law was the official extension of bilingual education to all sectors of the country where languages other than Spanish were spoken. Thus, Quechua and Aymara speakers from the highlands were in theory encompassed under bilingual educational policies for the first time, although the policies were not implemented, certainly not in a way that matches their full institutionalization in Peruvian Amazonia (see Chapter 4). This national mandate to establish bilingual primary schools for speakers of all of the country's indigenous languages stimulated a greater public awareness of the multilinguistic reality of the nation (see Varese, 1975). It also served as an antecedent to the reformed 1979 Constitution, which recognized all of Peru's indigenous languages as "official languages," although only in the specific "areas where they are spoken" (i.e., not as national languages and on the assumption that such languages are spoken only in rural areas).

This educational overhaul led the Velasco regime to question the existing relationship between the Peruvian state and the SIL. After two decades of work in Peru's Amazonian areas, the Velasco state recognized that SIL was essentially a foreign-operated, evangelical surrogate for the state. SIL held a virtual monopoly over access to native Amazonian communities via its expansive school system. The anti-yanqui sentiments boiled; and in 1970 the state gave SIL what it thought was its final contract, which was set to expire in 1976 and mark SIL's departure from Peru. SIL was given five years to transfer the supervision of native Amazonian community affairs (including education) to the newly created Division of Native Communities in the Ministry of Agriculture, headed by the pioneering Peruvian anthropologist Stefano Varese (Stoll, 1982: 202–207). Varese (1972b) helped expose the state's total absence in the Peruvian jungle; his advocacy in favor of Amazonian rights became a crucial part of the famous 1971 Barbados conference on the "liberation" of South American Indians.[3]

However, just when its days were numbered in Peru, SIL was saved from expulsion. In 1975 a considerably more conservative military coup replaced Velasco with General Morales Bermudez. He began a systematic scaling back of the "revolution" under the rubric of his Plan de Gobierno Tupac Amaru— yet another deeply ironic gesture in Peru's long history of political elites' appropriating neo-Incaic national icons. Bermudez renewed the political faith in SIL, and it was allowed to continue its translation work inside its Lima compound. SIL also continued to operate its bilingual teacher boot camp at Yarinacocha until just a few years ago. After nearly fifty years of operation as a North American–run pedagogical institute, Yarinacocha became the first National Intercultural University of Amazonia under Peruvian Law 27250 in the year 2000.

The third element in Velasco's military revolution was the attempt to channel populist support by the creation of a centralized "mobilization" agency. In 1971, in direct response to criticisms about the lack of popular participation during the early phases of the revolution, Velasco announced the creation of the Sistema Nacional de Apoyo a la Movilización Social (SINAMOS). SINAMOS quickly evolved into a hierarchically organized state agency of the first order. It was staffed with petty bureaucrats and applied academics whose job was to filter the many popular-sector demands placed on the military state by Andean indigenous peasants, urban workers, indigenous Amazonians, and other marginalized sectors. The result was a series of top-down, quick-fix solutions. One of the best examples is the Confederación Nacional Agraria (CNA), created with the help of SINAMOS. This was the military administration's attempt to centralize peasant desires and marginalize all other organizational efforts, particularly those of the much older Confederación Campesina del Perú (CCP) (see Matos Mar and Mejía, 1980).[4]

The contradictory nature of promoting popular mobilization so long as it was done through state-led initiatives and quelling it under other circumstances produced an increasingly divided Peru. In effect, the result was a successful coup to replace Velasco with Bermudez in the mid-1970s and then the steady dilution to scale back his overzealous nationalism and rein in his populist reforms. The new military state intended to transition back to democratic governance, but not before modifying much of Velasco's reformist legislation in accordance with Bermudez's Tupac Amaru Plan. SINAMOS closed its doors in 1978. Despite the language recognition gained by indigenous peoples in the reformed 1979 Constitution, more conservative measures dominated the Tupac Amaru agenda. Indeed, by 1980, with the "return" to democracy, Peru appeared to be back to where it started. Belaúnde Terry was elected for a second—and this time uninterrupted—term, and national development plans in the jungle started anew: new and better roads, more and more promotion of highland to lowland agricultural colonization, less and less Amazonian land titling.

Legalizing Amazonian Indigeneity: Native Rights to Land Then and Now

The Velasco reforms thus determined the fate of Aguarunia and the rest of indigenous Amazonia in very different ideological terms from those of the officially peasantized indigenous Andeans. Officially, Amazonians were no longer to be referred to as indios salvajes (in colonial Spanish) or chunchos (in Quechua). As of the early 1970s the official discourse painted Amazonian peoples as members of native communities—part of a state-sponsored ethnic terminology that stood in direct contrast to Andeans' official renaming from indigenous to peasant in the Andes. Stefano Varese's Division of Native Communities influenced the legislative content of the original Native Communities Law. The law was ratified in 1974 and initially implemented by SINAMOS personnel, which included other Peruvian anthropologists such as Carlos Mora and Alberto Chirif, close allies of Varese who left Peru in the mid-1970s and assumed academic posts in the United States.

One can still appreciate Varese's lasting influence on the state's effort to recognize native communities (see Varese, 1972b: 125–126). He rejected the use of the anthropological term "tribe" and substituted for it the term *grupo etnolingüístico* (ethnolinguistic group) on the grounds that the latter better described the territorial fragmentation of Amazonia and allowed for subclassification of language dialects. In fact, categorizing Amazonian peoples according to grupos etno-lingüísticos is still the preferred practice among the majority of academics and Amazonian activists working in the Peruvian context.[5] Varese defined a native community as "a stable socio-economic unit linked to a particular territorial area with a type of settlement that may be nuclear, semi-dispersed or dispersed, recognizing itself as a community distinct from other neighboring socio-economic units whether Native or not" (1972b: 126). Ultimately, this allowed the state to begin the process of recognizing existing communities. However, in the early phases of native community demarcation the sedentary and agrarian-oriented model of the Andean peasant community often won out. The result was a widespread inability of the Ministry of Agriculture to fully recognize the land-use patterns, resource needs, and migratory nature of many Amazonian groups or, at least, those sectors still heavily involved in hunting, fishing, and slash-and-burn horticulture (see Chirif, 1975; Mora, 1983; Uriarte, 1985). Law 20653 was the first recognition of the collective legal existence of Amazonian peoples. This, too, is a major contrast to the extensive colonial and early republican legislation—and intellectual writings—dealing with indigenous Andeans.

Varese promoted the idea of building a federated system of native community leadership, but Law 20653 did not recognize that part of his vision for Amazonia. The law recognized only individual native communities, each one an isolated administrative and territorial unit. The idea of recognizing a federated native community structure clearly countered the political elites' concerns for maintaining national integrity. And again the template of the Andean peasant community provided the state the precedent it needed to justify this divide-and-conquer effect. The response to community fragmentation in the Andes came when indigenous peasant syndicates sought to construct a system of nationwide alliances in organizations like the CCP, which originated in the 1940s, articulating the interests of different peasant communities; or when, in the context of Peru's civil war with the Shining Path in the 1980s and 1990s, peasant communities began to articulate a vision of rondas campesinas as a mode of self-defense and an expression of Andean communal autonomy at nationwide levels (see Starn, 1999).[6] A similar phenomenon occurred in the Peruvian Amazon. The state's creation of individual and isolated native communities resulted in Amazonian efforts to build a panregional movement to articulate native interests. The crucial difference is that in contrast to the various subtle ways in which indigeneity is smuggled into Andean peasant forms of resistance, pan-Amazonian organizing began as an explicitly indigenous, outwardly ethnic movement.

Ultimately, the state's continuing ideological and economic commitments to achieve the dream of Peruvian development, on loan from the World Bank and other global governance institutions, served to scale back Amazonians' customary land rights. Velasco's government continued to support the road-construction and internal-colonization schemes that Belaúnde had championed (see Smith, 1982). It also soon took on a massive petroleum pipeline project in the north right in the heart of Aguarunia that also extends into other parts of Jivaria, where Huambisa and Achuar live. Since the passage of the Native Communities Law, environmental degradation, bureaucratic mismanagement of land claims, and ceaseless agricultural migration have all intensified. The result is a host of Amazonian land conflicts that on a few occasions have turned violent, in significant part due to the state's active lack of interest in bringing about order (see Greene and Juep Greene, 2002).

Morales Bermudez's government devised ways to undo the perceived radicalism of the Velasco revolution via the Tupac Amaru Plan. The most telling cutback for indigenous Amazonia was the replacement of Law 20653 with a carefully modified version in 1978 that is still in effect. Ostensibly "clarifying" its legal precedent, the new Native Communities Law (Law 21175) in fact curtailed native community rights. It specified that native communities did not possess subsurface rights to mineral and hydrocarbon wealth and held only usufruct rights to forest resources, and it vamped up the promotion of agrarian and other "development" activities throughout the Amazonian region.

More important, the transition to Bermudez's reformed native community legislation in 1978 signaled a rapid decline in granting new native community titles that lasted essentially until the 1990s. During the initial two years of the 1974 Velasco legislation, the state granted 244 titles for potentially at least 1,000 Amazonian settlements with legitimate claims. For the entire six years following, the state granted only 128 more (see Mora, 1983). Under Belaúnde and even the populist leader Alan García, first elected in 1985, native community titling came to a screeching halt. Belaúnde was too concerned with implementing a development vision and completing his Carretera Marginal project. García's government was wrecked by multiple forms of instability due to the expansion of the Shining Path guerrilla movement to many parts of the country, political corruption scandals, and a massive inflation crisis.

Ironically, the state's reluctance to title Amazonian lands changed dramatically during the decade that began in 1990, despite President Fujimori's authoritarian and neoliberal tendencies. Examining Peru's national environmental policy context during the 1990s, Carlos Soria (2003) makes several important observations about the new neoliberal environmentalism of the Fujimori era. The liberalization of the economy swung the door wide open to foreign oil, forestry, and mining interests. Fujimori also stacked the deck by naming a mining company official to the newly created Consejo Nacional del Ambiente (CONAM) in 1994. According to Soria, however compromised CONAM was by natural resource interests, its creation and that of several other types of "sustainable development" policies are all clear signs that demonstrate the impact of international environmental activism in Peru.

Unsurprisingly, during the Fujimori era Amazonian native communities achieved their most tangible territorial victories since the Velasco era. In 1997 a national-level Aguaruna leader, speaking on behalf of the pan-Amazonian organization he represented, announced that recent efforts to gain more native community titles resulted in as many as four million new hectares granted to native communities (Inoash, 1997). Amazonian rights advocates attribute this directly to the impact of the ongoing eco-indigenous alliance that has been emerging since the late 1980s. Under the policy rubric of "sustainable development" and forest conservation, environmentally oriented NGOs and pan-Amazonian indigenous rights groups have worked together to title new territories (see Smith et al., 2003).

The trend in land titling within Aguarunia is a perfect example of these territorial gains and eco-indigenous alliances. After more than a decade of deliberate inattention from prior governments, native community titles granted during the Fujimori administration effectively doubled. Of the 186 native communities the Aguaruna held title to in 1999, some 80 were granted during the initial three years after the 1974 Velasco law. Another 90 were granted between 1991 and 1999 during Fujimori's two terms (the vast majority in 1998 and 1999). Remarkably, the state granted only 16 titles to the Aguaruna between 1978 and 1990 before Fujimori entered office.[7]

The more recent titling efforts took place thanks to cooperation between various indigenous organizations, conservation NGOs, and the Proyecto Especial de Titulación de Tierras (PETT), the division of the Ministry of Agriculture now charged with land titling. Indeed, many state officials now explicitly exhibit the widely popular idea of Amazonians as natural conservationists publicized by NGOs, international development institutions, and green corporations (see Conklin and Graham, 1995). Thus, a PETT official answered simply, "The natives protect the forest better than the colonists," when I asked why the effort to title more native communities was so widespread. This marks an important shift in state discourse about indigenous Amazonians. In the 1970s, when titling first began, the state fully expected Amazonians to transition toward sedentary agriculture and thus become more like Andeans. By the 1990s the impact of international environmental politics meant the state now expected Amazonians to conserve the forest, implying they should not now become agrarian Andeans, after previous decades of promoting the exact opposite ideology. Indeed, as the above state official's contrast between "natives" and "colonists," which here implies largely Andean migrants, makes clear, the state now recognizes uncontrolled migration to Amazonia as a form of environmental destruction even though the state plays a central role in promoting it.

Yet the state routinely fails to fully account for its own deep complicity in having created the contrast—natives versus colonists, Amazonian indigenes versus Andean peasants, environmental stewards versus environmental destroyers. In some parts of Amazonia, expanses of contiguous native communities now form de facto ethnic territorial blocs. But many parts of the Peruvian Amazon are rife with territorial fragmentation and latent with the potential for violent land and resource conflicts. This is certainly the case in Aguarunia. North of the Marañon in the Department of Amazonas between the Cenepa and Santiago Rivers, one finds large, contiguous areas of Aguaruna and Huambisa native communities. In other areas, particularly south of the Upper Marañon River and on the Upper Mayo River in the Department of San Martín, Aguaruna native communities are interspersed with growing migrant settlements. And even those living in the ostensible environmental harmony of forested areas are constantly under threat from illicit logging activities and mining and petroleum concessions.

Thus, if Fujimori's Peru went green, it did so via the path of neoliberalization. The state sought to place indigenous Amazonians as symbols of Peru's compliance with global conservation interests. But it did so while still lurching forward with the rampant privatization of natural resources and continuing state denial of the problems of territorial disorder that decades of mass migration into Amazonia unleashed in the region. The promises of more eco-ethnic empowerment are everywhere mixed with fewer restraints on neoliberal capitalism.

Dilemmas of Native Community Authority in Aguarunia

With Amazonian land-rights legislation emerged new forms of institutionalized, and largely male, authority in the native community institution.[8] SINAMOS typically initiated this administrative overhaul of Amazonian community life by designating native community *promotores* as liaisons with the military government's mobilization officials. Thus, Noé Cahuaza, a leader of the titled Aguaruna community Bajo Naranjillo, was contracted in 1976 as a SINAMOS promoter for the Aguaruna communities first titled in 1975 in the Alto Mayo region in the Department of San Martín. He remembers his duties in this way:

> Well, my work was to organize the communities because they still weren't organized well yet. I mean, the first thing was whether or not they had their little schools. But then organizing their territory still had to be done for titling. Then it was organized. Also the chief: how he should resolve problems, how he should convoke a meeting, do an assembly. They didn't know how to do an assembly. (personal interview)

Cahuaza's memory serves us well here since it was precisely this emphasis on the term "organization" that would infiltrate every aspect of native community politics. Soon thereafter the regional Amazonian federations that grew into the pan-Amazonian movement followed suit with the same "organization" mentality. The ideological and practical elements of organization that SINAMOS disseminated consisted of the establishment of the office of chief, an awareness of the chief's representational duties, and the mechanics of communal assemblies and elections.

Here again the military state, through its SINAMOS-trained promoters, viewed Andeans as the template for how to organize the recently recognized Amazonians. Native community governance structures were supposed to emulate those practices already considered routine in highland peasant communities. As in the Andes, simply by virtue of residing in a native community Amazonians began to be identified individually as *comunero* (a community member). Also as in the Andes, the basic institution of communal decision making in the native community became the *asamblea* (collective assembly of all the comuneros.) Although I can't speak to other areas in Amazonia, in Aguarunia the asamblea is a meeting of all male heads of household and, on decidedly rarer occasions, a few outspoken women.[9] Again, as in the Andes, the assembly is the body that elects community representatives to their various posts, as chief, vice-chief, treasurer, and so on. The degree to which the Andean model was imported is particularly telling. Aguaruna comuneros use the Spanish *jefe* and the Quechua *apu* completely interchangeably in reference to the elected community chief.

In his work with Sergio Chang from the Ministry of Agriculture, César Sarasara, a past Aguaruna president of the pan-Amazonian confederation CONAP, reflected on the compromises made as a result of the new governance structures imposed on native communities. "The first chiefs of the communities were persons considered elders, bearers of tradition [*tradicionalistas*], and with more experience in terms of the ethnic group" (Chang and Sarasara, 1987: 90). But this form of customary strong man, old man, visionary warrior leadership in the guise of a native community chief was fraught with problems. It was rife with complicated negotiations between older and newer understandings of what authority was. As quickly became clear, one of a chief's primary responsibilities was the same as that of the bilingual teacher, acting as an intermediary between his native community constituents and various external actors. The result, according to Chang and Sarasara, was that the elder generation of visionary warriors acting as chiefs became fundamentally dependent on those literate and bilingual Aguaruna living in the community. The local bilingual teacher was usually the first in line. After just a few short years of experimenting with this generational dependence model, most communities opted simply to replace the elder strong man chiefs with younger and younger communal representatives. In an apparently complete reversal of customary logic, the elder visionary warriors found themselves replaced with younger bilingual men, those who wielded the weapons of pen, paper, and money.

The case of the Aguaruna native community Bajo Naranjillo is a characteristic example of this reversal. Upon gaining title to their land in 1975, the Aguaruna in their first communal assembly elected Pancho Cahuaza as chief. Pancho was largely monolingual and illiterate, but he was the most respected warrior in his kin/river neighborhood. Pancho was in other words the most kakajam at that particular moment in that particular part of Aguarunia.

The bureaucratic duties of his new job as native community representative forced him to depend constantly on the assistance of two younger Aguaruna who in the customary order of things should have depended entirely on him. Pancho relied most on his son, Noé, who had received a primary education outside the community in Rioja; and his son-in-law, Adolfo Juep, an Aguaruna migrant to the Mayo River who first set up SIL-run bilingual schools in the early 1970s. Pancho's relation of dependency on these younger men was something completely foreign, something indeed that required a lot of getting accustomed to. Noé Cahuaza's appointment as a SINAMOS promoter put him in charge of teaching his own father how to hold a communal assembly. Similarly, Adolfo Juep took on various responsibilities that were the purview of the chief. For example, he carried out the first native community census to establish the population of Bajo Naranjillo.

Over the next two decades those Aguaruna elected to the office of chief in Bajo Naranjillo, like most everywhere else in Aguarunia, became progressively younger and younger. Everywhere it seemed that Aguaruna custom was being forced to replace older instantiations of authority with those mandated by a nation-state-inspired, Andean-inflected form of indigenous governance. Thus, in Bajo Naranjillo Pancho was followed by Robinson Wajai, who served two consecutive terms and was the last monolingual, illiterate member to assume the position of chief. After Robinson came two of Pancho's sons: Alfonso (in his early thirties) and then Noé (age twenty-nine). By the mid-1980s the revolution in authority was apparently complete. Santos Peas assumed the office of chief at the age of twenty, and two years later the community elected an even younger authority figure, Elias Peas, at the barely postadolescent age of nineteen. By standards in Aguarunia this was tantamount to completely turning custom on its head. A young person of nineteen may be on the path to becoming a man; but he is extraordinarily unlikely to have already become recognized as a successful visionary warrior.

As we can see from the case of Bajo Naranjillo, the authority of the native community chief manifests itself in a very different symbolic-pragmatic order from what the Aguaruna call "our custom." Chiefly authority finds its expression through those things most symbolic of Max Weber's coldhearted bureaucracy: the deed to land, the administrative record book, and the paper stamp that symbolizes the emergence of a rationalized, routinized order of political authority. And this is precisely why a generational inversion—turning custom on its head—seemed necessary if not inevitable in the move toward bureaucratizing Aguarunia. However, things are also necessarily and inevitably more complex than this—for every move toward institutionalizing indigeneity the Aguaruna encounter, they always seem to find another path that leads back to their practices of customization.

Customizing Land Conflicts and Native Communalism

By some standards one might see in these transformations of Aguaruna authority—brought on by the native community land-tenure system—a classic problem of modernization. Aguarunia is forced to trade in the old custom of elderly visionary war leaders for a new one of young, literate, bilingual intermediaries. Instead, Aguaruna authorities respond to that problem with a politics of customization. The modernization paradigm overlooks the fact that visionary warriors were in their own way already equipped to act as intermediaries. More important, it overlooks the fact that the younger generation of bilingual culture brokers purposefully decide to become a future generation of visionary warriors. The process begins with the need to get accustomed to native community customs imposed by Peru's Andeanist state. But it then morphs into an explicit political desire to customize those native community constraints in accordance with both the mental spaces and material places of Aguarunia. Following are a few examples.

Two extremes of customizing Amazonian land rights are occurring in Aguarunia—and many more examples are found somewhere in the middle. The one extreme *apparently* entails a forceful rejection of state law and market actors. The other extreme *apparently* entails a full embrace of expanding markets and capitalist consumerism. Although the examples I explore appear to be polar opposite approaches to state and market expansion, both are in fact forms of active negotiation with state and market articulated through the native community institution. Rather than interpret them as simple opposites—rejection versus acceptance—I see them as the diverse paths Aguaruna actors inevitably follow in their different projects to customize indigeneity. These diverse paths then map out a space of meaningful political engagements with Aguarunia's multiplicity of material conditions.

What is so useful about a term like "customization" is that it connotes both what comes before the arrival of global capital and the process of fragmentation from within global capital that has always been a part of its internal logic. There has never been a unified global market nor any homogeneous market processes. Capitalist markets have always been made up of diverse actors, events, and processes. That different Aguaruna actors respond differently to market expansion should not necessarily be interpreted as a sign of one sector of Aguarunia being completely beyond capital's logic and another having already fully succumbed to its false consumer consciousness. Less still should this diversity of Aguaruna responses signal that global capital only becomes glocal once it confronts the local customary logics of Aguarunia. If nation-state-promoted capitalism is itself internally diverse, then we should have every reason to suspect that interactions with state and markets in Aguarunia are equally heterogeneous.

Those Aguaruna actors who seemingly defy capitalism by rejecting recently arrived market actors do so with the objective of inserting themselves into *other* kinds of state and market relations. Those Aguaruna actors who seemingly embrace capitalism by exploiting all kinds of market opportunities do so convinced that the forms of capitalist consumption they engage in are a means to strengthen the autonomy of state-mandated Aguaruna communities. What customization comes to mean in this context is simply that if Aguarunia itself contains many partialities and is internally fragmented, so, too, are the forms of capitalist expansion and forms of statecraft that one encounters there.

Examples that would seem to warrant the label of market rejection abound in Aguarunia. In 2000, members of the Aguaruna native communities of Shaim and Pagata on the Upper Cenepa River took hostage several representatives of Newmont International, a North American mining corporation. They did so in open protest of damages caused by a company helicopter flying too close to an Aguaruna settlement and to voice their opposition to the Peruvian state granting the company a mining concession that overlapped with their titled native community territory. The comuneros of Shaim and Pagata also demanded a ransom (or from their point of view, a compensation payment) as a condition of the company representatives' release (Luisa del Río, 2000). Clearly, this was not a simple form of market rejection but a form of negotiated acceptance: a form of negotiating that aspect of a market one is willing to engage with while simultaneously demarcating that aspect of a market one refuses to tolerate.

Much more complicated examples of negotiated market rejection stem from land conflict cases between Aguaruna and migrant Andeans. The state has actively promoted Andean migration to the upper Amazonian areas of Peru since at least the first Belaúnde period in the 1960s. And the constant push toward expanding the commercial agricultural frontier written into the very title of the Native Communities Law makes this clear. The law has the dual intent of addressing the economic demands of poor Andeans in search of a productive plot of land and integrating Amazonia into Peru's largely agrarian economy. President Fujimori's various infrastructure projects, which included paving large portions of the Carretera Marginal, served to boost migration considerably in the 1990s. The result is that as the state tries to release one kind of market pressure in one region, it creates another kind of market pressure in another. In the case of Aguarunia, that market pressure corresponds to sometimes latent and other times open conflict between Aguaruna native communities and rural migrant populations in search of land.

The most spectacular instance of such conflict occurred in January 2002 in the far northeastern corner of the Department of Cajamarca in the Aguaruna native community of Los Naranjos (see Greene and Juep Greene, 2002). In the twilight hours of January 18 more than a hundred Aguaruna men from Los Naranjos and their allies from neighboring Aguaruna communities armed and adorned themselves for war. They then descended on the migrant agricultural settlement Flor de la Frontera, which was actually located inside the titled Aguaruna territory of Los Naranjos. The Aguaruna left fifteen dead colonists and sent the rest fleeing for their lives.

Mainstream press reports predictably stereotyped the Aguaruna assailants as members of an exotic Amazonian tribe, implying, when not forthrightly declaring, they were out of touch with the "civilizing" forces of market and state law. A CNN article painted them as members of a tribe that used "poison-darts"—even though Aguaruna used shotguns to commit the violence against the helpless migrants (see CNN, 2002). A Peruvian newswriter for one of Peru's best known magazines made no bones about classifying the Aguaruna of Los Naranjos as "savages" (see Gamarra, 2002).

Let me be clear. I make no excuses for nor can I even fathom the kind of violence that these Aguaruna men decided to use against the Andean migrants.[10] As I demonstrate later, they acted in significant part to call attention to the systematic way in which their state-granted rights were being violated and to question an illegal seizure of their property for someone else's market gain. In seeking to reveal state complicity in promoting uncontrolled market expansion and illegal invasions of native community land, however, they struck down those people holding the least power and resources to make change happen. The migrant land invasion was not an entirely innocent endeavor, and the migrants themselves were given repeated warnings. But they, too, were simply caught up in trying to negotiate a way through the diverse legal and illegal forms of market expansionism the Peruvian state promotes in hopes of rising above their own impoverishment.

When I asked Adolfo Juep of the community Bajo Naranjillo, far removed from the events, why the attack resulted in such aggression and why the migrants seemed so unable to offer any effective resistance, he invoked custom. "Well, because the Aguaruna went with the power of the ajutap, that is how they are protected." It was the ajutap's eternal source of ancestral power, he suggested, that guided their actions and explained the invincible customary force with which they reclaimed a state-granted indigenous right over their legally recognized land. In other words, this, too, was a war mission like other war missions Aguarunia has known. But in this case the ajutap was invoked as part of a broader politics of customization. It was an aggressive means of forcing the state to recognize its own complicity in Aguaruna violence and indeed of forcing the market to accommodate the interests of this sector of Aguarunia. Far from relying exclusively on "poison-darts," or rejecting the form of commercial agriculture the Andean migrants themselves were engaged in, these particular Aguaruna communities were explicitly hooked into regional coffee markets. Thus, the Aguaruna men acted in this case not out of an "uncivilized" indigenous ignorance of state and market but out of an explicit decision to aggressively customize the very rights of indigeneity that "civilization" had promised them. They acted not simply to reject the market. Rather the point was to purposefully force the state to recognize which aspects of market imposition they consider unwanted in this sector of Aguarunia without necessarily rejecting market interactions altogether.

In fact, the violent attack on Flor de la Frontera followed five years of legal claims, organized protest at regional and national levels, and public denouncements of the illegal occupation. By any account that pays attention to the details, the attack was the result of the mounting frustration the comuneros of Los Naranjos felt. It followed the state's and migrants' repeated refusals to take action in response to Aguaruna activists' explicit documentation that the location of Flor de la Frontera was inside territory demarcated as the native community Los Naranjos. Documents dating to 1998 show repeated Aguaruna allegations about the Los Naranjos case that directly implicate state officials. Indigenous leaders at all levels made state functionaries at the provincial and national levels aware of the occupation and requested appropriate legal action. At one point community leaders from Los Naranjos even convinced provincial police to attempt a removal of the migrants from the area. But the attempt was frustrated when the migrants immediately returned to the area after a provincial judge implicitly encouraged them to do so by expressing empathy with their search for a productive plot of land (see Greene and Juep Greene, 2002).

In several public documents Aguaruna activists explicitly warned that Los Naranjos community members would take the matter into their own hands if faced with continuing bureaucratic apathy. The national-level Amazonian organization AIDESEP published a document on behalf of regional Aguaruna activists just six months before the violent episode took place:

In other words, compatriots, brothers, the Peruvian State DOES NOT WANT TO DO JUSTICE FOR INDIGENOUS PEOPLES. For this reason, without any other legal option except our own, the option of our PRACTICES AND

CUSTOMS, the Aguaruna People have decided to give our support so that our brothers of Los Naranjos make their rights worth something. (AIDESEP and ORASI, 2001; capitalization in original)

The emphasis placed on "PRACTICES AND CUSTOMS" (*usos y costumbres*) explicitly intends to articulate Aguaruna customs, namely, their customs of conflict resolution, with an indigenous rights legislative framework. They cite what has become a common phrase in indigenous rights legislation not only in Peru's Native Communities Law but also in international agreements like Convention 169 of the International Labor Organization and the UN Declaration on the Rights of Indigenous Peoples.

The use of violent force to expel the agricultural migrants from Los Naranjos is, of course, not recognized as legitimate under any of these state or international legislative instruments for the practice of indigenous customs and practices. A congressional commission charged with investigating the events surrounding the Los Naranjos case found that the liberal political rights of the individual person (in this case the right to life) far outweigh any collective indigenous rights of the Aguaruna to custom or to their state-granted native community property (see Grupo de Trabajo Encargado . . . , 2002). The point is that the organizers of this aggressive action had decided to customize state and international indigenous rights law in accordance with the logic that when they are threatened, a violent reaction is justified. That's what Aguaruna activists meant when they said they were "without any other legal option except our own." That's what they meant when they said they supported Aguaruna community actors who were willing to "make their rights worth something."

Congressman Luis Guerrero Figueroa, who oversaw the investigation into Los Naranjos, visited the scene and helped author a final report that called for the arrest and punishment of the organizers of the attack. But in its report the commission also recognizes that "the State has an undeniable responsibility in the problem that occurred between colonists and Natives." It goes on to cite as prior warning the various public announcements Aguaruna activists made of their plan to use "custom," directly implying the use of force, as a means of dispute settlement (Grupo de Trabajo Encargado . . . , 2002: 27). The commission's report also identifies such land conflicts between indigenous Amazonians and migrant settlers as a widespread problem throughout Amazonia.

In this sense, Aguaruna efforts to customize their rights to native community land through armed action had the effect of forcing the state to recognize its own complicity in the violence. Unfortunately, two results are not conducive to positive change. In the short term was a needless loss of life among Andean migrants whose own attempt to negotiate state and market set them on a crash course with the more aggressive Aguaruna mode of customizing indigenous politics. In the long term the state, while willing to recognize its complicity in conflict-ridden market processes, rhetorically has yet to prove it is willing to act in ways that practically counter that complicity. Once Congressman Guerrero Figueroa filed his report, the issue of land conflicts in Amazonia was dropped, and latent tensions between indigenous Amazonians and migrant Andeans persist much as they have for the last several decades.

Other situations elicit different responses in Aguarunia. The Upper Mayo River valley, a highly productive agricultural area comprised of the northern provinces of Moyobamba and Rioja in the Department of San Martín, exemplifies what many think of as a full embrace of Peru's rural agricultural capitalism. By 1995 the Upper Mayo region was producing 73 percent and 91 percent, respectively, of all the rice and coffee grown in the entire department (Proyecto Especial Alto Mayo, 1998: 24). Most of it is destined for coastal and foreign markets. As a result the pressures on the fourteen titled native communities in the Alto Mayo region from agricultural migrants arriving in search of cultivable land are intense. A Ministry of Agriculture official I consulted with in 2000 estimated the number of migrants arriving in Nueva Cajamarca, the region's landing place for newcomers, at as many as fifty people a day in the Alto Mayo region.

As a result of this intense economic pressure the Upper Mayo region is riddled with conflicting and contradictory land politics. In 1999 I participated in an effort to map the region's native communities. It was funded by international aid agencies and carried out by Ministry of Agriculture officials in conjunction with the OAAM, which represented the majority of the native communities at the time. The mapping efforts identified multiple illegal occupations of titled native community territory by agricultural migrants (see Map 3). Since this pressure has built up over several decades, many of the Aguaruna communities in the area have grown accustomed to it. Indeed, they are already devising extremely complicated ways to customize it.

The case of the native community Bajo Naranjillo is most illustrative in this respect. Bajo Naranjillo is in reality two communities in one. The sector named Bajo Naranjillo is located alongside the Carretera Marginal about fifteen kilometers north of the expanding migrant town Nueva Cajamarca—named after the Andean province from which most of its inhabitants hail. Another sector,

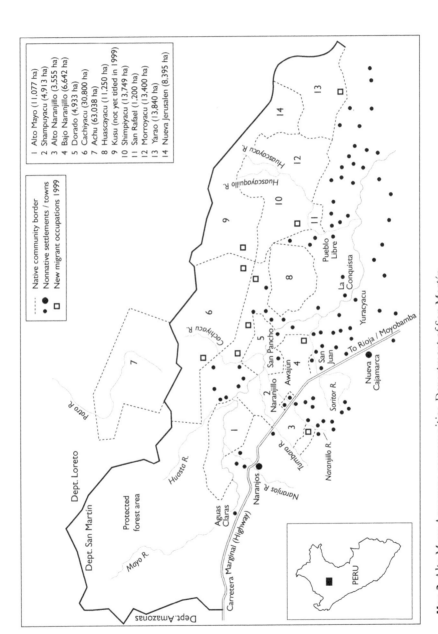

Map 3 Alto Mayo Aguaruna communities, Department of San Martín.

Legend:

Native community border
Nonnative settlements / towns
New migrant occupations 1999

1 Alto Mayo (11,077 ha)
2 Shampuyacu (4,913 ha)
3 Alto Naranjillo (3,555 ha)
4 Bajo Naranjillo (6,642 ha)
5 Dorado (4,933 ha)
6 Cachiyacu (30,800 ha)
7 Achu (63,038 ha)
8 Huascayacu (11,250 ha)
9 Kusu (not yet titled in 1999)
10 Shimpiyacu (13,749 ha)
11 San Rafael (1,200 ha)
12 Morroyacu (13,400 ha)
13 Yarao (13,840 ha)
14 Nueva Jerusalen (8,395 ha)

Dept. Loreto
Dept. San Martín
Protected forest area
Dept. Amazonas

Mayo R.
Huasta R.
Pidro R.
Cachiyacu R.
Huascayacu R.
Huascayaquillo R.

Aguas Claras
Naranjos R.
Carretera Marginal (Highway)
Naranjillo
San Pancho
Awajún
San Juan
Soritor R.
Tumbaro R.
Naranjillo R.
Nueva Cajamarca
To Rioja / Moyobamba
Yuracyacu
La Conquista
Pueblo Libre

PERU

also within the native community boundaries, named Soritor, is located about two kilometers off the highway. As a result of their integration into the regional market, members of Bajo Naranjillo and Soritor are now deeply economically dependent on commercial agriculture. But they are also deeply defensive about their desires for Aguaruna ethnic independence. Bajo Naranjillo and Soritor are divided for a reason having to do with patterns of migration internal to Aguarunia. Those in Bajo Naranjillo are largely either native to the Mayo River region or are Aguaruna migrants from the Marañon River who have married into Mayo families. Those living in Soritor are almost exclusively the extended family members of Marañon River Aguaruna who have not married into the Mayo group. Although the two band together on certain occasions, they also exist in a permanent state of latent tension, as described later.

One important detail discovered in the 1999 surveying expedition is that the migrant settlement Alto Peru, first settled just a few years after Bajo Naranjillo was granted title in 1975, is actually inside the southeastern sector of Bajo Naranjillo's native community limits. Most of the migrants living there possess their own individual deeds to the land. The same Ministry of Agriculture that granted these Bajo Naranjillo Aguaruna title to native community lands had superimposed individual property titles for the Andean migrants on one section of the communal land. This is a familiar scenario in Amazonia, where state officials possess only scattered geographic coordinates and incomplete maps and rarely conduct physical surveys to verify the legitimacy of new land claims.

In this case Ministry of Agriculture officials constantly evaded any discussion of removing the migrants or of recognizing the central role the state had played in creating the land conflict. Instead, they pressured and eventually were successful in convincing the comuneros of Bajo Naranjillo and Soritor to cede their communal claim and grant the migrants open-ended usufruct rights. To help justify this as a resolution to the problem, Ministry officials repeatedly made mention of the fact that the native community in question was already deeply engaged in *negocios* (doing business) with mestizos. In particular, they pointed to the fact that Bajo Naranjillo–Soritor, like several other native communities near the main highway, now rent out individual plots of their titled land to non-Aguaruna agriculturalists. At several points in the negotiations state officials made it clear that Aguaruna who lease communal land have essentially sacrificed any claim to social or territorial integrity as a native community. Implicit in every discussion was the rhetorical question, What's the difference in letting in a few more if you've already allowed yourself to be over-run? But to the Aguaruna involved, there was a difference.

The practice of Aguaruna communities in the Upper Mayo region collect-ing land rents from migrant agriculturalists first emerged in Bajo Naranjillo in the early 1990s. Since then it has spread to several other native communities in the area. Most agricultural plots are rented for rice, coffee, and, more recently, papaya cultivation. I see this as a perfect example of the desire to customize an approach that allows Aguaruna to appropriate the state's nationwide promotion of expanding rural agricultural markets even while being appropriated by it. In the minds of Aguaruna landlords, renting out native community lands for the apach's agricultural production solves three problems at once. First, it provides a constant, if variable, source of income in a context of rapidly shrinking forest resources. Second, it alleviates the feelings of market inadequacy the Aguaruna routinely express in the face of commercial agricultural practices they consider to be "apach custom" and thus not practices they are fully accustomed to nor in their minds very good at. Third, and relatedly, it provides them a sense of Aguaruna economic pride. They feel they have devised an effective way to beat the apach at their own economic game. Feeling ineffective in the commercial agricultural market, they successfully customized a different market venture by realizing they possess some prime native community real estate.

The case of Bajo Naranjillo–Soritor exhibits the complexity that these prac-tices of getting accustomed to and customizing mestizo markets entail in the Mayo region. By the mid-1980s this native community began to reorganize its internal administration of communal land to reflect the rapid growth of com-mercial agricultural plots and the influx of both Aguaruna migrants from the Marañon and Andean migrants from Peru's northern provinces. The leadership of Bajo Naranjillo designated seventy-five male heads of households as *titulares*, and each one was given 71 hectares for private familial use. Although the commu-nalist logic of the state still applies in theory, in practice Bajo Naranjillo–Soritor comuneros have taken it upon themselves to internally divide their state-granted land (see Map 4). The result is a form of de facto (from the point of view of the state) liberalist, patriarchal property holdings that the comuneros themselves consider de jure. In the late 1990s they consolidated this internal logic of com-munity land administration by codifying it and specifying inheritance rules in what they called the Internal Regulation for Aguaruna Native Communities.[11]

According to a census compiled by community members, Bajo Naranjillo–Soritor was producing approximately 545 hectares of rice and 178 hectares of

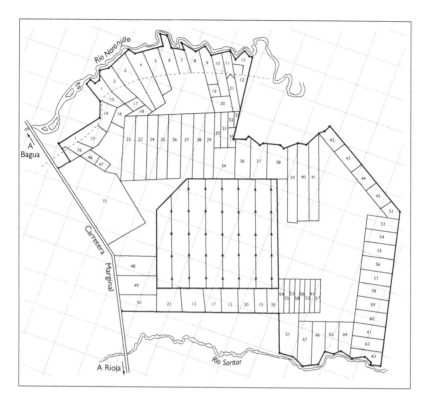

Map 4 Titled family plots in the native community Bajo Naranjillo. Map reproduced with permission of the native community Bajo Naranjillo.

coffee in 1997. Although community members cultivate and sell some of the coffee themselves, the irrigated rice production represents plots contractually leased to migrant mestizo agriculturalists. By 1999, when I was living in Bajo Naranjillo–Soritor, rental agreements had increased substantially. I estimate, based on rental contracts stored in the community office (which are not always accurate), that 900 hectares were rented out just for rice production in that year. This figure represents 12 percent of the community's total territory; when I presented the number to community members as a pie graph, they were simultaneously truly astonished by the amount, a bit embarrassed by the wealth it implied, and deeply proud of their accomplishment.

The native community chief is supposed to and usually does oversee the signing of rental agreements, because Aguaruna landlords are supposed to obey a communally regulated system of establishing fair rental prices. In 1999 the stated price for a roughly six-month rice-harvesting cycle was eight hundred soles per hectare. However, in the community's own records I found wild variation from the community price controls. Thus, the actual prices Aguaruna landlords were negotiating ranged from as high as one thousand soles to as low as one hundred soles.[12] Over the last several years prices have dropped considerably and stabilized (at the time of this writing) at around two hundred soles per hectare. The decrease is in part a product of the steady decline in market prices for rice over the last few years, but it also reflects the steady increase in internal competition among Aguaruna trying to secure renters.

Indeed, with 80 percent of the native community now internally designated as individually titled plots, this apparently radical liberalization of life in Bajo Naranjillo–Soritor has been taken to its logical extreme. Covered by forest as recently as the mid-1980s, the entire northeastern sector of the community is now a flat, open horizon of irrigated rice fields. Those fields are bisected down the middle with a well-maintained gravel road that (not in most people's memory) used to be an Aguaruna footpath (see Figure 9). The traffic of Aguaruna feet is now mixed with the traffic of hundreds of mestizo field hands bicycling their way to the rice fields and large Volvo semis extracting tons of rice sacks for

Figure 9 Rice fields of the native community Bajo Naranjillo. Photograph by author.

transport to the coast. Yet the road still belongs to the Aguaruna who live there because it traverses their native community—a fact the mestizo migrants and truck drivers are daily reminded of when they pay their toll to enter.

The emergence of this small class of Aguaruna landlords, forming a kind of rural real estate bourgeoisie, has created a host of new constraints that those involved in it seek to creatively customize. The most obvious problem is that the state now uses it as a weapon to shame those Aguaruna communities that do it and, more important, as a way to justify the state's lack of interest in resolving land disputes. It has also become a weapon of choice among those environmental activists who have become aware of this particular Aguaruna economic strategy. They see in it a kind of sacrilege, a violation of the secret pact that they think all Amazonian peoples signed in which the rights of indigeneity are conflated with dreams of an unaltered forest. All the complaints about it, of course, overlook an important fact. The decision to begin renting native community land began in a context where the ongoing destruction of forest and the rapid agriculturalization of everyday life were the projects of the Peruvian state. Indeed, in this particular region that process of market expansion, fueled by mass migration, is so advanced that becoming Aguaruna landlords was probably the wisest economic decision to make. As in the politics of customization displayed elsewhere in Aguarunia, the Aguaruna sought to make the best out of an inherently bad situation.

However, cashing in on their indigenous real estate opportunity has meant not only confronting a complicitous state and sour conservationists but also becoming accustomed to growing economic inequalities that are particularly notable in this Mayo River sector of Aguarunia. Thus, when I examined rental contracts for Bajo Naranjillo–Soritor in 1999, I also discovered a radical disparity in terms of the income generated. Certain family heads collected rent for as many as fifteen to thirty hectares. Others collected rent for only five or three hectares. And in some cases, there were families that rented no land whatsoever. Based on the numbers available from the contracts, we can assume a very rough average price of 500 soles per hectare during that year. A wealthy Aguaruna family with twenty hectares would have earned 10,000 soles (roughly $3,030 in 1999) about every six months for a rice-cultivation cycle. For rural Peru this is an extraordinary amount of money that far exceeds most of the main professional incomes (e.g., those of teachers, doctors, engineers, municipal authorities). Meanwhile, poorer Aguaruna families renting only three hectares would earn a mere 1,500 soles (roughly $455 in 1999) in the same period.[13]

This relatively new income gap is apparent on many levels, and during my time there community leaders were growing increasingly worried about it. Over the last decade or so those families administering more land rents have begun to accumulate material goods that act as markers of what Colloredo-Mansfeld (1999), inspired by Thorstein Veblen, calls a "native leisure class." In Bajo Naranjillo–Soritor the most visible signs of this brand of indigenous conspicuous consumption take the form of houses with cement foundations equipped with TVs, stereos, mountain bikes, DVD players, and a constant supply of nice clothes. In several cases it also includes privately owned cars and motorcycles, modes of personal transportation that are not at all common in most of rural Peru. To be fair, Aguaruna community members also invest a considerable amount of these rental profits in higher education for the younger generation. Indeed, to my knowledge there is no other similar concentration of Aguaruna families anywhere with the ability to consistently invest in the higher education of their children thanks to the money generated from land rents.

Unsurprisingly, those Aguaruna landlords with the most rental real estate in Bajo Naranjillo–Soritor belong to the families most clearly associated with the founding and titling of the community. For the most part this corresponds to either the direct descendants of one of the two original kakajams that lived in the area or the two original bilingual teachers who first relocated to the Mayo region from the Marañon River in the early 1970s and married into those families. Many of the more economically marginalized Aguaruna reside in the semi-separate *anexo* (annex, or satellite community) of Soritor; virtually everyone there is a relatively recent Aguaruna migrant from the Marañon River, where even fewer economic opportunities exist. Indeed, on many occasions they have expressed open resentment toward those in power in Bajo Naranjillo who have made a lot of money from renting their land. As one of the longtime leaders of Soritor once told me: "Sometimes we feel like unwanted guests on somebody else's land. In Bajo Naranjillo they have lots of rice. Here, we don't have anything."

But, considering the politics of indigenous customization, equally interesting questions are how, when, and why the Aguaruna rich and poor in Bajo Naranjillo–Soritor put aside their economic differences and express their ethnic solidarity. Unlike Aguaruna comuneros of the native community Los Naranjos, in a community like Bajo Naranjillo–Soritor armed resistance seems impractical. So near the highway and so engaged in daily transactions with apach society, they would risk a lot by engaging in such action. However, even though armed conflict appears impractical, it is far from unimaginable as a strategy of customization.

Faced with a form of land occupation that is outside their contractual control and contributes nothing to their rents, the residents of Bajo Naranjillo–Soritor do prove willing to band together to perform the visionary politics of Aguarunia. When Ministry of Agriculture officials pressured community leaders in 1999 to recognize usufruct rights to a small group of migrants living in the southeastern sector of the native community, the Aguaruna from Bajo Naranjillo–Soritor did not do so without first putting up a fight, nor without customizing the terms of their own indigenous land concession. Before deciding to recognize the migrants' right to use the land without paying any rent, community leaders from both Bajo Naranjillo and Soritor mobilized a cadre of notable strong men unafraid to make the situation appear as confrontational as possible. They were charged with going to *inspeccionar* (inspect) the site in the company of Ministry officials, the migrants, and the tagalong ethnographer. When they arrived en masse and well armed for their performative confrontation, they had exactly the effect they intended on nervous state officials and bewildered representatives from the migrant settlement (see Figure 10).

Figure 10 Aguaruna from Bajo Naranjillo–Soritor inspect a migrant occupation of native land with a show of force, December 1998. Photograph by author.

It seemed pretty clear that no one really intended to start a physical conflict that day. But that wasn't the point. The point was that under certain kinds of conditions, faced with certain kinds of confrontational odds, notable men work together. Aguaruna men representing haves and have-nots, Aguaruna men representing natives from the Mayo River and others mere migrants from the Marañon, Aguaruna men from disparate, even rival, Aguaruna families put their internal disputes on hold. The point—at least from the perspective of the projects of customizing indigeneity—was that in certain moments, in certain kinds of confrontational circumstances, the many diverse paths that traverse Aguarunia suddenly converge.

Paths meet roads. Roads break down borders. New borders emerge to renew the visionary logic of paths. Paths, roads, and borders: these are all signs of the divergent material conditions of living life in Aguarunia. They mark different territories with different customs, signaling different peoples with different trajectories. And yet somehow they're all still interconnected. Crisscrossed, convoluted, confused. Overlapping, superimposed, and sometimes far removed. These diverse dimensions of the native community institution and the chiefly form of indigenous authority it gave rise to are some of the most salient parts of contemporary experience in Aguarunia. But the emerging chiefs and members of native communities are not alone in this maze of intersecting paths, roads, and borders. There are also those Aguaruna activists who seek to transcend this fragmented terrain of the native community in search of some truly planetary opportunities to customize indigeneity. That was a job best left to those building a network of indigenous organizations, large and small. That was a job for the visionary warriors who began wielding the weapons of pen and paper not only from within Peru but also beyond it.

6 Warriors of Pen and Paper

The Customization of Organizational Encounters

*The idea came to me when I was little, approximately nine or ten years old.
My fellow Aguaruna lived in fear of the whites that we called Christians. . . .
So, because of this I got the idea that when I got bigger, I would be the person
to organize a military and start attacking them. And I would secede and
form another nation apart from the Peruvian one because I didn't identify
with a concept of the [Peruvian] nation. And even now I don't feel Peruvian,
of course not. I feel like I am Aguaruna.*
Adolfo Juep Nampin, cofounder of OAAM and OCCAAM (personal interview)

The true Aguaruna leader is not elected. He is born and then recognized.
A popular refrain repeated by many Aguaruna leaders to the author

The previous two chapters establish a context in which Aguaruna bilingual
teachers and native community activists began to position themselves to found
and ultimately spearhead Peru's pan-Amazonian movement. The twelve years
bookended by President Belaúnde's exile in 1968 and his return to power in
1980 were also the era of the first efforts toward an organized ethnic alliance
among indigenous Amazonians across the Peruvian landscape. Foreign missionaries had given the Amazonians the gift of bilingual literacy and with it a
new means of disseminating an interethnic consciousness. Velasco gave them
a "native community" consciousness and state territories to materially defend
and economically exploit. With both came ideological and practical struggles
to continue the work of getting accustomed to and beginning to customize a
politics of indigeneity.

The national and international dimensions of the pan-Amazonian movement led by Aguaruna activists beginning in the late 1970s were likely at the
time well beyond the imagination of any of these other actors—surrogate state
missionaries and military radicals, among others. Like popular social movements everywhere in Latin America, the Amazonians began to articulate new
political demands, often drawing on international sources of leverage (see

Keck and Sikkink, 1998). Increasingly vocal indigenous demands for political inclusion, territory, language, intellectual property, and, as a kind of ideological catch-all, cultural identity have come to redefine nation-states across the globe. Indigenous movements challenge and at the same time creatively engage the various ideologies of liberal citizenship, capitalist democracy, and national culture that have dominated in the nation-state form in the latter half of the twentieth century (see Alvarez, Dagnino, and Escobar, 1998; Warren and Jackson, 2002; Niezen, 2003).

By the late 1970s the direct forms of patronage over Amazonians held first by competing SIL and Jesuit missionaries and then by corporatist bureaucrats from the reformist military regime were rapidly receding.[1] Like other "underdeveloped" countries, Peru surfaced from the 1970s as a Third World debtor. Added to this was a growing preoccupation during the 1980s with the expansion of the state war against the Shining Path. By the time the violence and counterviolence subsided in the mid-1990s, the civil war had cost the lives of nearly seventy thousand Peruvians. Most of the violence and social instability occurred in the Andean provinces, Lima, and central Amazonian regions. The impact in the northern Amazonian provinces was marginal by comparison. Thus, most of Aguarunia was spared the radically transformative rupture of people's lives and psyches that occurred in a number of other places in the country.

The surprising win of Alberto Fujimori in the 1990 presidential election resulted in dramatic effects on the economy and politics of the country. Fujimori successfully decapitated the Shining Path by capturing its charismatic leader, Abimael Guzmán. But he did so through a brand of autocratic and secretive politics that ten years later led to his exile to Japan.[2] He responded to the hyperinflated economy, inherited from Alan García, with what became known as "Fujishock." This marked a dramatic turn to compliance with the International Monetary Fund (IMF) structural adjustment programs and other neoliberal trends in the world economy. The Peruvian government also strategically increased budget decentralization during Fujimori's second term. Fujimori's actions to distribute more municipal funds to provincial governments, spend money on rural infrastructure, and promote selected social services for the poor worked to prepare the poor to embrace his ambition to stay in office for a third term (Wise, 2003).

During this same period of the 1980s international advocacy networks expanded radically in Peru. This was part of a broader phenomenon of NGOs stepping in to do the work states and market actors did not do during the last two decades of the twentieth century (see Keck and Sikkink, 1998; Turner, 2003).

Issue-oriented NGOs—small, medium, and large—were a crucial part of this growth in the civil society sphere. Although the scope of NGO activities is diverse, the overwhelming tendency, as Keck and Sikkink note, is toward three interrelated themes and their various offshoots: human rights, gender, and the environment. The environment in particular—sparked by the global growth in concern about our collective ecological fate—is significant here. More than any of the other civil society agendas, it became a principal point of articulation for Peru's pan-Amazonian movement, so much so that one wonders where Amazonian indigeneity would be today without it.

Leaders in and of the Amazon

The network of indigenous organizations that Aguaruna activists have built over the last three decades has become the primary site for mediating inter-ethnic encounters on multiple scales within and beyond Peru. The political contours of Aguaruna organizations continue to shift periodically. Their appearance at any given moment should be viewed as a kind of still life of what in reality is an ongoing transformative process. Table 2 provides a glimpse into the state of Aguaruna organizational networks as I knew them at the turn of the twenty-first century. The sheer number of organizations, most of them legally registered, for a relatively small indigenous population is astonishing. Indeed, it has the effect of representing Aguarunia as if it were reducible to a flurry of memorizable acronyms. It is clearly a sign and symptom of Aguarunia's incorporation into the hegemony of bureaucratic shorthand practiced by nation-states, NGOs, and corporations. But to overemphasize this point would be to overlook how Aguaruna activists deploy their emerging acronymic indigeneity as part of a different kind of politics: a politics of customizing indigenous bureaucracy so that it meets the noninstitutional expectations of Aguarunia.

At both national and regional levels these organizations work on democratic principles of voluntary corporate affiliation and ethnic identity–based representation. The only major international organization that represents Amazonian peoples is the Coordinadora de Organizaciones Indígenas de la Cuenca Amazónica (COICA). Although its headquarters are now in Quito, COICA was founded in Peru and now has national-level member affiliates in nine Amazonian countries. In Peru there are currently two national organizations of indigenous Amazonians, AIDESEP and CONAP. In the late 1990s AIDESEP—the older and unquestionably more established organization—initiated an emerging pan-indigenous Peruvian organization, Coordinadora Permanente de los

Table 2 Amazonian and local Aguaruna/Huambisa organizations

Acronym	Name	Location	Initiation of efforts	Year of legal inscription	Primary indigenous founders
National level					
AIDESEP	Asociación Interétnica de Desarrollo de la Selva Peruana	Lima	1980	1985	CAH, CECONSEC, Congreso Amuesha FECONAU, FEDECOCA,
CONAP	Confederación de Nacionalidades Amazónicas del Perú	Lima	1986	1990*	CART, CONOAP, FECONAU, FECONAYA, FECONAYY, FENAMAD, OCCAAM**
Regional level					
CAH	Consejo Aguaruna Huambisa	Urakusa (originally Napuruka) / Marañon River	1977	1980*	Miguel Jempets, Francisco Juwau, Evaristo Nugkuag, Gerardo Wipio Deicat
FAD	Federación de Comunidades Aguarunas del Domingusa	Yumigkus / Domingusa River	late 1980s	1990	David Caicharo
FECONADIC	Federación de Comunidades Nativas del Distrito de Cahuapanas	Barranquita/ Cahuapanas River	1982	1993	?
FECOHRSA	Federación de Comunidades Huambisas del Río Santiago	Soledad / Santiago River	mid-1990s	?	Juan Noningo
FECONARIN	Federación de Comunidades Nativas Aguarunas del Río Nieva	Japaime Escuela (originally Tunduza) / Nieva River	late 1980s	1989*	Martín Reátegui
FEMAAM	Federación de Mujeres Aguarunas del Alto Marañon	Yamayakat / Marañon River	?	?	?
FENARA	Federación Nativa Awajun del Río Apaga	Atahualpa / Apaga River	1999	1999*	Tito Tuyasa Tunquia

Acronym	Full Name	River / Location	Founded	Legal Inscription	Leaders
FERIAM (previously OAAM and ORIAM)	Federación Regional Indígena del Alto Mayo	Bajo Naranjillo / Mayo River	2004	2006	Tito Nugkuag, Elias Peas
	Ijumbau Chapi Shiwag ("meeting of the people of the palm tree")	Santa Rosa / Yurapaga River	late 1970s	1986*	Francisco Shajian
OAAM (now FERIAM)	Organización Aguaruna del Alto Mayo	Bajo Naranjillo / Mayo River	late 1970s	1982*	Samuel Bazan, Noe Cahuaza, Adolfo Juep
OCCAAM	Organización Central de Comunidades Aguarunas del Alto Marañon	Yamayakat / Marañon River	1975	1983	Adolfo Juep, Salomón Katip, José Lirio
ODECINAC	Organización de Desarrollo de las Comunidades Indígenas Numpatkaim y Alto Comaina	Kusu-Chico/ Numpatkaim River	2002	2002	Antonio Mayan, Salomón Samaniego, Benito Tetsa, Wilson Tetsa
ODECOFROC	Organización de Desarrollo de las Comunidades Fronterizas del Cenepa	Mamayaque / Cenepa River	mid-1990s	1996*	Francisco Quiaco, Carlos Tijiats
ONAPAA	Organización Nativa Aguaruna de la Provincia de Alto Amazonas	Sachapapa / Potro River	?	1987*	?
ORASI	Organización Regional Aguaruna de San Ignacio	Naranjos / Chinchipe River	1990	?	Francisco Shajian, Carlos Ukuncham
ORIAM (now FERIAM)	Organización Regional Indígena del Alto Mayo	Shampuyacu / Mayo River	early 1990s	1992*	Santos Adan, Ruben Wajajai

*Legal inscription verified.

**CART (Central Ashaninka del Río Tambo); CONOAP (Consejo de Comunidades Nativas Nomatsguenga y Asháninka de Pangoa); FECONAYA (Federación de Comunidades Nativas Yanesha); FECONAYY (Federación de Comunidades Nativas Yine Yami); FENAMAD (Federacion Nativa del Río Madre de Dios).

Pueblos Indígenas del Perú (COPPIP). This followed decades of political and ideological separation—the native community Amazonians versus the peasant community Andeans. The explicit purpose was to seek alliances with newer Andean organizations, particularly those invested in ecological concerns and eager to reappropriate a publicly politicized form of Andean indigeneity to counter the various submerged forms of indigeneity that dominate in Peru's Andean milieu. Thus, AIDESEP built an alliance with the Coordinadora Nacional de Comunidades Afectadas por la Minería (CONACAMI), an organization with growing support that works to counter the negative impact of mining activities in Andean communities. However, this story, still very much in the making, of emerging Amazonian-Andean alliances is not one I try to detail here (see Greene, 2006).

CONAP and AIDESEP compete for regional-level organizational affiliates, federated clusters of titled native communities that are in essence the basic sociopolitical building block of the pan-Amazonian movement. Amazonian leaders typically document their institutional affiliations. This proves important because sometimes only by demonstrating evidence of a solid grassroots base can an organization establish a sense of legitimacy in the eyes of international advocacy groups, funding agencies, and the state itself. Many of the Amazonians' financial and political supporters hold romantic assumptions about indigenous peoples' struggles, which—in perfect synchrony with the universalizing assumptions of indigeneity—they assume to be the same everywhere. This often leads to major disappointment when indigenous organizational actors fail to speak with a "unified" voice and instead make internal dissent visible. As a result, moments of representational crisis and corporate restructuring come and go, subject to a complicated flow of customizing Amazonian politics and politicizing Amazonian customs.

Expansion of the movement and the number of organizations can be explained by two general trends: the birth of organized movements in previously unorganized areas and the ongoing internal restructuring of older organizations. For example, just five pioneering organizations (Consejo Aguaruna Huambisa; CAH), Shipibo (Federación de Comunidades Nativas del Ucayali; FECONAU), Amuesha (Congreso Amuesha), Ashaninka (Central de Comunidades Nativas de la Selva Central; CECONSEC), and Cocama-Cocamilla (Federación de Comunidades Nativas Cocama-Cocamilla; FEDECOCA) among the Aguaruna peoples confederated to form the national-level association AIDESEP in 1980. By 2001 AIDESEP represented forty-seven regional organizations. Most of this expansion is due to the emergence of more recent organizations in areas or among ethnic groups not previously organized. As the case of Aguarunia demonstrates particularly well, the expansion of the movement is also due to new organizational structures that break off from older and larger ones. This constitutes a kind of bottom-up decentralization effort that reflects an imperative to customize these emergent forms of institutional power by redistributing them at more and more localized levels.

Regional organizational leaders and delegates elect their Lima representatives. Management of more significant budgets at the national level, however, requires that these organizations privately contract administrative, legal, and technical support staff. At the regional level a quorum of affiliated native community chiefs (who are elected by their own communal assemblies) votes to elect organization leaders. At every level the constituency elects a board of directors (president, vice-president, treasurer, one or more spokespersons, and so on) to the organization for terms of two to four years depending on the electoral principles stated in the statute.

Dean (2003) discusses the profound gender imbalance found in Amazonian organization politics, where leaders are overwhelmingly men. In broad terms his argument is correct. However, considerable variation occurs across different ethnic groups. As can be appreciated from Table 2, all but one of the recognized founders of every Aguaruna organization are men. An exception, the recently founded Federación de Mujeres Aguarunas del Alto Marañon (FEMAAM), an exclusively female-run Aguaruna organization, would appear to challenge this logic.[3] And there are other Aguaruna women involved in Aguaruna politics worth noting. An all-male electorate of community chiefs elected Amanda Lunginote in 2000 as the first female president of a well-established Aguaruna organization in the Nieva River area (Federación de Comunidades Nativas Aguarunas del Río Nieva; FECONARIN). They intended it as an experiment in female leadership. Furthermore, regional and national organizations alike now often reserve a formal or informal position within their organizations for a representative of *asuntos femininos* (women's issues).

The relatively recent inclusion of female representatives and women's issues is in part a function of the extent of school-based education, state or NGO campaigns and other influences in a given area. Thus, the handful of Aguaruna women leaders I have met are all fluently bilingual and typically hold higher degrees of education and access to the apach world beyond Aguarunia than does the average woman in a native community. The increasing inclusion of women is also a direct reflection of outside advocates, allies, and financial supporters requiring indigenous organizations to speak directly to women's issues. As a result, many indigenous men in leadership positions, whatever their personal opinions, have come to factor it into the organizational profile.

The Actors: Amazonians and Their "Experts"

Most Aguaruna activists recognize OCCAAM as the oldest regional-level Aguaruna organization. The immediate precursor to OCCAAM was a small *comité de producción* (an agricultural production committee) founded in the mid-1970s in the native community Yamayakat, the site of Roger Winans's Nazarene school from decades earlier. The principal actors were a handful of SIL-trained bilingual teachers. Originally, their outlook was a predominantly economic one: how best to commercialize cacao. The famed bilingual teacher Daniel Dánduchu acted as the first president of the committee. But by most accounts the real impetus behind the organization was a teacher named Salomón Katip. In an interview in 2000, he described the moment of OCCAAM's founding as a process of solidifying the internal pacification of Aguarunia but as a means of redirecting some familiar warlike sentiments toward an emerging mestizo enemy:

> I remember that they [the Aguaruna] seemed like children. With all the [internal] conflicts there wasn't any peace either. But when the organization was started, only then was there peace. It spread all the way to Nieva. Then we [bilingual teachers] met thinking it would be more mature to work united and not to fight among ourselves. And that our true enemies are the mestizos, against whom we should struggle. Better that we fight with those demonic lost souls [*iwanch*—refers to mestizos].[4] That's what I said.

Although its mission has expanded considerably since its creation, OCCAAM has always maintained an economically interested orientation. Katip's statement makes clear that the economic aspirations are inextricable from a larger political concern. Competitive engagement in the market translated into a new kind of war tactic for a new enemy whose battlefield was the market. The apach, or mestizo, thus became a kind of generic symbol in Aguarunia. "Mestizo" represents all those processes of neocolonial incorporation into capitalist markets and state institutions that Aguaruna organizations were founded to confront. As discussed in the previous chapter, the point of the confrontation is not usually to reject the processes outright but to actively negotiate them, to customize them, in ways that make them accord with the realities of Aguarunia.

By 1977 several Aguaruna activists in the native community Mamayaque at the mouth of the Cenepa River began their own efforts to build an organization, which they called the Consejo Aguaruna Huambisa. As its name reveals, the Consejo aimed to institutionalize a movement toward a Jivaroan organization that allied the Aguaruna with their customary rivals, the Huambisa. Gerardo Wipio Deicat, working as a bilingual teacher in communities on the Marañon, was one of the original participants in this process. But the main catalyst was Evaristo Nugkuag. Faced with a critical shortage of funds while pursuing his university education in Lima, Nugkuag returned to the Upper Marañon River area and began to lead the Consejo. Several external influences were present at the Consejo's inception. The most direct influence came from a team of Spanish and Peruvian development experts, named Grupo Desarrollo del Alto Marañon (Grupo DAM). In fact, Santiago Manuig, president of the Consejo from 1989 to 1993, clarified to me in an interview that the Consejo appropriated its institutional focus—with designated areas for education, legal/territory issues, health, and economy—directly from Grupo DAM's original four-part development agenda.

The Consejo and OCCAAM are the oldest Aguaruna organizations in the Department of Amazonas; however, several other initiatives were under way in other areas by the end of the 1970s. After relocating to the Mayo River in the Department of San Martín to found SIL bilingual schools, Adolfo Juep became the main catalyst for the OAAM. One of Juep's SIL classmates from Yarinacocha, Francisco Shajian, engaged in similar long-distance political action. Originally from the Upper Marañon area, Shajian was sent to found an SIL school on the Lower Marañon River in the Department of Loreto. There he founded Ijumbau Chapi Shiwag, the only organization to date that carries a name in the Aguaruna language and, tellingly enough, has no acronym. Aguaruna activists simply shorten it to Chapi Shiwag, meaning "people of the palm tree."

This brief sketch of the four oldest Aguaruna organizations only begins to reveal the multiply configured layers of political action that produced the movement. Processes at the national and international levels were central in allowing these more regional ethnic organizations to take on a wider pan-Amazonian political project. The Barbados conference of 1971 calling attention to the plight of indigenous South Americans was crucial in this respect. By late 1976 domestic and foreign intellectual activists in Peru, each working in different areas of Amazonia with different ethnic groups, came together in informal meetings in the capital city. They spontaneously named themselves the Grupo de Investigadores de la Selva. And in their first internal communiqué, they labeled themselves the "inheritors of the current of thought illustrated by the Barbados Symposium" (Grupo de Investigadores de la Selva, 1976).[5]

A French biologist, two American anthropologists, and two Peruvian anthropologists working in SINAMOS at the time were the main protagonists.[6] By most accounts I have heard, the Grupo also became a space for indigenous Amazonian self-representation at the national level through accident rather than conscious intent. In an interview, Richard Smith, one of the leading protagonists, recalled that the Grupo originally formed out of a fear of persecution for their political views from repressive state regimes (the norm in 1970s Latin America). They set out to establish a safety and communication network among like-minded professional intellectuals and development activists working in Amazonia. The Grupo did, however, recognize in its first meeting a commitment to the "liberation of the Indian ethnic groups" and "concepts of action different from classical anthropology," especially for "those that have lived through the moments of organizing Indian communities in the last few years" (Grupo de Investigadores de la Selva, 1976). This commitment to advocacy—in addition to a more questionable desire to "show off" regional indigenous leaders to their colleagues, according to Smith—prompted some members to start bringing native community representatives to the meetings. Originally, these representatives consisted primarily of community-based Aguaruna, Amuesha, Ashaninka, and Shipibo-Conibo activists, since by that time each of these ethnic groups had established regional organizational initiatives.

The professional experts' logic soon backfired. The indigenous leaders came to the Lima meetings to complain about more than common enemies, such as the Peruvian state, that they shared with the Grupo. They also came to complain about the development work and research in which these self-identified Amazonian experts were engaged. The tension soon produced an institutionalized split. Peruvian anthropologists in the Grupo, principally Carlos Mora and Alberto Chirif, founded a nonprofit organization, Centro de Investigaciones y Promoción Amazónica (CIPA). In response, Amazonian leaders decided to found their own indigenous-directed organization, one that declared a kind of semi-independence from the Grupo and CIPA. The organization now known as AIDESEP was born.[7]

The original spirit of collaboration between AIDESEP, CIPA, and the other independent Grupo members soon became distorted by personal, institutional, and ethnic agendas that failed to coincide. In the early years CIPA obtained international funding, rented an apartment they called the *casa nativa* where AIDESEP members and other Amazonian natives could stay while in Lima, and began working on land and legal issues. CIPA personnel also created opportunities for a select few Amazonian leaders, principally the Aguaruna leader Evaristo Nugkuag, to gain greater international exposure. Thus, Nugkuag attended a conference with several recently established indigenous rights NGOs (Cultural Survival, International Working Group on Indigenous Affairs [IWGIA], and Survival International) at the University of Wisconsin in the late 1970s. He then went to the Netherlands in 1980 for the Russell Tribunal on the Rights of Indians, which many other indigenous leaders in Latin America identify as a catalyst for international networking (Brysk, 2000: 87). From Nugkuag's perspective the emerging structure of this new enterprise appeared to mimic a familiar pattern of dependency that the experts were, in theory rather than in practice, working against:

> They got the money. But why did mostly CIPA get the money in 1978? They just constituted themselves as CIPA as a result of our meeting in Lima. We [natives] had carried the needs [of communities] already planned out and agreed upon. . . . So, seeing that the needs were great and anticipating from then on to serve us better, they form their NGO and get money. . . . And they buy their own office, they buy their car, they had salaries, they had loans to make [i.e., titled] communities. So we needed, we wanted to know: How's it going to be? How much is there? You know. We wanted them to inform us with details. And later we said they should permit us to have an indigenous person that works there too to learn. . . . They didn't want that. They said . . . CIPA and international cooperative agencies understand each other. . . . So we looked for our own organization to represent us. That was a meeting with a heated discussion, on an afternoon like today. And that's when it emerged and we made AIDESEP. So, CIPA lost us, various communities, various federations, but they had their car, their house, their office, etc., etc. (personal interview)

AIDESEP was not legally registered as a nonprofit until 1985. Before then Nugkuag presided over the organization informally without any direct funding and with tensions increasing because of the pattern of paternalism he noted in these domestic and foreign Amazonian experts. AIDESEP's exposure grew exponentially in the mid-1980s thanks in part to the reappearance of Richard Smith. He returned to Lima after a few years' absence to set up a South American office of OXFAM America. OXFAM almost instantly became one of AIDESEP's direct sources of financial support. Some see in this simply a change of guard, AIDESEP emerging from its dependence on a domestic Peruvian NGO into dependence on an internationally financed NGO. Others see it as a distinct moment of financial liberation: since the mid-1980s AIDESEP has attempted, whenever possible, to pursue a path of internal financial management even if constantly forced to depend on international forms of financial support.

OXFAM's most significant contribution to the expansion of the Amazonian movement and AIDESEP's exposure in it began in 1984. Working with representatives from AIDESEP, OXFAM organized a meeting among emergent Amazonian indigenous organizations from four other countries: Colombia, Bolivia, Ecuador, and Brazil. The result was the creation of the now widely recognized international Amazonian organization COICA. As leader of AIDESEP, Nugkuag also took the lead in representing COICA following the 1984 meeting. COICA's activities were coordinated from Lima until the early 1990s when, partly in response to concerns over the concentration of leadership in Nugkuag's hands, COICA transferred its headquarters to Ecuador (see Smith, 1996).

The purpose behind the meeting that gave rise to COICA was to expose Amazonian representatives from different countries to the activities of the still young Work Group on Indigenous Populations formed at the United Nations in 1982 (Conclusiones de la Reunión de Trabajo . . . , 1984). As such, the 1984 encounter marks a starting point for widespread discussion, dissemination, and adoption of the internationally politicized term "indigenous" by Amazonian representatives. Many of them were more familiar with other kinds of colonial terminology, each one reflecting the peculiar histories of their countries of origin (see Smith, 1996).

For centuries in Peru the term *indígena*—as in the colonial *tributo indígena* (indigenous tribute)—referred almost exclusively to highland Andean peoples. This logic was institutionalized again during the height of the appropriately named indigenista era of the 1920s, when President Leguía constitutionally recognized the comunidad indígena as the communal land system for Andeans. This Andean-centric view of who an indígena was in Peru was only really officially declared defunct when in 1968 the Velasco state decided to ideologically transform Andeans into campesinos. As the names from older Amazonian federations founded in the wake of the Native Communities Law of 1974 reveal, Amazonians had grown accustomed to the term *nativo*. The state adopted the language of nativism in order to replace pejoratively interchangeable Spanish and Quechua terms, such as *indio salvaje* and *chuncho*, that were commonly used to refer to Amazonians, and still are in some popular discourse. The state also clearly did so to differentiate Amazonians from the historically Andeanized image of who an indígena is and what region an indígena is from in Peru. Notably, many of the newer Amazonian federations now substitute the term *indígena* for *nativo*. This is a direct consequence of Amazonians' recognition of the term's international cachet. The sense is that being a nativo in Peru is comparable to being an indígena outside, if not always inside, Peru. This act of explicit appropriation of the international language of indigeneity was another essential step in consolidating the concentric layers of indigeneity in which the Aguaruna, as Amazonians and not Andeans, are enmeshed in Peru.

By the mid-1980s CIPA and AIDESEP, the original Amazonian experts and their Amazonian invitees, were competing for international funding to run their respective organizations. According to participant-observers like Smith (1996), this was a direct result of the impressive, if also controversial, influence that Nugkuag exerted in Peru's transnational Amazonian movement. During much of the 1980s he was working at regional, national, and international levels. He was often found simultaneously representing the Jivaro bloc via the Consejo Aguaruna Huambisa, Peruvian Amazonia via AIDESEP, and much of lowland South America via COICA. Without a doubt one of his most important achievements in this respect was the explicit alignment of the Amazonian indigenous agenda with that of powerful environmental organizations. This alliance formally took shape during Nugkuag's tenure as COICA president with the signing of the 1990 Iquitos Declaration. Amazonian leaders and all the major international environmental organizations publicly declared that they were engaged in a shared struggle, just in time for the "sustainable development" policy era (see Greene, 2006).

Controversies also began to erupt over international awards Nugkuag received, his constant international engagements with institutions as powerful as the World Bank, and the perception that the amount of institutional power he wielded was too great. The populist president Alan García (1985–1990) unwittingly contributed to this moment of controversy in the Amazonian movement during his famous Rimanakuy tour of the Peruvian provinces in 1986 (see Figure 11). García's Rimanakuy, meaning something like "to talk to each other" in

Quechua, constituted a series of town-hall-style meetings convoked to gauge provincial people's needs and capture voter's imaginations. The Rimanakuy held in the central Amazonian city of Pucallpa was reserved for hundreds of representatives from native communities. During the meeting several Yanesha and Aguaruna activists met to discuss their disaffection from AIDESEP and to plan another national-level organization (CONAP, 1987). They soon discovered that Peruvian NGOs like CIPA, a constant object of AIDESEP's criticism, were more than happy to provide the assistance necessary to realize that plan.[8]

During a meeting in May 1987 fifteen regional Amazonian federations banded together to create CONAP with the assistance of a handful of interested Peruvian NGOs. Aníbal Francisco Coñivo, a Yanesha leader, spearheaded the effort and became CONAP's first president. José Lirio, who had recently stepped down from office in the Aguaruna organization OCCAAM, became vice-president. In an interview Lirio recalled that CONAP was formed partly as a result of "misgivings among leaders." This was implied not only by tensions with AIDESEP but also by the long-standing rivalry between the regional

Figure 11 President Alan García during his 1986 Rimanakuy meeting in Pucallpa. Photograph reproduced with permission of Carlos Mora Bernasconi.

Aguaruna organizations OCCAAM and CAH. But Lirio insisted that the real impetus for his participation in the creation of CONAP was "to create a representative organization better than AIDESEP because we said AIDESEP did not have a political presence." In Lima newspapers AIDESEP immediately rejected the legitimacy of CONAP and interpreted it as an attempt by their nonindigenous NGO rivals in Lima to fabricate a "pseudo confederation" (see AIDESEP, cited in CONAP, 1987: 10). CONAP's founders, however, did not stand down. And for the next several years both organizations' news bulletins became a forum for launching allegations and counter-allegations about claims to legitimacy in a war over Amazonian indigenous self-representation.

The national-level crisis of representation reverberated at the regional level. For example, a crisis of the Upper Mayo River Aguaruna organization OAAM was a direct result of the struggles between AIDESEP and CONAP. OAAM's founders quickly grew suspicious of Santos Adan, who upon being elected to preside over OAAM in 1985 made a decision to affiliate the organization with AIDESEP. An open conflict resulted when Adan refused to relinquish power at the end of his two-year term. Original founders of OAAM, Noé Cahuaza and Samuel Bazan, attended the first CONAP congress in 1987. Instead of listing themselves as representatives of OAAM, they chose the more generic "representatives from Upper Mayo communities" (CONAP, 1987). Later that same year they decided to work around Adan, who refused to call a new election. Convoking a quorum of native community representatives affiliated with OAAM without Adan's participation, Cahuaza and Bazan succeeded in naming Jaime Pijuch the new OAAM president.

For the next several years the AIDESEP/CONAP wounds festered, and OAAM's crisis continued unabated. Adan, acting as president of OAAM, refused to give up the OAAM record book and official seal and continued to work with AIDESEP. Pijuch, also acting as OAAM president, started a new record book and filed for an official affiliation with AIDESEP's Lima rival, CONAP. As one can appreciate from their periodic news bulletins, CONAP and AIDESEP both claimed OAAM as their exclusive affiliate from 1988 to about 1990 (see CONAP, 1988a, 1988b, 1989; AIDESEP, 1988, 1989, 1990). The conflict was finally resolved in June 1991 when Noé Cahuaza, acting as president of the anti-Adan OAAM faction, invited community heads, state officials, and NGO representatives to the community Bajo Naranjillo and publicly denounced Adan's activities as those of the "pseudo-president of OAAM" (OAAM, 1991; Cahuaza Noashampi, 1991).

The national-level struggle over Amazonian self-representation went into a latent stage once it became clear to AIDESEP leaders that their CONAP rivals were simply not going to back down. CONAP has never been able to match the financial and political resources of AIDESEP, whose international funding contacts are stronger and whose grassroots base is larger. But CONAP's image has transformed considerably with changes in leadership. In 1995 a savvy, university-trained Aguaruna leader, César Sarasara, replaced the original Yanesha founder. He was reelected twice and served as president until 2007, despite similar allegations that he represented the style of top-down leadership Amazonians had witnessed from Nugkuag in AIDESEP during the 1980s and early 1990s. To his credit, Sarasara built the CONAP into a respectable competitor of AIDESEP. As I document elsewhere, this has much to do with his successful negotiation of a high-profile international bioprospecting venture that catapulted CONAP to a kind of international stardom in the realm of indigenous intellectual property rights issues (see Greene, 2004b).

Customizing International Indigenous Engagements

Academic discussions surrounding indigenous movements abound with talk of ethnic-state politics, neoliberal multicultural reforms, the intensification of advocacy networking, rights claims, representational politics, the waxing of identity and the waning of class, and so on (see Brysk, 2000; Warren and Jackson, 2002; Van Cott, 2000; Albó, 1991; Niezen, 2003; Hale, 2002). Although always occurring at local and national scales, the phenomenon of contemporary indigeneity is routinely described as imbricated in international politics and processes. My interest, however, is not merely in documenting the ways in which indigeneity is abstracted to the level of nation-state and globe. I'm also interested in the projects of customization that Aguaruna activists put into political practice to make indigeneity more concrete. How do contemporary organizational politics in Aguarunia reveal something about the particular modes of purposeful action Aguaruna activists use to customize the indigeneity imposed on them? How do such actions reverberate through the material space and the mental plane I call Aguarunia?

We might start with what many Aguaruna activists consider the obvious. The names of regional Aguaruna organizations reveal that most of them take a river as the basis for their sense of political, corporate locality (see Table 2). Contemporary Aguaruna activists explain this as an outgrowth of customary associations between rivers and endogamous kin groupings headed by strong men figures. As Octavio Shakaime, a well-known educator in the town of Nieva, once put it, "The river basin is the foundation because customarily things were managed according to river basins and names of rivers."

The exceptions to the adoption of river names for organizational structures are worthy of note. Organizations such as the Organización Regional Aguaruna de San Ignacio (ORASI; named after the province of San Ignacio in the Department of Cajamarca) represent Aguaruna organizational initiatives that articulate ethnic identity claims within state administrative categories. The most significant exception to the "river rule" is the Consejo Aguaruna Huambisa, which initially sought to speak broadly for the entire Jivaro collective, at least on the Upper Marañon and its main tributaries, Chiriaco, Cenepa, Nieva, Domingusa, Santiago. However, according to Nugkuag, the principal founder, the Consejo originally assigned each river sector its own representative, a design that also reflects the customary organization by corporate river groups. But such a structure proved insufficient to appease the hunger for decentralization in Aguarunia. By the end of the 1980s virtually every major river sector was complaining about a perceived monopolization of power and resources in the Consejo and maneuvering to create its own river-based organization. Nowadays each major river sector except Chiriaco has its own Aguaruna, or in the case of the Santiago River, Huambisa, organization.[9]

River-based autonomy is directly related to the singular importance attributed to charismatic strong men who many Aguaruna activists believe are the very foundation of the Aguaruna's contemporary ethnic organizations. For example, when I asked him to reflect on the fragmentation of the Consejo into individual river organizations, José Lirio, founder of OCCAAM, gave this response:

> The very structure of living, the very social structure of the Aguaruna people did not permit having an organization that centralizes all the native communities because the communities' social nature does not permit it. It was undoable because it couldn't be adjusted right; there was no piece to make it operate correctly. Most importantly: How are we going to find an authentic fit? It doesn't come from that one [the Consejo]. That's why OCCAAM maintained the hegemony that I and everyone else consider superior. We knew that in the future each river basin should have its own organization. That was already known then [when the Consejo and OCCAAM were started]. Because, in the old days Cenepa had a *pamuk* [another type of strong man warrior] or kakajam. Nieva

had a pamuk or kakajam. Santiago and the other rivers of the Jivaro peoples have representatives called pamuk or kakajam. (personal interview)

His invocation of pamuks and kakajams, related terms for the visionary strong man figure that predominates in Aguarunia, is more than merely meta-phorical.[10] Those who have *fundador* (founder) status within a particular orga-nization often continue to stand in for the organization in everyday discourse even when no longer occupying a formal role. Aguaruna speakers thus resort to a familiar practice of equating the name of a notable visionary leader with the river neighborhood he is thought capable of mobilizing (see Figure 12). I can't recall the number of times I heard people make an implicit reference to OCCAAM by saying "José Lirio *aentsjiyai*" (José Lirio's people) or to OAAM as "Adolfo Juep *aentsjiyai*" (Adolfo Juep's people). This is despite the fact that the former has not been in an elected post in OCCAAM since the mid-1980s, and the latter, although he was central in founding OAAM, never sought a formal office in it. Similarly, Evaristo Nugkuag's name is so frequently conflated with the Consejo at the regional level and AIDESEP at the national level in everyday discourse throughout Aguarunia that one is led to believe he has yet to relin-

Figure 12 Meeting of OCCAAM founders and leaders, 2003 (Adolfo Juep, Ricardo Apanú, Salomón Katip, and José Lirio). Photograph by author.

quish power in either organization. However, records from the two organizations show that his official status as an elected authority in the Consejo has alternated with that of multiple others since its foundation, and he has had no formal role in AIDESEP since the late 1980s.

The implication from the point of view of Aguarunia and the political imaginary with which it operates is clear. These fundadores are customizing themselves into reincarnations of the strong, biography-worthy warriors of the Aguaruna past. Up-and-coming leaders elected to take charge of the organizations they founded are forced to operate under the fundadores' shadow. Even those who have held such positions of authority confirm this. For example, Santiago Manuin, a two-term past president of the Consejo, stated to me directly, "He [Nugkuag] doesn't let others work in peace." The extent to which a newer leader can pragmatically prove his own visionary status—and thus crawl out from under another leader's aggrandized name—is thus a matter of constant political negotiation.

Customizing the Visionary Warriors' New Path

There are a number of other examples of the creative reworkings of indigeneity within Aguaruna organizational politics and the customization of strong man leadership it entails, two of which I will examine in detail.

The first example comes from the early years of the CAH. Founded about 1977, the Consejo was finally legally constituted a Peruvian nonprofit organization in 1980. According to its own statute the organizational mission is to "unify the actions of the Aguaruna and Huambisa communities" (Article 3.a), "be the element that reinforces ethnic identity" (Article 3.f), and "be the spokesperson of its members with other social sectors of the country" (Article 3.g). In Article 23 the statute also states that the president of the Consejo "can be called the waisam" and the vice-president the "kakajam."[11] This gesture effectively promotes the idea that the men occupying these roles should be more than simply indigenous activists and seek to become a new kind of visionary warrior. As founding member and first waisam president, Evaristo Nugkuag put the Consejo's vision into practical political action and catapulted the new organization onto the stage of international indigenous rights activism. He did so by successfully confronting a major foreign film project that set down on Aguaruna soil in the 1970s just as the Consejo was coming into being and Nugkuag was rising to the occasion.

The Aguaruna's new enemy was the internationally renowned German filmmaker Werner Herzog. Herzog's long cinematic obsession with Europe's sordid quest to spread civilization led him on a crash course with the Consejo's vision-ary indigenous politics. Herzog arrived in the Peruvian jungle in the late 1970s with plans to film *Fitzcarraldo*, which he initially hoped would be a commercial success and instead became a cult classic (see Goodwin, 1982). The movie de-picts the life of a nineteenth-century rubber baron of Irish origin who arrived in the Peruvian Amazon to realize his own egomaniacal fantasies. Infamous for his desire to civilize the Amazon by building an opera house in Iquitos that would be the envy of Europe, Carlos Fitzcarrald hoped to finance this dream by expanding his extractivist activities. His most notorious endeavor was an attempt to haul a cargo boat overland to reach an unreachable river network by using pulleys, logs, and, of course, indigenous laborers. The feat proved futile and cost the lives of several hundred laborers in the process.

Herzog thought he had located the perfect site to film Fitzcarrald's failed boat-on-land trick in the Aguaruna native community Wawaim on the Cenepa River. He planned to recruit Aguaruna men to work as laborers and extras in the filming. Discussions began in Wawaim and surrounding communities in February 1979 when Herzog's film crew from Wildlife Films announced an ap-proximate arrival date. The community members were divided on the matter from the start. Those willing to acquiesce knew this meant the possibility of earning temporary wages. However, discontent grew among other community members who perceived the film company's attitude as a familiarly paternalis-tic one completely out of tune with the expectations of Aguarunia. In early July representatives of the film crew arrived in Wawaim to present permits granted by a municipal council in Iquitos and the Peruvian Commission of Cinematic Promotion. Yet neither of these Peruvian entities held any direct authority over what were by then titled native community lands (Cultural Survival, 1979). The opposing faction of Aguaruna took action by sending a letter to the Ministry of Agriculture (the ministry that handles native community titles) and circulat-ing a petition that eventually found its way to the North American indigenous rights NGO Cultural Survival.

Wawaim community leaders clarified their position against Wildlife Films in a provincial newspaper published in the small town of Jaén. They believed that Herzog sought to "relive moments of exploitation and abuses of the man [Fitzcarrald] that caused the death of so many natives by working rubber. These scenes will later be shown in foreign countries and present us like savages; ask-ing help especially from those of us that have long hair. It's the fault of people like this that come to do business with our customs that we are frequently shit on and exploited by people that come from outside" (*Nor Oriente*, 1979a). They went on to justify their decision to reject the filming activities by demanding recognition of their property rights in accordance with the then recent Native Communities Law. Nugkuag, acting as president of the recently founded Consejo, took charge of the struggle at the national and international levels. In an August 1979 letter to Cultural Survival, Nugkuag depicts the Consejo as a defender of the rights of fifty different Aguaruna and Huambisa native communities and declares outright: "We now know that Fitzcarrald and Herzog are like each other" (Consejo Aguaruna Huambisa, 1979).

Faced with international exposure and Aguaruna opposition, the film crew set up camp on the banks of the Marañon anyway. Technically they were just outside the boundaries of local native communities but definitely still inside what Aguaruna on the Cenepa and Upper Marañon considered their river neighborhoods. The film crew also hired several willing Aguaruna laborers to work at the camp as armed guards. This the Consejo and affected community leaders from Wawaim interpreted as a classic divide-and-conquer strategy and simply, in their words, "more provocation" (*Nor Oriente*, 1979b). In an interview Nugkuag remembered that even though the crew set up camp outside Wawaim, they still insisted on entering the native community because it was near a site Herzog considered essential for some of the movie's most important scenes. "When they were on the state-owned land, they still continued with the same thing. Then, they wanted to cut a trail through the community. The community didn't want them to move there."

The saga dragged on without resolution into October and November. Tensions rose dramatically when the Aguaruna in protest became privy to an article published in the popular Lima magazine *Caretas*. The article crudely characterized the conflict as a battle of "indios y gringos" and clearly sided with the plight of the German filmmaker (see *Caretas*, 1979). *Caretas* depicted Nugkuag as the leader of a constitutionally "unrecognized" organization that was akin to a "separatist movement." More outrageous still was the claim that the Consejo's protest consisted merely of "lies, defamation, slander, and violence." To complicate things further, Aguaruna bilingual teachers active on the scene reported ongoing events in provincial newspapers. In one report a teacher noted increasing unrest when native community members realized the movie crew continued to film scenes in the area after the original permits had expired and new ones had been denied by the Peruvian government in hopes of avoiding the conflict (Samaniego, 1979a). Enough was enough.

In the twilight hours of December 1, 1979, a party of at least three hundred warriors carried out an elaborately organized takeover of the film crew's camp (*Nor Oriente*, 1979c).[12] The few film crew members and Aguaruna guards present at the time chose wisely not to resist, and as a result there was no violence. A small group escorted the prisoners, hands tied, downriver to Santa Maria de Nieva in the crew's own boats. Others stayed behind and lit fires that burned the entire installation to the ground (see Goodwin, 1982). Herzog finally accepted his defeat in Aguarunia and moved on to another site in the central Peruvian jungle to finish his cinematic production, which was finally released in 1982.

Les Blank's *Burden of Dreams* is a documentary about the various obstacles encountered in the making of *Fitzcarraldo* that is equally if not more famous than Herzog's motion picture itself. But the conflict in Aguarunia is given short shrift in Blanc's documentary. Furthermore, most of the written accounts of the takeover resulted in short commentaries on the conflicting interests (Brown, 1982; Goodwin, 1982). The various commentators portray Aguaruna leaders as indigenous rights advocates eager to defend their newly recognized native community rights at all costs. And they typically represent Herzog as the well-intentioned but clearly bourgeois artist who can't be bothered with indigenous community dynamics. True enough.

But seen from the point of view of Aguarunia, the past gets retold in different ways. Aguaruna actors often recount this particular experience of the indigeneity that has been imposed on them with a narrative about the cunning bravery of ready warriors eager to defend themselves from an outside threat. Immediately following the takeover of Herzog's film camp, a bilingual teacher from Cenepa, Salomón Samaniego, and a few other Aguaruna writers acted as war correspondents for the Jaén daily, *Nor Oriente*. They retold the story step by step for a more provincial Peruvian audience and with a decided interest in customizing the news reports to consider the world as it looks from inside Aguarunia. The result was the publication of a multiple-part series titled "Asalto a la Compañía," firsthand reports authored by Aguaruna and provincial press writers working together for the weekly paper. The series provides considerable detail on the events and direct quotations from those involved, although often without mention of specific names or places.

Elder men pressured younger native community leaders to cooperate in the military action as a result of their growing impatience with the apparent failure to remove the film crew through diplomatic means (*Nor Oriente*, 1980a). The elders, better schooled in the arts of war, took charge of leading the younger, less experienced down the path to battle since they were best equipped to take the front guard (*Nor Oriente*, 1980b). The day before the takeover eight Aguaruna spies had arrived at the film crew's camp pretending to ask for jobs in order to inspect the layout (*Nor Oriente*, 1980c). They returned to give a report to the organizers of the military action; that night more than three hundred warriors carved out secret paths through the forest to avoid anyone detecting their arrival.

They arrived around four in the morning, quietly encircled the camp, and waited for dawn. "Their attention and all their thoughts were on the attack," the Aguaruna correspondents reported to *Nor Oriente* (1980c). They were divided into two roughly equal halves. The front line consisted of unarmed men who surprised the film crew by their sudden, simultaneous entrance from all sides of the camp just as day broke. Unarmed and first seeking a nonviolent solution, they maintained readiness to signal to the rear guard. Armed and ready for action, the second group waited just inside the forest perimeter in case a confrontation broke out with the film camp's watchmen, most of whom were fellow Aguaruna kinsmen eager to earn a day's wage (*Nor Oriente*, 1980c).

For those who arrived expecting a fight, the easy victory over foes that failed to resist proved disappointingly anticlimactic. Thus, certain members of the war party opposed the idea of an immediate withdrawal once the crew had been bound and sent downriver. According to *Nor Oriente* reporting they complained, "It was impossible to have come from so far away, suffering so much, for such a small thing and, reliving old traditions in regards to enemies, the idea of setting a fire immediately surfaced" (*Nor Oriente*, 1980d). Thus, the camp was set ablaze before they returned home.

In the political imaginary of Aguarunia an aggressive act is immediately followed by fear of a revenge attack. So the Aguaruna men involved employed a customary method to protect the network of participants in the raid. For several days after the events they designated specific people to act as lookouts in the various mestizo settlements, river ports, and military outposts on the Marañón in order to monitor the enemy's movements. These "messengers" reported back to the principal organizers of the takeover through the customary system of verbal relays: person to person, house to house, river to river (*Nor Oriente*, 1980e).

Retelling the Herzog affair as an Aguaruna war story was not the only means of customizing this spectacular event. Over the long term good war stories don't make good narratives of the past without the naming of good war heroes. In retrospect, more than twenty-five years after the events, almost every Aguaruna I have had the chance to ask has named Evaristo Nugkuag of the Consejo as the *autor intelectual* (principal designer) of the raid. The *Caretas* article that helped spark the event had previously cited testimony from Aguaruna laborers in the film camp pinpointing Nugkuag as the individual making plans for an attack (see *Caretas*, 1979: 36). It is true that the Consejo, with Nugkuag as its main leader, had emerged with a considerable amount of enthusiastic community support when Herzog's crew arrived on the scene. Salomón Samaniego (1979b), one of the Aguaruna war correspondents who provided firsthand descriptions of the events, depicts Nugkuag as "our leader," implying he was leading all of Aguarunia.

However, according to the textual record Nugkuag, in his role as representative of the Consejo, was carrying out duties of formal written protest of the Herzog affair in Lima on the day of the raid. He acted as surprised as everyone else when the news first surfaced (see Marka, 1979). When I touched on this topic in an interview, Nugkuag made no mention of having organized the military action. But he clearly supported the idea that community members were right for refusing to help Herzog repeat what he called "a dark history" of abuses against indigenous Amazonians. When I asked if the Herzog affair is what won the Consejo its occasionally "rebellious" image, he responded as the voice of the organization: "Yes, the Consejo is an organization that likes to become well informed. Only then does it give an opening, give an opportunity. It's only when they want to deceive us. That we won't accept."

Clearly, I haven't had the opportunity to ask all the relevant people about the Herzog affair. Many of the ones I have identify Nugkuag as the responsible party in part because of their distance from him and the indigenous organization with which his name is conflated. However, that, too, makes perfect sense given that one's internal enemies are oftentimes more likely than one's own allies to pinpoint a single strong man that represents an undoubtedly diverse social group (see Taylor, n.d.).[13] But the question of Nugkuag's precise role is not relevant in terms of understanding this event as a spectacular instance of Aguaruna activists customizing their condition of indigeneity. One of the true hallmarks of a strong man leader is also his cunning, particularly when mixed with the admirable ability to mobilize others in his stead. Knowing when to keep secret and when to reveal one's ambitions is a quality virtually every creditable leader possesses. Thus, one of my closest confidants, and a career Aguaruna organizer, once forthrightly declared to me that he was only "eighty percent trustworthy." This, he said, was a lesson I should always carry with me while traveling in Aguarunia. From then on, usually when more serious matters arose, I tried to lighten the tension a bit by asking which percent I was talking to: the twenty or the eighty. He always laughed. And we left it at that.

The point is that regardless of Nugkuag's real or fictionalized role in the Herzog affair, the fact is that he is often portrayed as the main protagonist. This means we are dealing with something more than a modernization paradigm or a standardized historical narrative. We are dealing with a political imagination specific to Aguarunia and the peculiar attention it places on the visionary power of notable men, men who are making history their own even if that history has also been made for them. There simply is no fixed line, no neatly periodized temporal difference, between life as the biography-worthy warriors of times past and the indigenous rights activists of times present and future. The versions of indigeneity found in Aguarunia have always been more ambiguous, creative, and customized than that.

Customizing Intellectual Property Claims in the Bioprospecting Era

A second example deals with another renowned Aguaruna leader, whose political ascension is intimately tied to the return of Nugkuag to the CAH after more than a decade of indigenous rights work in AIDESEP and COICA. First elected in the mid-1990s, César Sarasara was a three-time president of AIDESEP's Lima-based rival Amazonian organization, CONAP. Sarasara is originally from the Nieva River area, but he has long-standing ties to the organization OCCAAM that in conjunction with Jesuit aid facilitated his university studies in Lima. He also has strong ties to Upper Mayo River communities in the Department of San Martín because he chose to do research there for his BA thesis in business administration.

In a coauthored report that became the basis of Sarasara's BA thesis, Sarasara and Sergio Chang, a Ministry of Agriculture official, analyze the Aguaruna practice of ipaamamu (see Chang and Sarasara, 1987), which they identify as the "fundamental institution of the Aguaruna ethnic group." They also view it as something common throughout the various Jivaroan groups. They do so in part by dispelling any notion that it is equatable to the system of reciprocal labor obligations known in the Andes as the *minga* (25). Thus, they view it as a distinctly Amazonian kind of cultural practice. Communal work efforts, like the building of a new house, are referred to with the same term. But Chang and Sarasara argue that the "ipaamamu has a more profound significance and binds the total-ity of the Aguaruna ethnic group's social, economic, and cultural life" (26).[14]

Since the term *ipaamamu* derives from the verb *ipaamat*, "to invite," it is commonly translated as an "invitation" to participate in a specified collective encounter at the behest of the person who convokes the meeting. In Chang and Sarasara's account the ipaamamu's association with communal work is completely overshadowed by its association with those meetings specifically convoked for the purpose of going to war. "In Aguaruna myths and legends one always finds forms of ipaamamu to confront a common enemy and overcome difficulties" (28).

To illustrate this point, they recount the great war initiated by a *tsukanka* (toucan) against a predatory *unkaju* (crab), which occurred in the time when animals and humans were capable of everyday social intercourse (29–32). The unkaju inhabited a lake, protected by his obedient fish guardians. On the shores of the lake soldier ants informed the unkaju when humans approached so that he could cause the water to rise, and thus easily drown, capture, and devour his prey. All attempts to defeat the unkaju had failed until a toucan decided to convoke a large ipaamamu to address this common threat. Only animals of relatively minor status and little physical strength attended, including a variety of small birds (like the colorful *shiik*), a species of wild turkey called *mashu* (which has a red beak), and the *tuwich* (a species of small armadillo). This un-impressive show of force caused the women present to mock them and predict that they would meet a quick demise.[15]

But the participants gathered to drink *ayahuasca* (datem) and soon acquired individual visions. Acquiring visions led to a well-organized plan to successfully overcome their common enemy. Upon arriving at the lake where unkaju lived, they first diverted the ants' olfactory attention by wetting the point of a stick with tuwich's sweat and placing it at a safe distance from their approach route to the lake. Tuwich and the other underground dwellers' expertise in digging served to construct tunnels to tactical positions underneath the unkaju's dwell-ing at the bottom of the lake. When shiik gave the order to attack, tuwich and his subterranean posse punched through the lake bottom to drain the water so that unkaju could not raise the water level. When unkaju was finally exposed, mashu rushed in to make the kill by stabbing unkaju with his knifelike beak. This of course explains why mashu's beak is now red.

The importance of the death of unkaju for understanding the ipaamamu is threefold. First, it illustrates that collective action is highly circumstantial, delimited by a temporary need to accomplish a specific task, in this case defeat a specific enemy. As Chang and Sarasara (1987: 33) note, the ipaamamu is "an institution of transitory character, of short duration, that ends when the proposed objective has been accomplished." Nowhere does the ipaamamu give rise to organizations of a more durable institutional, or even quasi-institutional, type. As Chang and Sarasara state, "After confronting the problem, they [those involved] did not maintain a sense of continuity and practically disappeared, whether with the celebration of success by the parties or with their dispersion as a result of defeat" (33).

Second, the reasons for the temporary and task-oriented nature of this practice are found in the widespread emphasis on the preeminence of the individual notable man. Individual notable men rather than abstract political collectives become the heroic actors in Aguarunia. The ipaamamu thus represents a necessary coordination of unique individuals, each with his specific talents and defects, not an expression of a primordial collective solidarity. Durkheim would be disappointed. According to Chang and Sarasara this reflects "an overconfidence about self-sufficiency and an arrogance about personal freedom. This gives rise to a profound self-love among the Aguaruna, who only come together to help others in cases of indispensable need, or when the problem cannot be solved by the individual or the individual with his family" (33). Thus, the unkaju was only defeated following a meticulously planned effort that relied on the host inviting participants with unique, individualized abilities relevant for the task at hand: tsukanka to mobilize an army, tuwich to dig tunnels and sweat, mashu to stab unkaju with his beak.

The third important aspect is Chang and Sarasara's location of the source of that rugged Aguaruna individualism in the quest for visionary experience. It is the repeated acquisition of visionary experience that allows individuals to reach their "total maturation" (50; see Chapter 4). They acknowledge that this process of socializing people to become unique individuals is subject to the ongoing, flexible negotiations within what I call networks of rivers, paths, and strong men (see Chapter 3). An ipaamamu is thus determined not only by the particularities of individual talents but also by a social organization that imbues certain individuals, those with accumulated visionary experience and practical demonstration of its efficacy, with the social prestige necessary to mobilize subordinate others.

Sarasara's work on the significance of the ipaamamu was not, however, merely an intellectual project. With his rise to national indigenous leadership he began to put it to use in a politics of customizing indigeneity that sought to institutionalize the ipaamamu. After years of working with the Ministry of Agriculture in Bajo Naranjillo, Sarasara launched a political campaign in 1995. It resulted in his successfully taking over the directorship of the national confederation CONAP. Sarasara's election to CONAP in the mid-1990s would change things considerably. With his business background and entrepreneurial outlook he aimed to engage directly in issues of indigenous economic development.

Sarasara's vision for expanding economic projects in Aguarunia is most evident in CONAP's role in successfully renegotiating a multimillion-dollar bioprospecting venture to investigate and potentially commercialize Aguaruna medicinal knowledge. CONAP came upon the deal after Evaristo Nugkuag, having returned to the Consejo, had caused a great controversy throughout Aguarunia by rejecting the deal (see Greene, 2004b). In fact, Sarasara's acting as CONAP's representative to salvage this project largely accounts for his rise to international indigenous fame. By the time Sarasara emerged onto the national and international scenes, indigenous rights activism and environmental advocacy had come to focus on a new problem: indigenous claims to traditional biodiversity knowledge as a novel form of collective intellectual property. Particularly intense in ecological hotspots like Amazonia, indigenous rights debates coalesced around the problem of how to recognize and compensate indigenous peoples for the market uses of their traditional knowledge. Ironically, then, Sarasara came to occupy this position after leaders like Nugkuag had already played a significant role in establishing such eco-ethnic politics with alliances between Amazonians and international conservationists in the 1980s.

It was in this context that a team of ethnobotanical researchers from Washington University arrived in Peru in 1994 to negotiate an entrance into Aguaruna native communities. Led by Walter Lewis, the team arrived with a financial award from the International Cooperative Biodiversity Group (ICBG), a grants program run by the National Institutes of Health (NIH). The program was clearly a product of the United Nations' sustainable development and Convention on Biological Diversity era. The ICBG program's stated methodology was to form mutually beneficial partnerships between U.S. botanical researchers, pharmaceutical corporations, Southern biodiverse countries, and in some cases specific indigenous populations. The ICBG's goal was to search for potential drug discoveries in order to promote a sustainable economic use of biodiversity and foster benefit sharing with Southern countries and indigenous peoples simultaneously. Thus, in the ICBG-Aguaruna research agreement the four partners were Searle (previously the pharmaceutical division of Monsanto), Washington University, two Peruvian universities acting as a "host country partner," and the "Aguaruna people" (the category used in the agreements).

The ICBG team began negotiations with Evaristo Nugkuag in 1994 in hopes of working with the Consejo as a contractual partner. At first Nugkuag signed a "letter of intent" to participate that promised annual payments during field collections and potential future royalties in the somewhat unlikely case that a commercial drug product based on Aguaruna knowledge ever made it to market. However, he and his constituents in the Consejo grew suspicious when they became aware of a separate license agreement signed between Searle and Washington University to which the Consejo was not a direct party. Contact with an international NGO, known for its heated criticism of biopiracy, helped deepen the distrust. In their estimation the ICBG program appeared to be a thinly disguised attempt to exploit indigenous knowledge and Peruvian biodiversity. Relations between the ICBG team and the Consejo soured completely when Nugkuag found out that the researchers had already begun botanical collections while working with the Ministry of Agriculture. The project spiraled into controversy after the ICBG researchers attempted to renegotiate the project with the Consejo's longtime competitor, OCCAAM, and immediately received harsh public criticism from the Consejo. NIH temporarily froze the project.

This time, however, the Consejo's campaign of protest backfired. A faction of Aguaruna leaders from OCCAAM and two other regional organizations that had broken away from the Consejo opposed Nugkuag's tactics. They were eager to renegotiate the deal in their favor. And they risked expanding the controversy by openly contesting Nugkuag's attempt to speak in representation of Aguaruna native communities. To further their chances for successful renegotiation, regional Aguaruna activists put the ICBG researchers in touch with the Amazonian confederation CONAP and thus with César Sarasara.

As a national-level Aguaruna representative, Sarasara soon became the central actor in charge of sealing this major bioprospecting deal and was given the responsibility of protecting Aguaruna intellectual property interests in the process. In December 1995 CONAP convoked various regional Aguaruna organization representatives in the Marañon River port of Nieva to discuss the ICBG project. The assembly granted Sarasara, along with two legal advisors, the authority to represent the interests of three regional Aguaruna organizations (OCCAAM, Federación de Comunidades Aguarunas del Domingusa [FAD], and FECONARIN) in the ICBG negotiations. After several months of draft agreements and a final negotiation at Searle's St. Louis headquarters, Sarasara and his advisors closed the deal on behalf of a quasi-incorporated consortium of entrepreneurial Aguaruna organizations that elsewhere I term CONAP and Affiliates (see Greene, 2004b).[16]

The renegotiations resulted in a royalty and annual payment scheme that was more profitable for the Aguaruna than that first promised the Consejo. The most interesting outcome of the agreement was a "know-how license" based on a model of computer software licensing. In contractual terms CONAP and Affiliates, constituting the indigenous signatories, licensed to Searle the traditional medicinal "know-how" of the entire Aguaruna collective for an initial four years of research. And like software licensing, this license guaranteed that CONAP and Affiliates did not forfeit any proprietary claims to their medicinal know-how even while Searle utilized it.

The successful renegotiation of the ICBG deal proved to many that Sarasara was capable of rivaling Nugkuag at the complicated game of international deal making. It also made evident his interest in implementing an aggressive market-based model of Aguaruna leadership rather than being constantly on the defensive against market processes and actors (see Greene, 2004b). The result was a dramatic rise in CONAP and Affiliates' status as legitimate indigenous institutions and a corresponding decline in the power of Nugkuag and the old protest model of the Consejo. Much of that symbolic power crystallized in the charismatic and savvy leadership of Sarasara, another notable, individual leader, who in the years following the agreement found himself in more and more press interviews, received a prize from the International Society of Ethnobiology, and became a coauthor on a scientific paper.

Dealings with international bioprospectors, however, did not simply represent a shift in representative legitimacy among the diverse Aguaruna organizational actors. Nor did Sarasara's exceedingly market-friendly approach represent a simple politics of indigenous modernization. It represented an opportunity for Sarasara to implement his vision, to follow his path, and thus to customize this encounter in terms deeply rooted in the mind-set of Aguarunia. Sarasara seized the opportunity to try to institutionalize what he had already claimed was not institutionalizable: the ipaamamu. He did so based on his own long-standing conviction, his personal vision, in fact, that the ipaamamu constitutes the customary essence of what it means to be Aguaruna—and a bit by logical extension, Jivaro. Thus, CONAP titled the meeting in Nieva in

1995 to deliberate over the bioprospecting project the "Congreso-Ipaamamu to Strengthen and Consolidate the Aguaruna and Huambisa People and the ICBG Project." The official declaration from the meeting states:

> The indigenous Aguaruna and Huambisa peoples recognize the importance of research and inventories on and conservation and sustainable use of the biological diversity from our region. Therefore, they are ready to cooperate with state and private institutions dedicated to these objectives if previous consent is given in accordance with the traditional organizational system of the Aguaruna and Huambisa peoples, the Ipaamamu. (ICBG, 1996: appendix 1)

Following Sarasara's initiative, the ICBG Biological Collecting Agreement contractually validates the ipaamamu as the method through which other Aguaruna or Huambisa non-parties can solicit consideration and participation in the ICBG project. Article 7 states, "Additional organizations or communities representing Aguaruna or Huambisa People may wish to participate in this Agreement," and stipulates, "Applications for inclusion of such organizations shall be made to and approved by the IPAAMAMU" (ICBG, 1996: 22). Remarkably, the international policymaker at the NIH in charge of the ICBG program credits the Aguaruna's customary use of the ipaamamu with having been *the* element crucial to the project's successful renegotiation (see Rosenthal, 2006).

In fact, the 1995 ICBG ipaamamu in Nieva allowed Sarasara the opportunity to initiate a new institutional practice. The following year CONAP began to convoke semiannual assemblies of Aguaruna and Huambisa regional federations under the rubric of the ipaamamu. Each time the goal was to address contemporary problems and identify common enemies. These ranged from talks about the Peru-Ecuador border conflict (see Greene, 2008) to petroleum activities in indigenous territories, for a total of six ipaamamu thus far.[17]

The one held in Nieva on November 2, 1996, is of particular interest here. Sarasara used the occasion to explicitly articulate his vision of the ipaamamu to Jivaroan leaders from various regional organizations and open a public discussion about the customary practice he has been theorizing since the 1980s. According to the paraphrased notes taken by the ipaamamu secretary, Sarasara gave the first word to Martín Reátegui, his brother-in-law and close familial confidant. According to the meeting minutes Reátegui declared:

> When we make agreements like the ICBG project it is a grand IPAAMAMU. It is our history that we make. So, IPAAMAMU means to call, to invite to solve

an existing problem. Before, the Santiago, Cenepa, Marañon, Nieva, Domingusa rivers, each one had its leader, the kakajam. The kakajams understood each other and now we have regained our ancestral position according to [river] sectors. We convoke the IPAAMAMU to solve problems or big issues that involve everyone. So, he who is called to the meeting constitutes the IPAAMAMU. We live with this vision that our forefathers left us. (CONAP, 1996; capitalization in original)

José Lirio, listed as an "advisor to CONAP" in the meeting minutes, added to this by stating that nowadays, "the biggest enemy that we have is poverty." Further, he suggested that "we need to formalize the IPAAMAMU to forge a path for our children." Several others chimed in to reinforce the general consensus that concluded the session: "The IPAAMAMU Jibaro is the maximum instantiation of consultation and decision making of the traditional system of organization of the indigenous Jivaro peoples" (CONAP, 1996). For his own contribution to the discussion Sarasara returned to the story of the unkaju and recounted how a motley crew of unassuming but vision-enhanced forest creatures killed the monstrous underwater crab that preyed on humans. The meeting secretary paraphrased Sarasara:

> The IPAAMAMU, according to tradition, refers to the UNKAJU that lived exterminating the Aguaruna or the Jibaro Nation. He was only eliminated through the IPAAMAMU. Today, we will not kill people, but we will overcome our problems through the IPAAMAMU. With the IPAAMAMU the Jivaro People won this territory. Today, as their children we are here. The IPAAMAMU means surmounting a problem with everyone, the Aguaruna killing problems. (CONAP, 1996; capitalization in original)

In short, he returned the discussion to a level of discourse meant to reverberate throughout Aguarunia and into the larger concentric circles of Jivaria. In doing so, he articulates a vision that sounds as much like the voice of a contemporary kakajam preparing his followers for war as it does a modernized ethnic politician preparing a constituency for its encounter with an imposing indigeneity. Today's enemies are different from those in the past, but they are still common enemies. Today's enemies go by other names, names like poverty, state formation, international research and development, anthropology, and what have you.

But just like the old ones, Sarasara suggests, the new enemies must also be killed. He doesn't mean it in the viscerally graphic and violently mortal sense.

But he means killed nonetheless. To do that, Aguaruna activists must become more than abstract ethnic agents, messengers of an overly generalized identity politics. They must become visionary warriors engaged in their own projects of customizing indigeneity. They continue to make war, but they make it by other means, with weapons fit for other times. They become warriors of the pen and visionaries forging new paths that also allow them to talk to paper.

. . . A Path Out

Throughout this journey in Aguarunia I have sought to demonstrate something about the importance of paths. I invoke paths here as they are often invoked within Aguarunia as simultaneously material and metaphorical phenomena, as a distinct way of thinking about life and a distinct way of living it. Paths represent both a form of territorial groundedness and a philosophy of visionary intellectual development. Paths are a method for describing organic social relatedness and a theory of open-ended social intercourse. They divide and connect things in Aguarunia: remote rivers and heavily trafficked highways; tropical Amazonian forests and towering Andean landscapes; acquirers of ancestral visions and agents of a politicized indigeneity.

The particular paths I have followed through Aguarunia inevitably represent only a partial description of an exceedingly diverse reality. This is just one of the many routes I might have taken. But I chose it for a reason. If envisioned together, even these particular, and at times completely divergent, paths represent the possibility of a convergence into collective projects to customize indigeneity. Rather than rooted in ideas of primordial communalism, these projects are expressed through a collective agreement about the importance of indigenous individualism. This does not make of it a hypothetically absolute individualism of the liberal Enlightenment kind but instead a unique form of coordinated individualism. Aguaruna projects of customizing indigeneity anticipate the need for individual—if also mostly masculine— visionaries to combine their unique talents. They express a desire to form a collective alliance in times of critical need. They anticipate a historical necessity for one's own path to come together with the paths others have forged during life's confrontational moments.

This particular form of coordinated individualism prevalent among these notable Aguaruna activists is deemed necessary at least until a common enemy has been identified and the foreignness the enemy represents has been in some manner neutralized. That moment Aguaruna activists define as now, a moment we might see as constituting their particular historical present and defined by their particular absorption into the violent abstractions of indigeneity that modernity imposes on them. From the perspective of Aguaruna activists this historical present consists of an ongoing time of conflict and crisis with the apach—an imposing foreign presence that takes many forms ranging from the gringo anthropologist and Peruvian state official to the European NGO and the poor Andean migrant. This is not the result of a failure to perceive any significant differences among these different actors, as the irinku is but a subset of the apach. But it is the result of prioritizing a sense that what these diverse actors share is a basic unfamiliarity with what it means to be Aguaruna.

Seen from within Aguarunia, these coordinated projects of customizing indigeneity revolve around turning the logics of visionary warfare into a workable politics of indigenous opposition. Yet by doing so, they confront a structure of historical hierarchies and a series of violent abstractions that the generic condition of indigeneity imposes on its ethnic subjects. The result is a complex articulation of political demands and desires that give rise to a heavily constrained form of cultural creativity, but a form of cultural creativity nonetheless. Aguaruna activists in many ways must simply represent themselves to more powerful actors as the generic indicators of indigeneity such actors expect. But they do so by constantly clarifying, sometimes subtly and other times explicitly, the specific indicators by which their own peculiar indigenous experiences might be measured.

I have sought to define these contextual dimensions of the abstracted world of indigeneity in which Aguaruna activists operate and to begin delineating the concentric layers of indigenous identification to which they have been forced to grow accustomed in a country like Peru. Their indigenous identities are expressed not only through global abstractions—à la the West versus the Rest—but also within much more specific varieties of lived historical experience. First and foremost among these has been the Peruvian nation-state's curious colonial mixture of Andean-inflected history that is also deeply European centered. Such experiences give rise not to easily generalizable forms of indigeneity in Peru but to multiple, diverse, and explicitly regionalized forms. These range from elitist Peruvian ideals that focus on an imaginary return to a civilized Inca era to persistently pejorative ideologies about the wildness of Peru's lowland inhabitants, alternately labeled chunchos, indios salvajes, Jivaro, and, ultimately, native Amazonians.

Thus, Aguaruna activists' experiences with indigeneity in Peru are lived within the comfortable confines of a space and a place called Aguarunia. And Aguarunia is concentrically related to the slightly more abstracted spaces and places of Jivaria and Amazonia. The first is a marker of a shared ethnocultural experience and an incipient political sentiment that spans the northern Peruvian border region. The second is a marker of a much more widely regionalized indigenous experience. Amazonian indigeneity is constantly counterposed to, but at the same time constantly being influenced by, Andean indigeneity, long the historical template for all forms of indigeneity in Peru. I say these Aguaruna activists are confined because they are actors in a history loaded with relations of power, a history they did not make themselves. I say these activists are comfortable because they are also historical actors imbued with the power to make that history their own. Having grown quite accustomed to the foreignness of their experiences with indigeneity, they now engage in projects to customize it from deep within and also well beyond Peru.

The motivations behind these projects to customize indigeneity are not as simple as staking out a categorical opposition to the notions of modernity, history, and global capitalism. Such terms are as abstract and meaningless as the notions of cultural difference and alterity that inhere inevitably in the idea of indigeneity when detached from context. The point for Aguaruna activists engaged in projects of customization is not so much about a choice of becoming either modern or indigenous, globally capitalist or locally subaltern, cultural peoples without history or historical actors without culture. That is a choice based on a vision that many a social theory of modernization has advanced. Yet it is less a vision than an illusion. And the illusion is sustained by seeking solace in concepts that have no context, fixing essential identities while forgetting the political processes of identification, and looking for timeless insights while overlooking the practices of lived experience.

Nor is my final point that if faced with such an illusionary choice—generic sameness on one side, generic difference on the other—Aguaruna activists must therefore resolve themselves to the happily-ever-after life of the dialectical hybrid: thus to become alternatively modern. Surely there are other alternative paths to the single teleological path that modernization presents. Just as surely there must be other paths than that of the alternatively modern, the mytho-praxeological cultural historian, and the glocalized capitalist. To construct these as the primary alternatives to indigeneity's modern illusions is really to have no alternatives at all. Or, perhaps I should say it is to have three, strikingly similar, alternatives to the one dialectical opposition that makes them possible: the alternation between the generalizable difference of localized indigenous subalternity and the equally generalizable sameness of a global capitalist modernity.

To define these projects of customizing indigeneity either way—alternatives versus modernities on the one hand; no alternatives to alternative modernities on the other (see Kelly, 2003)—is to miss the point about the importance of paths. Paths always divide and connect. They have a way of closing off spaces and opening them up at the same time. And they simultaneously reach into the past and point toward the future. This is certainly something Bikut, Aguarunia's version of Socrates, knew long ago. And it explains why Aguaruna activists' projects of customizing indigeneity make such good sense to them now. The real importance of paths today is knowing how to make them one's method for talking to paper. Considerations of modernity and its alternatives, history and its culturalness, capitalism and its localities—and indigenous identity and all its essentialisms—take a distant second.

I had occasion to speak of such things with César Sarasara, one of Aguarunia's notable national-level activists, although not in so many words. I returned to Peru in 2003 with the intention of convoking meetings to discuss this research project with those most interested in the experiences of Aguarunia (see the Epilogue). I stopped in to Sarasara's Lima office to coordinate a few things regarding the meetings. Despite various ups and downs in our own relationship, he attended me with a notable patience that particular day.

To compensate a bit for his absence at the meetings I was proposing, he pulled me aside into a small conference room and asked me to give him a short report on what the text was about. I did the best I could insofar as I am capable of saying anything in the extemporaneous fifteen-minute presentation format. Sarasara had nothing by way of direct comments about my summary of the research. Nor did he pose any specific questions. Instead, he paused for a moment, then stood up, and approached the eraser board. And he began to draw circles. There were four of them (see Figure 13).

Feeling caught somewhere between the roles of student-in-the-classroom and ethnographer-in-the-field, I began to take notes on his lecture. Circle A, he said, was a representation of an "indigenous culture in a specific state." "Just at a particular moment," he added. Circle B, he continued, was "another moment," the moment at which a foreign, Western culture begins to "influence" the indigenous culture, producing a "fragmented" result. Hence, the squiggly lines. The various ninety-degree angles in circle C represented a "moment of restructuring," that moment in which the indigenous culture and the foreign culture begin to come more into alignment with one another. Finally, he said, the perfectly symmetrical design of circle D—depicting the perfect balance between the "FGI" (indigenous form of governance) and the "FGO" (Western form of governance)—represented a final moment. This was the moment of a "synthesis of indigenous governance."

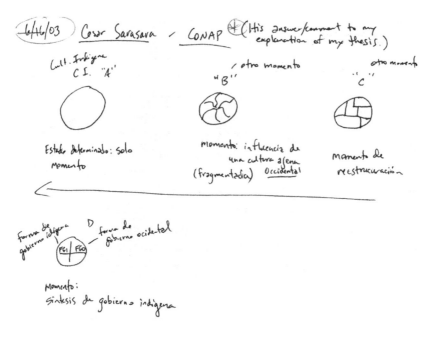

Figure 13 Sarasara's circles (taken from the author's field notes).

He never mentioned exactly where the Aguaruna were, if anywhere, on this time-line, and I never thought to ask. The truly interesting thing about the incredibly lin-ear temporal path he drew and his apparently straightforward dialectical reasoning was the comment that followed. One might expect, much as I did while listening to his lecture about the circles, that Sarasara was suggesting D as the final telos, as the final destination to which this path of circles leads. Instead, he suggested something entirely different. The "key question," he said, was whether or not D, the "synthesis for indigenous governance," was actually desirable as a destination. In his estima-tion, moment D *"no tiene mucha garantia"* (didn't come with much of a guarantee). To back this up with some evidence, symbolic of the international dimensions of the indigeneity in which he lives, he recounted his recent visit to Canada. He had visited a few indigenous territories while there. When native Canadians debate be-tween "being indigenous and being Western," it seems only to produce an "internal struggle," he said. But when they "struggle to recover A," this initial site on the path he was imagining, that's when "they feel more like themselves." Pointing me to his own intellectual and political vision, he said, "In the case of the Aguaruna, I think we have to recover the ipaamamu."

Still operating under the enlightened ignorance of my own academic skepticism, and growing a bit anxious about these gestures toward an Aguaruna essentialism displayed in circle A, I couldn't help questioning him on the temporal path he had graphically depicted on the board. "But César, what about A?" I asked. "It's not like Aguaruna culture doesn't have its own history before A or internal conflicts. Surely it is affected by other indigenous cultures like the Huambisa or whomever."

"Of course," he answered. "But that's not what matters to us right now." Gesturing toward the circles drawn on the board, he added, "What matters to us right now is this." And then he immediately remarked on the indigenous differences—and the differences within indigeneity—I had implicitly pointed to. "It seems that the Huambisa are good boatmen. But the Aguaruna are much better at forging paths."

Indeed, perhaps it is this ability to recognize the importance of paths—the particular sites they lead to without leading to any one site in particular—that really matters in Aguarunia. At least, and even especially, right now.

Epilogue
Field Notes on Customizing Anthropology

My journey through Aguarunia began in earnest in 1998. I spent a considerable period (the latter half of 1998; all of 1999) researching in a handful of Aguaruna communities on the Upper Mayo River in the Department of San Martín. I did so initially on the basis of a contractual research agreement I held with a local organization, the Organización Aguaruna Alto Mayo, and a national-level indigenous confederation, the Confederación de Nacionalidades Amazónicas del Perú. Following a brief stint back in Chicago I returned to Peru in the spring of 2000 for another fourteen months. This time I spent sporadic periods ranging from a couple of weeks to a month or more making brief visits to several Aguaruna native communities in the Department of Amazonas as well as various small migrant settlements and provincial towns (including Chiriaco, Nieva, Imazita, and Jaén), where many of my Aguaruna collaborators live, work, and transit. During this latter period I also intensified my work with Amazonian organizations in Lima and conducted archival work, mostly in the libraries of the Summer Institute of Linguistics and the Centro de Antropología y Aplicación Práctica de la Amazonia Peruana (CAAAP). I have made several follow-up visits to Peru almost every year since 2001. I never really learned to function fluently in the Aguaruna language. I usually characterize my conversational abilities as something approaching the high-tourist level. But I did have the opportunity to work with some of the most amazing translators I could imagine. Without their constant help the occasional analytical insights I provide into the deeper meanings of speaking Aguaruna would have been impossible.

As I write this, I am now approaching the ten-year mark after I first began to forge my own path into and out of Aguarunia. This calls for a bit of reflection on the methods of anthropological engagement I have used. In essence, my entrance began as what we in *irinkinum* (where gringos are) call a career path. It initiated with an application to graduate school in anthropology and continues, at least for now, through what others have come to call engaged or activist scholarship (see Hale, 2008; Rappaport, 2005; Warren and Jackson, 2002; Duneier, 1999). What is indexed by the word "scholarship" in the social sciences is fairly clear—a basic commitment to the pursuit of insight into the social dimensions of the human condition. Terms like "engagement" and "activism" add to this a concern with how academic practices and institutions are part of rather than separate from relations of power. The desire to address such asymmetries results in engaged scholars taking steps, however small and sometimes purely symbolic, to be a bit more self-reflexive. It also requires one to think about modifying one's methods. This usually takes two forms: a decision to get involved in advocacy efforts and an attempt to construct more dialogic means of doing scholarship in the first place.

As Craig Calhoun (2008) notes, activist scholarship has been around for as long as the idea of scholarship has existed, even if it does not necessarily constitute the institutional norm of science-centric academe. It is fair to say that within anthropology, calls for engagement have intensified since at least the 1960s. This follows directly from the postcolonial critique of the discipline and the postmodern critique of scientific positivism. According to Charles Hale (2008: 3) the visibility of feminist and minority intellectuals doing activist scholarship based on a politics of personal connection to marginalized communities is central. This is true because a central ambition of activist scholarship is to contribute to a de-whitening of the academy. Yet, as Hale's collaborator, Jemima Pierre (2008: 132), points out in the same volume, any minority scholar's activist status, like his or her minority status, is a highly contextual matter. So, too, I think are the ideas and identities associated with whiteness.

Because engaged scholarship is nothing new and inequalities prove to be persistent, it's not at all clear what, if any, good engaged scholarship does. The uncertainty about its utility is compounded by the fact that scholars—particularly those anthropologists who continue working with so-called subaltern populations—appear not to know when, if ever, to stop apologizing for the past. And the continued debate about something called engagement lends itself to a certain degree of predictability if not at times quasi standardization among those who practice it. No matter how many times academics point out the contradictory limits of their activism, words like "advocacy" and "dialogue" continue to surface and continually resonate with a call for a utopian egalitarianism. These central tropes of engagement thus risk becoming as fetishized by academic activists as the concept of informed consent has within Institutional Review Board (IRB) meetings. Just imagine activist academics trying to monitor each other's engagements in the way that IRB officials try to comply with federally mandated and highly bureaucratized human subjects' protection by ignoring the actual complexities of research in context.

This brings us to a fairly interesting dilemma. Express no self-reflexivity, no will to advocate for subaltern others, and no methodological dialogism at all, and you will be labeled the (white) privileged, positivist, neo-imperialist academic. Express too much, and you will be tagged as the navel-gazing, self-dramatizing, hyper-PC ethnographer who fails to give the scholarly community what it really wants: less of the endless diatribe against academic practice and more and better academic analysis. Both criticisms are persuasive. The irony is that these ostensibly divergent paths easily lead to the same sad site of scholarly self-absorption. And so the current challenge—easier said than done—appears to be one of avoiding this damned-if-you-do, damned-if-you-don't scenario. The engaged anthropologist is encouraged to search for a new path even while forced to face the facts. Finding one is anything but guaranteed. Some scholars, just like some activists, will inevitably interpret too much or too little into one's practices and politics of academic engagement. As a means of making these general remarks a bit more concrete, I offer the following as a final reflection on my experiments in anthropological engagement in Aguarunia.

A Few Experiments in Engagement

I initially approached the design of this research into Aguarunia as a matter of contractual arrangement. I consulted and sought agreements with various indigenous authorities from a national-level Amazonian confederation all the way down to the level of the individual native community. The contractual approach was in many ways a necessary first step toward respecting the institutional ambitions of the indigenous organizations I was researching. Too much faith in the contractual approach ultimately obscured the many other dimensions of engagement that emerged in my research. Some of this was due to my occasional tendency to put research interests above all else. Some of it was due to indigenous authorities that routinely compete over jurisdictional claims and have little means to enforce their decisions on Aguaruna individuals at the community level.

Ultimately, I abandoned a strictly contractual approach. I did so in part out of a realization that experiences like the one described in the opening section, "A Path In . . . ," did little to instruct me on how to act effectively in different contexts with different kinds of Aguaruna actors. Nor did the contracts I originally signed contemplate the complicated, contradictory relationships that were bound to develop: from hiring university students in Lima as Aguaruna-language tutors to briefly visiting native communities where I was not sponsored by indigenous organizations but went by local invitation. In terms of the day-to-day contingencies that ethnography in Aguarunia entailed, *like ethnography everywhere*, it was simply impossible to draw a firm boundary between research and not-research. That in my estimation is what good anthropology is and should be.

My attempts at direct indigenous rights advocacy have taken the form of either mediation with state and development institutions or efforts to write for broader publics beyond the academy. I am always pleased to receive the occasional positive comments from collaborators. But my actions seem rather insignificant when compared to the flow of communications I receive from various collaborators in Peru. Generally they accompany a request for *apoyo* (support). The term tends to connote everything from specific sums of cash and translation help to international development contacts and precise forms of legal, immigration, and agricultural advice I usually can't deliver. As a result, I am often at odds with the abstractly appealing idea of calling what I do engaged anthropology. And yet I feel somehow obliged to. Apparently, I am not alone (see Graham, 2006).

The fact that certain Aguaruna individuals, communities, and organizations accepted my research while others so roundly rejected it has always puzzled me. This is no doubt a dilemma as old as ethnography itself. But it bothered me enough that I eventually decided to carry out an experiment designed to make myself at least minimally accountable to others invested in Aguarunia and indigenous rights in Peru.

What followed was an opportunity to hold a public debate about my research. I planned a return visit to Peru with the intention of holding meetings to present the research, along with a written summary in Spanish, and host open discussions. After consulting with César Sarasara of CONAP and Diogenes Ampám of AIDESEP, I organized two debates: one in the native community Bajo Naranjillo in the Department of San Martín and one in the small river port town of Nieva in the Department of Amazonas. We invited various Aguaruna activists, organization representatives, and community leaders. We also invited NGO representatives and provincial state officials involved in the areas where I had worked. A typical outcome: numerous invitees never showed, and several people were welcomed upon their arrival without prior invitation.

There were two comments from the Bajo Naranjillo meeting that I find interesting. The first came from Noé Cahuaza, a longtime leader of the community Bajo Naranjillo. He took the opportunity to clarify an important point about their past relations with foreign researchers. This followed a criticism of a U.S. anthropologist who worked in some of these same Aguaruna communities in the 1970s and whose absence since the 1980s is sometimes a point of contention. Interesting to me is the way that Cahuaza staunchly defended him. Carrying out research projects is no longer just done by foreigners, Cahuaza said. Younger Aguaruna, especially those in university training, also must now engage in research to become, as he put it, "*profesionales*" (professionals). On that basis alone everyone should realize that research is "indispensable" and represents something that the Aguaruna now also aspire to do.

Another memorable comment came from an environmental activist who was present in Bajo Naranjillo. As a prelude to a comment about the importance of conserving the forest, she declared to the participants: "In my opinion . . . if the forest disappears, Aguarunaness [*lo Aguaruna*] will disappear." I find this significant not because it reveals something about her individually; rather, it is revealing of the ways in which Amazonian indigenous rights rhetoric and conservationist discourses result in an ideological overlap and simultaneously produce alternative interpretations of what is at stake in real political terms. Aguaruna reactions to the comment were thus diverse. In reviewing the footage, I noticed one young Aguaruna activist shake his head in agreement as she spoke of forest conservation and its necessary linkage to Aguaruna struggles. But following the meeting, and in reference to her foreign nationality, another Aguaruna remarked to me and others, "Yeah, but I bet if the forests in France disappear, the French would just keep right on going. Being French."

The Nieva meeting was different because I had never met a majority of the participants and only maintained casual contact with others. The four women present in Nieva sat together throughout the meeting. Their participation was noticeably different from that of their female counterparts in Bajo Naranjillo, where almost all of the women present either sat in silence or stood to the side preparing the lunch that followed the meeting. In Nieva each of the four women present represented the gender exceptionalism of Aguaruna women leaders I discuss in Chapter 6. A remark I made during my presentation, that Aguaruna custom generally associates the male gender with public leadership roles via their conflation with visionary war leaders, sparked their interest. During a break in the meeting I noticed that they gathered together, designated a spokeswoman (Rebecca Detén), and came up with a list of items she should cover in her commentary.

Detén's intervention was almost entirely gender inflected, aimed as much at the Aguaruna men present as it was at me, the foreign, male researcher. Generally speaking, she emphasized the fact that women have always played an important role in men's leadership but simply not been recognized for it. Until more recently, with the impositions and opportunities that a Western educational system represents, women's input was typically offered in the home. It was then expressed to others outside the home through a husband or another male relative. In other words, Aguaruna men have a tendency to act like every Aguaruna woman's appointed "spokesperson" (to use her word). In point of fact this is something many Aguaruna men readily recognize—but usually only when women point it out for them. I find her intervention salient for two reasons. Along with perhaps two or three others her comments inspired me to significantly modify specific parts of the manuscript draft, creating a form of intertextual dialogue that went beyond the bounds of the debate experience itself (see Chapter 3 in particular). Despite this, her comments still stand as a substantial critique of the book, which is overwhelmingly—and at times too comfortably—told from a masculine point of view. This is a fact I make no particular apologies for, but it is a fact worth recognizing.

Certain comments in the Nieva meeting played on my original suggestion that everyone ask me directed questions. Yet it was precisely the founders who were the most reluctant to do so. Instead, they used this as an opportunity to continue perfecting their ability for authoritative verbal displays. At one point Evaristo Nugkuag spoke continuously, without interruption, for twenty-seven minutes in one of the most fluid, spontaneous, and convincing political voices I've ever heard! And I was not the only one captivated by his abilities for political discourse. It's no wonder he has been such a visionary force and respected rival in Aguaruna politics. For the founders the meeting was less about a dialogic interrogation of my research than it was another occasion on which to impart their vision, in part by demonstrating their verbosity, to all those present.

Levy Tiwi, who in my estimation was the most directly confrontational of the bunch during the Nieva meeting, asked a series of tough questions. At one point he asked why I chose to work in a community like Bajo Naranjillo, which he characterized as "mixed between colonists and natives," as opposed to a community "where purer indigenous peoples live." Deciding more or less spontaneously to take an explicitly confrontational strategy to answer his question, I said the following:

> Frankly, from my point of view, I see it as somewhat dangerous to distinguish like that. . . . [As if] there are pure indigenous peoples, that live far off, that eat jungle meat, that practice their customs, and there are modern indigenous peoples, or better said, those already Westernized. Well, you all, even you [gesturing toward Tiwi] are speaking that way. Several of you are using that kind of discourse. But instead, even better, I would ask a question of you. What is the basis of Awajún identity? Does being Awajún mean simply living far off in the forest, isolated, removed, practicing ancestral customs, however ancestral customs are defined? That would mean that an Aguaruna can't be the mayor of a town [gesturing to Merino Trigoso, the Aguaruna mayor of Condorcanqui], or couldn't be a businessman who sells his product in the market. So, I guess I would return the question to you: What does it mean to be Aguaruna? . . . For me identity isn't based on something merely biological, that I have such and such a percentage of indigenous blood. . . . It's also a political project, an ideological and historical project that its believers undertake because they think the struggle serves a purpose.

There was no immediate response to my question or the commentary that bookended it. Instead, there was a brief silence. I've come to recognize this comment as one of the few times I've been able to display effectively my own authoritative voice in direct response to an Aguaruna challenge to do so. It is one of the clearest examples I can think of where I really "dialogically engaged." I don't mean it in the idealized advocatory sense of anthropologists working toward a better world for the subalterns. I mean it in the sense of customizing my own anthropological practice by responding in kind to an invitation to engage in the conversational combat that the notable men of Aguarunia so enjoy.

I don't have any incontrovertible proof that my Awajún interlocuters recognized my response as such. But Martín Reátegui, founder of FECONARIN, later referenced my statement in the middle of his lengthy discourse. "What you just said is that the Awajún cannot remain as Awajún. . . . Maybe this transformed Awajún that we speak of today is a new Awajún with a different knowledge, that must now look toward the future very, very differently." His remark revealed just how extraordinarily complicated it is to even phrase one's understanding of being Awajún. This is a problem I—author and anthropologist looking for my own path through Aguarunia—share with those who identify as Awajún.

Needless to say, the nine armed and unnamed men from Achu who figure prominently in my depiction of a Path In to Aguarunia at the outset of this book were not invited to my research presentations. They exhibit a certain predisposition toward gringos that made them unlikely to attend. In my experience this is a predisposition widely shared among many other segments of Aguarunia, where some prefer to reject any form of dialogic encounter the engaged anthropologist comes to offer. They follow paths that I'm explicitly forbidden to follow. Yet I have no reservations about writing them into my anthropological representations here. I'd be willing to bet they, too, represent me on occasion, perhaps over a good bowl of manioc beer and with stories about the time they tried, and nearly succeeded, to take an irinku hostage in Cachiyacu.

And thus I'd like to recall from Chapter 1 my invocation of Jean Jackson's (1989) pointed question as a way to think about the paradoxes of engaged anthropology: "Is there a way to talk about making culture without making enemies?" My response is simple. *Sometimes making culture is about learning to live with making enemies.* This is a lesson I learned on the paths I was allowed to follow through Aguarunia —and a lesson from which other anthropologists might benefit.

In reality, there are much more subtle forms of refusal to engage in dialogue worth mentioning. Jeremias Juep was always a mysterious figure: so close to people I know so well, so estranged from me. He attended the Bajo Naranjillo meeting and sat in silence. His comments about the affair were unknown to me until I began to review the more candid footage from after the event that my wife had recorded. He launched his own peculiar critique of my anthropological enterprise:

Mamais: Hello, uncle.
Jeremias: Hi.
Mamais: Are you chatting?
Jeremias: Yes, chatting.
Mamais: What are you talking about?

Jeremias: I was saying that anthropology deals mainly with just doing research. It's like a declaration of some sort, like a declaration of the truth. National anthems are also like that. They declare something about truth and heroes. History is the same way. It deals with declarations of truth and heroes. But it seems these fields of study aren't that difficult. They just stop at that. That's all they do. Like the hummingbird that announces things. They just announce things.

Poetic somehow. But also disconcerting. I never got the chance to ask Jeremias exactly what he meant. He died in 2006. I've always wondered what he imagined as the relation between the heroes that anthropologists are wont to declare and the apparent lack of heroism he finds in anthropologists that do little more than declare things. I guess I'm okay with being compared to a hummingbird. *Jempe* is one of the most cherished messengers of Aguarunia. But I don't relish the idea that the message I deliver is equivalent to the triumphant nationalism state leaders put to bad marching band music. The path he imagined me following is simply a bit beyond my grasp.

My Path Revealed

I present these inconclusive conclusions on my various modes of engagement in Aguarunia as a final thought for two reasons. I hope to come clean about the complexities of engaging in the often idealized anthropology of engagement. I also hope to reveal a bit about how Aguaruna projects of customizing indigeneity have influenced my project to customize anthropology.

I've learned some things of notable importance from these many notable men—and a few notable women—during my travels in Aguarunia. These are things that bear directly on questions of scholarly engagement and the advocatory dialogues at the center of such debates. When engaged in dialogues of a more confrontational sort, one must actively persuade others with an authoritative voice. It's really not enough to sit back and hope that one day a methodological dialogism will spontaneously, or even necessarily, lead to a liberating consensus. Implicitly, this is a point all academics, who are no strangers to the arts of persuasive display and the realities of constant disagreement, can agree on. Yet the more empathetic tendencies and egalitarian standards engaged anthropologists hope to set often result in giving the exact opposite impression. Perhaps we should be careful not to shy away from the directly confrontational and competitive aspects of dialogic engagements.

Perhaps we should even try to become a bit less apologetic about our own sense of authority.

To the sometimes utopian visions and inherent idealism implied in scholars advocating for subaltern liberation, experience in Aguarunia tells me something different. To be recognized as a visionary, you first have to prove the vision's effectiveness in practice. Having the vision in the first place is a necessary step in finding the right path. But it is only through emerging continually successful in outlasting life's confrontational encounters that it becomes a path of one's own. This leaves me with a rather paradoxical parting impression. Finding my own path through Aguarunia is something that is starting to take shape and something of a permanent work in progress.

Chuu! Jintá wetajai!

Reference Matter

Notes

Chapter 1

1. When was the last time someone taught a serious course on the history of anthropology without mention of the various postcolonial critiques of "classic" anthropology (à la Hymes, 1972; Asad, 1973; Clifford and Marcus, 1986)?

2. In fact, Niezen's use of the term "indigenism" in place of "indigeneity" is revealing to anyone familiar with the specific connotations of such terms in the Latin American context. "Indigenism," when translated (*indigenismo*), connotes the history of elite literature and state policy on indigenous populations. For this reason, I opt for the term "indigeneity" throughout the text.

3. Special thanks to an anonymous reviewer who helped provide the precise conceptual language to encapsulate my ideas here.

4. Thanks to Quetzil Castañeda, who encouraged me to pursue this connection.

5. This does not necessarily account for other parts of the Amazon. Gow's (1991) important work in the Urubamba valley also discusses the complex continuities between discourses of "Indianness" and "mixed blood."

6. Quetzil Castañeda, pers. comm., 2008.

7. The ethnonym that predominates throughout the text is "Aguaruna," although in certain places the term "Awajún" replaces it. Generally, this reflects an attempt to use the term "Awajún" when in a context where some other voice in the text vocalizes it. I use "Aguaruna" because it is still widely used by many Aguaruna leaders and because it's the term I've grown most accustomed to. A few leaders I know insist that the "real" name of the ethnic group is Awajún because when speaking in Awajún, people use this term to refer to themselves. However, given the lack of full consensus and having met several leaders who explicitly acknowledge that "Awajún" is a phonetic modification of "Aguaruna," which in turn they acknowledge comes from a Spanish-

Quechua hybrid term, many consider this is a terminological difference not much worth the struggle. See also Chapter 2 and Greene (2008).

8. In this book I focus primarily on the Aguaruna, with only occasional comparative references to other Jivaroan groups. I do so in part because of the degree of depth I hope to achieve in recounting Aguaruna political efforts and because it was primarily Aguarunia that constituted the context for this research. I've met several Huambisa leaders and students in various places but never visited a native community that identifies itself as Huambisa, nor do I focus on Aguaruna-Huambisa relations. I'm sad to confess that after having read much about the Shuar and Achuar, I've yet to even visit Ecuador.

Chapter 2

1. Readers interested in a valiant attempt to paint a fuller picture of customary practice for a Jivaroan group should consult Philippe Descola's (1994) work. And those to whom the ideas of a truly pan-Amazonian identity appeal, whether articulated through a perspectivist ontology or a sociology of aesthetic conviviality, might consult the works of Eduardo Viveiros de Castro (1998) and Overing and Passes (2000).

Chapter 3

1. Some of these ways include possessing a vast knowledge and powerful array of medicinal plants, cultivating particularly memorable kinds of manioc, preparing notably appetizing kinds of manioc beer, and so on.

2. As an example, a shaman from the Alto Mayo during the 1970s and 1980s began to repeatedly occupy the office of chief in his home community Alto Naranjillo and travel frequently to other communities in the area. He eventually took a second wife and started another household in Huascayacu. Because he was a shamanic practitioner, his curing expertise was often sought. But at the start of the 1990s he was brutally killed by his new in-laws on the path to Huascayacu. Several people insisted to me that his death was a consequence of his apparent ambition in occupying the role of communal chief and taking up a second residence in another community.

3. Thus, many Aguaruna note that shamans are rarely invited to attend communal assemblies and gatherings (and rarely show up on their own initiative), another reflection of their isolation within communities. The Aguaruna organization OAAM published an internal statute that prohibits shamans from making their curative practice mobile. It states that communal authorities will take no responsibility for any harm that comes to shamanic practitioners should they choose to exercise such occupational travel.

4. In this discussion of anen I am deeply thankful to Adolfo Juep for being one of the most committed and creative translators I could imagine.

5. I was able to make recordings of several varieties of anen typically through an

exchange of this sort, either goods for anen or money for anen. However, I never did the more ritualized transmission involving tsaag. The contemporary concern over the potential collective property rights that many indigenous people claim over this kind of musical heritage of course weighs heavily on the anthropologist's mind these days, despite the individual Aguaruna property that anen arguably constitute (see Brown, 2003; Greene, 2004b). Samuel Kasep (Chimpa) of the community Alto Naranjillo put this concern into an entirely different perspective for me. On one of the days in which Chimpa generously allowed me to record anen considered effective for playing with female sentiments, someone present suggested that I must want to record these songs to gain a certain advantage over the female gender in my own country. Chimpa snapped back. On the contrary, he said, none of the songs being recorded would have any use since I had undergone none of the ritual prescriptions associated with the transmission of anen. No matter how well I memorized them, they would be completely ineffective given the mechanized form by which I would learn them (he appears to be a Benjaminian at heart). To strike the appropriate balance between revelation of these secret possessions and contemporary indigenous leaders' concerns over collective cultural property, I present them only in their translated English form (from the original Spanish translation done by various Aguaruna assistants). I do so under the assumption that there is an extremely low probability that anyone anywhere would have the resources, time, interest, and abilities to reverse the translation and thus uncover their original form.

6. The plant *tsuak* (another variety of baikua, *Datura*), which Aguaruna translate simply as "medicine," is thought to cure fractures and serious diseases and even resuscitate those on the verge of death. Botanically, the difference between the two plants is minimal (see Brown, 1978). Although some Aguaruna I have asked label them "different varieties" of the same plant, both serve the purpose of "reconstructing" the self (i.e., there is no hard-and-fast distinction between curing the self with tsuak and seeking to enhance it with baikua). Although I have not witnessed anyone take baikua, I have witnessed someone take tsuak. It is prepared in much the same way as baikua.

Chapter 4

1. For example, many Aguaruna activists, students, and educators are familiar with Michael Brown's *Una Paz Incierta*, which expresses this view of Jivaroan resistance. One common difference I've noticed is the emphasis that Northern academics place on the Logroño rebellion of the late 1500s, whereas the various Aguaruna accounts of the colonial period often don't make specific mention of it. For their part the academics typically cite Juan de Velasco (or Michael Harner's [1972] citing of Juan de Velasco), who recounts the apparently extraordinary size of the rebellion. But again, more recent accounts (cf. Taylor, 1994; Guallart, 1990) downplay the "resistance" angle. They present evidence that Velasco highly exaggerated the population

numbers. Despite downplaying Jivaroan resistance, both these accounts confirm the general idea that Jivaroan populations lived virtually isolated from contact with the national society until the turn of the twentieth century.

2. Here, due to a simple lack of space, I leave out any discussion of the multiple causes and consequences of the long-standing Peru/Ecuador border dispute and the emergent binational indigenous politics currently practiced by the Aguaruna and their various Jivaroan counterparts on both sides of the contested border (but see Greene, 2008).

3. Presumably this Jesuit (whoever he was) stayed in Aguarunia rather briefly. The only place I have seen him referenced is in Winans's (1989) autobiography. The Jesuits who would later go on to install Catholic missions in the area generally credit Father José Martín Cuesta with making *la primera entrada* (the first incursion) into Aguarunia decades later in 1945 (see Cuesta, 1992; Guallart, 1997).

4. For example, in 1969 JAARS pilots logged a total of 2,427.4 hours of flight time. Among other private parties, the flight traffic for the same year was divided between SIL-related personnel (31.17 percent), Peruvian military personnel (18.08 percent), and oil company personnel (16.05 percent) (Hefley and Hefley, 1972: 107).

5. For example, so far as I know the original Nazarene missionaries, Roger Winans and his wife Esther Carsons, were the first to attempt to write an Aguaruna dictionary and grammar in the 1920s and 1930s. But that document contains only a few dozen vocabulary words and remains an obscure textual relic, inaccessible to everyone except the persistent researcher willing to dig through Lima archives (see Personel de la Iglesia del Nazareno en esa Tribu, 1946). In 1958 Mildred Larson of SIL compiled three thousand vocabulary words and published the first comprehensive Aguaruna/ Spanish dictionary for use in the bilingual schools. The expanded edition, completed by Gerardo Wipio Deicat, an Aguaruna educator, is still the most widely used dictionary in Aguaruna schools.

6. Although the Nazarene mission continued to run its school in Yamayakat, it would eventually be replaced entirely by the SIL bilingual schools and resign itself to a more straightforwardly evangelical agenda. As the SIL school system grew, the schools themselves began to produce new recruits for bilingual teacher training. Through Nazarene contacts the most educationally advanced Aguaruna were also routinely sent to coastal cities to live with, and of course do chores for, Nazarene pastors in Chiclayo and Trujillo. There they also pursued a secondary education that was still unavailable in most Amazonian territories. Many of these young Aguaruna educated in the late 1950s and 1960s went on to become the next generation of SIL-trained bilingual teachers and eventually some of the first political organizers.

7. I use a contemporary spelling over the earlier one, Dánduchu rather than Dantuchu.

8. In fact, Efraín Morote Best was part of a line of infamous Peruvian leftists. His

son, Osmán Morote, rose to one of the highest ranks in the guerrilla group Sendero Luminoso under Abimael Guzman in the 1980s.

9. I emphasize "less" here since one cannot definitively declare organized military resistance a thing of the past. Nor can it be easily separated from organized Aguaruna politics. To the contrary, there are several recent instances of it (as discussed in the following two chapters).

10. I say "his" advisedly. Female bilingual teachers were virtually unheard of until more recently in bilingual education. The fact that gender asymmetry played such a major role in the phenomenon of new bilingual teacher-leaders points to the fact that aspects of custom (namely, the dominance of men) continued to manifest within the educational programs.

11. I am not suggesting that these ethnic intermediaries are entirely new to the Aguaruna's relations with the dominant society. Neighboring indigenous groups mediated their contact with the Spanish at various stages during the colonial period, which is also the reason they were attributed the hybrid Quechua-Spanish ethnonym Aguaruna (also see Taylor, 1994). The point is that the kind and scale of mediation performed by bilingual teachers were unheard of before the birth of bilingual education.

12. The expressions *jaanu* and *yamayajanu* are part of a standard refrain that accompanies all male nampet and that has no significance other than as vocal filler during the song.

Chapter 5

1. This was originally Ley 20653, Ley de Comunidades Nativas y de Promoción Agropecuaria de las Regiones de Selva y Cejas de Selva, later replaced by Ley 22175, Ley de Comunidades Nativas y de Desarrollo Agrario de las Regiones de Selva y Cejas de Selva. See the atlas published by Brack et al. (1998) for the most recent comprehensive account of indigenous Amazonian populations.

2. This is also clear from the only prior attempt by the Peruvian state to deal with Amazonian land rights, Supreme Decree 03 of March 1, 1957. In addition to a small forest reserve this decree granted individual members of a native settlement (over the age of five) ten hectares each on the assumption that the individuals would transition quickly to a sedentary agrarian lifestyle (see Chirif and Mora, 1977: 39). In practical terms Decree 03 had little impact. Only 114 reserves out of potentially at least 1,000 at the time were recognized.

3. The 1971 Barbados conference was organized by the Ethnology Department of the University of Berne in Switzerland and the World Council of Churches. Several anthropologists from the conference drew up a public declaration, the Declaration of Barbados: For the Liberation of the Indians. The declaration set new ideological criteria for states, missionaries, and anthropologists, in terms of their relations with

South American indigenous populations, by stressing the need for liberation and autonomous Indian leadership (see Dostal, 1972).

4. This should not be taken to imply that the CCP is itself an independent agent. It has long been influenced by Peru's various leftist parties, particularly the Partido Unificado Mariateguista (PUM).

5. As an example, the common usage of the term *Jivaro* designates an umbrella ethnolinguistic group that is then dividable into Aguaruna, Huambisa, Shuar, Achuar, and sometimes Candoshi. However, this classification is highly controversial because it corresponds to peoples living on both sides of the Peru/Ecuador border with differing opinions about the colonial term *Jivaro* (see Greene, 2008).

6. Of course, on this front the state also sought to fight back by coopting rondas with military and police influence. The cooptation is in many ways symbolized by Fujimori's decision to constitutionally legitimize rondas campesinas in his revised 1993 Constitution.

7. I compiled this data from the *Directorio de Comunidades Nativas del Perú* published in 1999; and titling data collected from the Ministerio de Agricultura, PETT, in Tarapoto, Department of San Martín, in late 1998.

8. In future references to the position of chief I use the male pronoun advisedly. The occupation of the office of chief is an almost exclusively male-gendered activity throughout Peru and certainly so in Aguarunia. Of the fifteen or so native communities that I have visited, no woman has ever been elected to serve in any capacity within the communal authority structure. I have heard of one exception: Raquel Kaikat, once the vice-president of the Consejo Aguaruna Huambisa, was elected chief of her community Ajachim on the Marañon River a few years ago. Ironically, it is not at the level of individual communities where women have gained access to positions of authority but rather in the various indigenous organizations that group native communities together at regional levels and federate them at national levels, a gender dynamic I discuss further in the following chapter.

9. In a few communities some women insert themselves into public affairs by attending communal assemblies and demanding a vote. In my experience the women who do so are those either without husbands (e.g., separated or widowed) or educated outside the community (some of the recently trained female bilingual teachers participate in this way). Women in some of the more geographically accessible communities get involved in other activities brought in by outsiders (e.g., Club de Madres, a state program, or the *cursos de capacitación* [training courses] that NGOs often bring).

10. Another indication of my unease here is found in my substitution of the word "migrant" for the word *colono*. Although I seriously doubt these migrants referred to themselves as "colonists," Aguaruna activists and community members routinely do. In fact, eventually even the state officials charged with investigating this case used this term to refer to migrant populations entering Amazonia.

11. In rare cases women have assumed de facto responsibilities for plots of commercial agricultural land (they retain all the customary rights to subsistence gardens where manioc, plantains, and other food and medicinal plants are cultivated). Albertina Nanchijam for many years administered her plot as if she were a titular after her husband's death because her sons were not living in the community (her eldest son nevertheless retained formal status as titular). Celestina Cahuaza has recently become a de facto titular of ten hectares as a result of her separation from her husband (she is bilingual and employed by the community's health post). These are the only cases I know of women administering economically productive plots in the Alto Mayo.

12. Variable pricing also reflects the accessibility of the field, past deals with the rentee, whether or not it needs further mechanization before planting, "package deals" of several hectares rented to one rentee, and so on.

13. This does not account for other possible income that might be available from other cultivation activities (coffee) or from salaried jobs, such as bilingual teachers or municipal positions.

Chapter 6

1. As Amazonian organizations grew in power and prestige, they asserted more control over education in native communities. In 1988 the Ministry of Education and an Italian NGO backed the national-level Amazonian organization AIDESEP in its efforts to experiment with and improve the pedagogical training and curriculum development of bilingual education in the Department of Loreto. AIDESEP's educational initiative, Formación de Maestros Bilingues de la Amazonia Peruana (FORMABIAP), is now one of the most widely used resources for teacher training and curriculum materials for the jungle's bilingual schools.

2. Fujimori has since made a failed effort to return to Peru via Chile, where he was detained and eventually extradited by the Peruvian government. At the time of this writing the Peruvian state is conducting his trial for various human rights abuses and corruption charges.

3. The fact that it is newer is also why I know relatively little about it. I have not had the opportunity to seek out FEMAAM leaders.

4. SIL's translation work has prompted many Aguaruna to translate *iwanch* as "devil." This is just a thin veil for the evangelical imperative that guides their linguistic work. *Iwanch* is one of Aguarunia's complex terms for "soul." Here Salomón is drawing on the idea of monstrous lost souls, also called iwanch, that roam the forest and occasionally attack the innocent: a metaphor he employs to demonstrate how many of the Aguaruna conceptualize mestizos in their midst.

5. I am deeply indebted to Richard Chase Smith for providing me open access to many of his personal archives, which contain numerous unpublished but highly significant documents from this era.

6. These were, respectively, Dominique Temple, Richard Chase Smith, Carolyn Heath, Carlos Mora, and Alberto Chirif. Several other notable activist figures later joined in these meetings, including Frederika Barclay, Margarita Benavides, Lucy Trapnell, Fernando Santos, and Thomas Moore. Members of Grupo DAM also began to participate.

7. The original name of the organization was Comité de Coordinación de Comunidades Nativas de la Selva Peruana (COCONASEP). In 1980 the name was changed to AIDESEP.

8. Another important supporter for the formation of CONAP was the Consejo Indio Sudamérica (CISA), which had received considerable criticism from AIDESEP (see Smith, 1996).

9. Several Huambisa communities on the Santiago River, under the leadership of Juan Noningo, decided to withdraw from the Consejo—in part because of decentralizing tendencies and in part because of interethnic tension between Aguaruna and Huambisa. They formed their own organization in the mid-1990s, now known as Federación de Comunidades Huambisas del Río Santiago (FECOHRSA). Thus, some leaders refer to this as the moment when "CAH lost its H," although some Huambisa communities still affiliate with the Consejo. More important, the ethnic separation ostensibly represented by the Consejo-FECOHRSA split is infinitely complicated because of the levels of intermarriage and joint residence in what state records nonetheless depict as mutually exclusive Aguaruna or Huambisa native communities.

10. Although both terms connote a warrior with visionary experience and repeated success in battle, pamuk is also often considered to be a superior rank to kakajam.

11. Waisam, like kakajam, is another customary term used to reference visionary warriors, although it has more specific connotations of one who knows how to use the plant wais, both as a purgative and as a way to manipulate future events.

12. The number of warriors is hard to confirm. I met a mestizo resident of Nieva who claimed to have been among the workers present at the time of the Aguaruna assault. His estimate of the size of the war party was six hundred.

13. In particular, I have never had the opportunity to ask Aguaruna from the Cenepa River region, who, so far as I can tell, were the primary actors involved in actually carrying out the raid. Were I to ever get the chance (a rather unlikely scenario given how reluctant most communities in Cenepa have proven to be about speaking with outside visitors), I would in fact expect a different account and probably for other strong men to emerge as prominent actors in the recounting.

14. Chang and Sarasara (1987: 26) also note that the ipaamamu is an "eminently masculine institution" since it corresponds to predominantly male activities and labors (burning a new garden, constructing a house, organizing for war, etc.). Women do in fact play a complementary role as hosts since a central feature of any ipaamamu is the serving of manioc beer. The person who formally "invites" is typically a male head

of household. The exceptions I have found to this general rule consist of women who have become heads of household by virtue of a marital separation or being widowed.

15. Chang and Sarasara (1987: 64) cite this critical observational role played by women as proof that although they are officially considered to act outside the sphere of the ipaamamu, they make critical suggestions and remarks that enter into the way men organize particular activities.

16. The OAAM was not part of the original agreement since the organization was outside the original collection areas. It was added in 1999 when the ICBG team decided to expand the collections to the Alto Mayo area in the Department of San Martín, where OAAM is located.

17. The first organizational ipaamamu was held in 1990 (CONAP, 1996) before Sarasara was head of CONAP (although he was already a participant). I have no information about its content. The second would not be realized until 1995 in the middle of the ICBG negotiations, at which time Sarasara explicitly sought to modify it into a recurring institutional practice of CONAP and its Aguaruna affiliate organizations.

References

Abercrombie, Thomas. 1998. *Pathways of Memory and Power*. Madison: University of Wisconsin Press.

Abu-Lughod, Lila. 1991. "Writing against Culture." In *Recapturing Anthropology*, ed. R. Fox, 137–162. Santa Fe, NM: School of American Research Press.

AIDESEP (Asociación Interétnica de Desarrollo de la Selva Peruana). 1988. *Voz Indígena* (April 7): 19–20.

———. 1989. *Voz Indígena* (May 8): 23–24.

———. 1990. *Voz Indígena* (August 9): 25–27.

AIDESEP (Asociación Interétnica de Desarrollo de la Selva Peruana) and ORASI (Organización Regional de los Aguarunas de San Ignacio). 2001. "El Estado Peruano es Cómplice de los Usurpadores de Tierra Indígenas." Communiqué. August 13. http://barrio peru.terra.com.pe/losnaranjos/documentos/doc_10.htm (accessed February 15, 2002).

Albó, Xavier. 1991. "El Retorno del Indio." *Revista Andina* 9 (2): 299–345.

Alvarez, Sonia, Evelina Dagnino, and Arturo Escobar, eds. 1998. *Cultures of Politics/ Politics of Cultures*. Boulder, CO: Westview Press.

Asad, Talal, ed. 1973. *Anthropology and the Colonial Encounter*. New York: Humanities Press.

Belaúnde Terry, Fernando. 1994. *La Conquista del Perú por los Peruanos*. Lima: Minerva.

Bourdieu, Pierre. 1977. *Outline of a Theory of Practice*. Cambridge: Cambridge University Press.

Brack, Antonio, Carlos Yáñez, Carlos Mora, and Alonso Zarzar. 1998. *Atlas de Comunidades Nativas*. Lima: Biblos S.A.

Brown, Michael F. 1978. "From the Hero's Bones: Three Aguaruna Hallucinogens and Their Uses." In *The Nature and Status of Ethnobotany*, ed. Richard Ford, 117–136. Anthropological Papers, 67. Ann Arbor: Museum of Anthropology, University of Michigan.

———. 1982. "Art of Darkness." *The Progressive* (August): 20–21.

———. 1984. *Una Paz Incierta*. Lima: Centro Amazónico de Antropología y Aplicación Práctica.

———. 1986. *Tsewa's Gift*. Washington, DC: Smithsonian Institution Press.

———. 1989. "Dark Side of the Shaman." *Natural History* (November): 8–10.

———. 2003. *Who Owns Native Culture?* Cambridge, MA: Harvard University Press.

Brysk, Alison. 2000. *From Tribal Village to Global Village*. Stanford, CA: Stanford University Press.

Cahuaza Noashampi, Noé. 1991. "Carta de la OAAM." *El Trueno* 43 (October): 3.

Calhoun, Craig. 2008. "Foreword." In *Engaging Contradictions*, ed. Charles Hale, xiii–xxvi. Berkeley: University of California Press.

Caretas. 1979. "Disparos contra Herzog." *Caretas* 580 (December 3): 34–37.

Carneiro da Cunha, Manuela. 1997. "Points of View on the Amazon Forest: Shamanism and Translation." Robert Hertz Lecture, Association pour la Recherche en Antropologie Sociale, Paris, July 9.

Chakrabarty, Dipesh. 2000. *Provincializing Europe*. Princeton, NJ: Princeton University Press.

Chang, Sergio, and César Sarasara. 1987. *Organizaciones Sociales y Economicas en las Comunidades del Grupo Etno-linguistico Aguaruna*. Lima: Ministerio de Agricultura, INADE, Proyecto Especial Alto Mayo.

Chavez Kuja, Alfonso, and Cesar Sanchium Kuja. N.d. "Historia del Grupo Etnolinguistico Aguaruna." Unpublished thesis, Pedagogical Institute, Yarinacocha, Peru.

Chirif, Alberto. 1975. "Occupación Territorial de la Amazonía y Marginación de la Población Nativa." *América Indígena* 34 (2): 265–295.

Chirif, Alberto, and Carlos Mora. 1977. *Atlas de Comunidades Nativas*. Lima: SINAMOS.

Chumap Lucia, Aurelio, and Manuel Garcia-Rendueles. 1979. *Duik Muun: Universo Mitico de los Aguaruna*. Lima: Centro Amazónico de Antropología y Aplicación Práctica.

Clifford, James. 1994. "Diasporas." *Cultural Anthropology* 9 (3): 302–338.

———. 2007. "Varieties of Indigenous Experience: Diasporas, Homelands, Sovereignties." In *Indigenous Experience Today*, ed. Marisol de la Cadena and Orin Starn, 197–224. Oxford: Berg.

Clifford, J., and G. Marcus, eds. 1986. *Writing Culture: The Poetics and Politics of Ethnography*. Berkeley: University of California Press.

CNN. 2002. "Settlers Killed in Clash with Peru Tribe." January 18. www.cnn.com/2002/WORLD/americas/01/18/peru.tribe.reut/index.html (accessed January 27, 2002).

Colby, Gerard, and Charlotte Dennett. 1995. *Thy Will Be Done: The Conquest of the Amazon: Nelson Rockefeller and Evangelism in the Age of Oil*. New York: HarperCollins.

Colloredo-Mansfeld, Rudi. 1999. *The Native Leisure Class*. Chicago: University of Chicago Press.

Comaroff, John, and Jean Comaroff. In press. *Ethnicity, Inc.* Chicago: University of Chicago Press.

CONAP (Confederación de Nacionalidades Amazónicas del Perú). 1987. *Runcato: Voz Nativa del Ucayali.* May 31.

———. 1988a. *CONAP.* June/July, 1 (1).

———. 1988b. *CONAP.* October/November, 1 (2).

———. 1989. *CONAP.* August/September, 2 (3).

———. 1996. "Congreso Ipaamamu Jibaro." November 2. Notes from assembly in Santa Maria de Nieva, Peru.

Conclusiones de la Reunión de Trabajo por los Derechos Humanos de los Indígenas Sudamericanos de la Cuenca Amazonica. 1984. Meeting Results: Workshop held March 26–31, Lima, Peru.

Conklin, Beth. 2002. "Shamans versus Pirates in the Amazonian Treasure Chest." *American Anthropologist* 104 (4): 1050–1061.

Conklin, Beth, and Laura Graham. 1995. "The Shifting Middle Ground: Amazonian Indians and Eco-Politics." *American Anthropologist* 97 (4): 695–710.

Consejo Aguaruna Huambisa. 1979. Letter of Protest about Herzog Affair to Cultural Survival. August 16.

Cuesta, José Martín. 1953. "Campaña de Alfabetizácion en la Selva Peruana." *El Comercio* (February 28): 5, 18.

———. 1992. *Entre el Condor y el Marañon: Memorias Misioneras.* Lima: Salamanca.

Cultural Survival. 1979. "CIPA, the Aguaruna and Werner Herzog." *Cultural Survival Newsletter* 3 (3): 10–12.

Dean, Bartholomew. 2002. "State Power and Indigenous Peoples in Peruvian Amazonia." In *The Politics of Ethnicity,* ed. David Maybury-Lewis, 199–238. Cambridge, MA: Harvard University Press.

———. 2003. "At the Margins of Power: Gender Hierarchy and the Politics of Ethnic Mobilization among the Urarina." In *At the Risk of Being Heard,* ed. B. Dean and J. Levi, 217–254. Ann Arbor: University of Michigan Press.

Degregori, Carlos Iván. 1998. "Movimientos Etnicos, Democracia y Nación en Perú y Bolivia." In *La Construcción de la Nación y la Representación Ciudadana en México, Guatemala, Perú, Ecuador, y Bolivia,* ed. Claudia Dary, 159–226. Guatemala City: FLACSO.

de la Cadena, Marisol. 2000. *Indigenous Mestizos.* Durham, NC: Duke University Press.

de la Cadena, Marisol, and Orin Starn. 2007. "Introduction." In *Indigenous Experience Today,* ed. Marisol de la Cadena and Orin Starn, 1–32. Oxford: Berg.

Descola, Philippe. 1994. *In the Society of Nature.* Cambridge: Cambridge University Press.

Dirección de Comunidades Campesinas y Nativas. 1999. *Directorio de Comunidades Nativas del Perú.* Lima: Proyecto Especial Titulación de Tierras, Ministerio de Agricultura.

Dostal, William, ed. 1972. *The Situation of the Indian in South America.* Geneva: World Council of Churches.

Drysdale, Robert, and Robert Myers. 1975. "Continuity and Change: Peruvian Education." In *The Peruvian Experiment*, ed. Abraham Lowenthal, 254–301. Princeton, NJ: Princeton University Press.

Duneier, Mitchell. 1999. *Sidewalk*. New York: Farrar, Straus and Giroux.

El Comercio. 1991. "Violencia en la Selva." August 22, 1904. Reprinted in *El Siglo XX en el Peru a traves de "El Comercio."* Tomo I. Lima: Ausonia, S.A.

Escobar, Arturo. 1995. *Encountering Development: The Making and Unmaking of the Third World*. Princeton, NJ: Princeton University Press.

Flores Galindo, Alberto. 1988. *Buscando un Inca*. Lima: Editorial Horizonte.

Friedman, Jonathon. 1999. "Indigenous Struggles and the Discreet Charm of the Bourgeoisie." *Australian Journal of Anthropology* 10 (1): 1–14.

Gamarra, Luis. 2002. "Morir Bajo las Hojas." *Caretas* (January 24). www.caretas.com .pe/2002/1705/articulos/aguarunas.phtml (accessed February 3, 2003).

Gaonkar, Dilip. 2001. "On Alternative Modernities." In *Alternative Modernities*, ed. D. Gaonkar, 1–23. Durham, NC: Duke University Press.

García, Maria Elena. 2005. *Making Indigenous Citizens*. Stanford, CA: Stanford University Press.

García-Cancilini, Nestor. 2001. *Consumers and Citizens*. Minneapolis: University of Minnesota Press.

Gilroy, Paul. 1995. "Roots and Routes: Black Identity as an Outernational Project." In *Racial and Ethnic Identity: Psychological Development and Creative Expression*, ed. H. Harris, H. Blue, and E. Griffith, 15–30. New York: Routledge.

Goodwin, Michael. 1982. "Herzog: The God of Wrath." *American Film* (June): 36–73.

Gow, Peter. 1991. *Of Mixed Blood*. Oxford: Clarendon Press.

———. 1996. "River People: Shamanism and History in Western Amazonia." In *Shamanism, History and the State*, ed. N. Thomas and C. Humphrey, 90–114. Ann Arbor: University of Michigan Press.

Graham, Laura. 2006. "Anthropologists Are Obligated to Promote Human Rights and Social Justice." *Anthropology News* 47 (7): 4.

Greene, Shane. 2004a. "Paths to a Visionary Politics: Customizing History and Transforming Authority in the Peruvian Selva." PhD diss., University of Chicago.

———. 2004b. "Indigenous People Incorporated? Culture as Politics, Culture as Property in Pharmaceutical Bioprospecting." *Current Anthropology* 45 (2): 211–237.

———. 2006. "Getting over the Andes: The Geo-Eco-Politics of Indigenous Movements in Peru's 21st Century Inca Empire." *Journal of Latin American Studies* 38 (2): 327–354.

———. 2007. "Entre lo Indio, lo Negro, y lo Incaico: The Spatial Hierarchies of Difference behind Peru's Multicultural Curtain." *Journal of Latin American and Caribbean Anthropology* 12 (2): 441–474.

———. 2008. "Tiwi's Creek: Indigenous Movements on, around, and across the Contested Peruvian Border." *Latin American and Caribbean Ethnic Studies* 3 (3): 227–252.

Greene, Shane, and Mamais Juep Greene. 2002. "Settlers Clash with Aguaruna in Peru's Amazon." *Cultural Survival Quarterly* (Spring): 71–72.

Grupo de Investigadores de la Selva. 1976. No title. Document commemorating meetings held during November and December.

Grupo de Trabajo Encargado de la Investigación de los Hechos Ocurridos en la Provincia de San Ignacio. 2002. *Informe del Grupo de Trabajo Encargado de la Investigación de los Hechos Ocurridos en la Provincia de San Ignacio.* Lima.

Guallart, Jose María. 1990. *Entre Pongo y Cordillera.* Lima: Centro Amazónico de Antropología y Aplicación Práctica.

———. 1997. *El Vicariato de San Francisco Javier del Marañon.* Lima: Centro Amazónico de Antropología y Aplicación Práctica.

Gupta, Akhil, and James Ferguson. 1992. "Beyond 'Culture': Space, Identity and the Politics of Difference." *Cultural Anthropology* 7 (1): 6–23.

Hale, Charles. 2002. "Does Multiculturalism Menace? Governance, Cultural Rights, and the Politics of Identity in Guatemala." *Journal of Latin American Studies* 34 (3): 485–535.

———. 2008. "Introduction." In *Engaging Contradictions*, ed. Charles Hale, 1–30. Berkeley: University of California Press.

Harner, M. 1972. *The Jívaro: People of the Sacred Waterfalls.* Garden City, NY: Anchor Books.

Hebdige, Dick. 1981. *Subculture: The Meaning of Style.* New York: Routledge.

Hefley, James, and Marti Hefley. 1972. *Dawn over Amazonia.* Waco, TX: Word Books.

———. 1981. *Uncle Cam.* Milford, MI: Mott Media.

Hendricks, Janet. 1993. *To Drink of Death.* Tucson: University of Arizona Press.

Herder, Johann Gottfried. 1803. *Outlines of a Philosophy of the History of Man.* Translated by T. Churchill. 2d ed. London: Luke Hansard.

Hodgson, Dorothy. 2002. "Introduction: Comparative Perspectives on the Indigenous Rights Movements in Africa and the Americas." *American Anthropologist* 104 (4): 1037–1049.

Hunt, Shane. 1975. "Direct Foreign Investment in Peru: New Rules for an Old Game." In *The Peruvian Experiment*, ed. Abraham Lowenthal, 302–349. Princeton, NJ: Princeton University Press.

Hymes, Dell, ed. 1972. *Reinventing Anthropology.* New York: Pantheon.

ICBG (International Cooperative Biodiversity Group). 1996. "Biological Collecting Agreement." Signed with CONAP, OCCAAM, FAD, FECONARIN, Washington University, Peruvian University Cayetano Heredia, Museum of Natural History at the National University of San Marcos. St. Louis.

Inoash, Gil. 1997. "Perspectivas Generales de la Situación Indígena Amazónica." In *Desarrollo y Participación de las Comunidades Nativas.* Lima: Defensoría del Pueblo, CAAAP, USAID.

Jackson, Jean. 1989. "Is There a Way to Talk about Making Culture without Making Enemies?" *Dialectical Anthropology* 14 (2): 127–144.

Keck, Margaret, and Kathryn Sikkink. 1998. *Activists beyond Borders*. Ithaca, NY: Cornell University Press.

Kelly, John. 2003. "Alternative Modernities or an Alternative to 'Modernity.'" In *Critically Modern*, ed. B. Knauft, 258–286. Bloomington: Indiana University Press.

Knauft, Bruce. 2003. "Critically Modern: An Introduction." In *Critically Modern*, ed. B. Knauft, 1–54. Bloomington: Indiana University Press.

Koselleck, Reinhart. 1985. *Futures Past: On the Semantics of Historical Time*. Cambridge, MA: MIT Press.

Kroeber, A. L., and Clyde Kluckhohn. 1952. *Culture: A Critical Review of Concepts and Definitions*. New York: Vintage Books.

Kuper, Adam. 1999. *Culture*. Cambridge, MA: Harvard.

Larson, Mildred. [1963] 1985. *Kistian Chicham Unuimatai*. Yarinacocha, Peru: Ministerio de Educación and Instituto Lingüístico de Verano.

———. 1981a. "Training to Train: The Key to an Ongoing Program." In *Bilingual Education: An Experience in Peruvian Amazonia*, ed. Mildred Larson and Patricia Davis, 335–350. Dallas, TX: Summer Institute of Linguistics.

———. 1981b. "Promoting Bilingual Education through Teachers' Conferences." In *Bilingual Education: An Experience in Peruvian Amazonia*, ed. Mildred Larson and Patricia Davis, 179–187. Dallas, TX: Summer Institute of Linguistics.

Larson, Mildred, and Patricia Davis, eds. 1981. *Bilingual Education: An Experience in Peruvian Amazonia*. Dallas, TX: Summer Institute of Linguistics.

Larson, Mildred, and Lois Dodds. 1985. *Treasure in Clay Pots*. Palm Desert, CA: Person to Person Books.

LeTourneau, R. G. 1960. *Mover of Men and Mountains*. Chicago: Moody Press.

Luisa del Río, Maria. 2000. "Newmont sobre Cenepa." *Jempe, Boletín de Noticias del SAIPE* 10 (August–September): 16–18.

Mamdani, Mahmood. 2001. "Beyond Settler and Native as Political Identities: Overcoming the Political Legacy of Colonialism." *Comparative Studies in Society and History* 43 (4): 651–664.

Mann, Charles. 2005. *1491*. New York: Knopf.

Marka. 1979. "Herzog vs. Aguarunas." *Marka* (December 6): 34.

Marx, Karl. [1852] 1978. "The Eighteenth Brumaire of Louis Bonaparte." In *The Marx-Engels Reader*, ed. R. Tucker, 594–617. New York: Norton.

Matos Mar, José, and José Manuel Mejía. 1980. *La Reforma Agraria en el Perú*. Lima: Instituto de Estudios Peruanos.

Mendez, Cecilia. 1996. "Incas Sí, Indios No: Notes on Peruvian Creole Nationalism and Its Contemporary Crisis." *Journal of Latin American Studies* 28:197–225.

Miller, Daniel. 1998. *A Theory of Shopping*. Ithaca, NY: Cornell University Press.

Mora, Carlos. 1983. "Reflexiones acerca del Problema Territorial de las Comunidades In- dígenas de la Amazonía." *América Indígena* 43 (3): 569–584.

Morote Best, Efraín. 1957. "Tres Temas de la Selva." *Tradición* 7 (17–18): 3–21.

———. 1961. "Trabajo y Escuela en la Selva Peruana." In *William Cameron Townsend en el Vijesimoquinto Aniversario del Instituto Lingüístico de Verano*, 301–312. Cuernavaca, México: Tipográfica Indígena.

Niezen, Ronald. 2003. *The Origins of Indigenism*. Berkeley: University of California Press.

Nor Oriente. 1979a. "Terror en el Cenepa." August, 4th week.

———. 1979b. "Mas Provocación." La Voz de Nuestra Jibaría Column, September, 1st week.

———. 1979c. "Arde la Selva." La Voz de Nuestra Jibaría Column, December 8.

———. 1980a. "El Rechazo a Herzog." La Voz de Nuestra Jibaría Column, January 12.

———. 1980b. "El Asalto a la Compañía (2)." La Voz de Nuestra Jibaría Column, Janu- ary 19.

———. 1980c. "El Asalto a la Compañía (3)." La Voz de Nuestra Jibaría Column, Janu- ary 26.

———. 1980d. "El Asalto a la Compañía (5)." La Voz de Nuestra Jibaría Column, Feb- ruary 9.

———. 1980e. "El Asalto a la Compañía (6)." La Voz de Nuestra Jibaría Column, Feb- ruary 16.

Novick, Robert. 1988. *That Noble Dream*. Cambridge: Cambridge University Press.

Nugent, José Guillermo. 1992. *El Laberinto de la Choledad*. Lima: Fundación Friedrich Ebert.

OAAM (Organización Aguaruna Alto Mayo). 1991. Oficio No. 001–OAAM-91. Commu- niqué resulting from OAAM meeting about new OAAM leadership and denounce- ment of Santos Adan. Bajo Naranjillo, San Martín, Peru.

Overing, Joanna, and Alan Passes. 2000. "Introduction." In *The Anthropology of Love and Anger*, ed. Joanna Overing and Alan Passes, 1–30. London: Routledge.

Pagden, Anthony. 1998. *Spanish Imperialism and the Political Imagination in Latin Amer- ica*. New Haven, CT: Yale University Press.

Personel de la Iglesia del Nazareno en esa Tribu. 1946. *Un Estudio Sobre los Aguaruna*. Monsefu, Peru: Imprenta Nazarena.

Pierre, Jemima. 2008. "Activist Groundings or Groundings for Activism?" In *Engaging Contradictions*, ed. Charles Hale, 115–135. Berkeley: University of California Press.

Poster, Mark. 1997. *Cultural History and Postmodernity: Disciplinary Readings and Chal- lenges*. New York: Columbia University Press.

Povinelli, Elizabeth. 2002. *The Cunning of Recognition*. Durham, NC: Duke University Press.

Proyecto Especial Alto Mayo. 1998. *Programa Sobre Manejo Ambiental en el Valle del Alto Mayo*. Moyobamba, Peru: PEAM.

Ramos, Alcida. 1998. *Indigenism: Ethnic Politics in Brazil.* Madison: University of Wisconsin Press.

Rappaport, Joanne. 2005. *Intercultural Utopias.* Durham, NC: Duke University Press.

Rasnake, Roger. 1988. *Domination and Cultural Resistance.* Durham, NC: Duke University Press.

Robertson, Roland. 1995. "Glocalization: Time-Space and Homogeneity-Heterogeneity." In *Global Modernities,* ed. M. Featherstone, S. Lash, and R. Robertson, 25–44. London: Sage.

Rosenthal, Joshua. 2006. "Politics, Culture, and Governance in the Development of Prior Informed Consent in Indigenous Communities." *Current Anthropology* 47 (1): 119–142.

Rubenstein, Steven. 2001. "Colonialism, the Shuar Federation, and the Ecuadorian State." *Environment and Planning D* 19:263–293.

———. 2007. "Circulation, Accumulation, and the Power of Shuar Shrunken Heads." *Cultural Anthropology* 22 (3): 357–399.

Sahlins, Marshall. 1985. *Islands of History.* Chicago: University of Chicago Press.

———. 1993. "Goodbye to Tristes Tropes: Ethnography in the Context of Modern World History." *Journal of Modern History* 65:1–25.

Samaniego, Salomón. 1979a. "Werner Herzog Quiere Reivindicarse." *Nor Oriente,* La Voz de Nuestra Jibaría Column, November 17.

———. 1979b. "El Incendio del Campamento." *Nor Oriente,* La Voz de Nuestra Jibaría Column, December 22.

Santos-Granero, Fernando. 1992. *Etnohistoria de la Alta Amazonia.* Quito: Abya-Yala.

Sapir, Edward. 1984. *Selected Writings of Edward Sapir in Language, Culture, and Personality.* Berkeley: University of California Press.

Scott, James. 1998. *Seeing Like a State.* New Haven, CT: Yale University Press.

Serrano Calderón de Ayala, Emilio. 1995. *David Samaniego Shunaula: Nueva Crónica de los Indios de Zamora y del Alto Marañon.* Quito: Abya-Yala.

Silverblatt, Irene. 2004. *Modern Inquisitions.* Durham, NC: Duke University Press.

Slater, Candace. 2002. *Entangled Edens.* Berkeley: University of California Press.

Smith, Richard Chase. 1982. "The Dialectics of Domination in Peru." *Cultural Survival,* Occasional Paper 8, October.

———. 1996. "Las Políticas de la Diversidad: COICA y las Federaciones Etnicas de la Amazonia." In *Pueblos Indios, Soberania y Globalismo,* ed. Stefano Varese, 81–125. Quito: Abya-Yala.

Smith, Richard Chase, Margarita Benavides, Mario Pariona, and Ermeto Tuesta. 2003. "Mapping the Past and the Future: Geomatics and Indigenous Territories in the Peruvian Amazon." *Human Organization* 62 (4): 357–368.

Soria, Carlos. 2003. "Avances en el Derecho Ambiental en el Perú." Paper presented at the Seminario de Abertura do Curso de Doutorado em Direito, Universidade Federal de Pará, October 24.

Starn, Orin. 1999. *Nightwatch.* Durham, NC: Duke University Press.

Stern, Steve. 1982. *Peru's Indian Peoples and the Challenge of Spanish Conquest.* Madison: University of Wisconsin Press.

Stoll, David. 1982. *Fishers of Men or Founders of Empire?* London: Zed Press with Cultural Survival.

Summer Institute of Linguistics. 1966. *Twenty Years with the Summer Institute of Linguistics and Wycliffe Bible Translators, Inc. among Peru's Peoples.* Yarinacocha, Peru: Summer Institute of Linguistics.

———. 1978. *Initik Augmatbau: Historia Aguaruna Primera Etapa, Segunda Parte Tomo I.* Lima: Summer Institute of Linguistics and Ministerio de Educación.

Taussig, Michael. 1987. *Shamanism, Colonialism, and the Wild Man: A Study in Terror and Healing.* Chicago: University of Chicago Press.

Taylor, Anne Christine. 1993. "Remembering to Forget: Identity, Mourning and Memory among the Jivaro." *Man* 28:653–678.

———. 1994. "Estudio Introductorio." In *Conquista de la Región Jívaro (1550–1650),* ed. A. C. Taylor and C. Landázuri, 1–32. Quito: Marka.

———. 1998. "Jivaro Kinship: 'Simple' and 'Complex' Formulas." In *Transformations in Kinship,* ed. Maurice Godelier, Thomas Trautmann, and Franklin Tjon Sie Fat, 187–213. Washington, DC: Smithsonian Institution Press.

———. 2007. "Sick of History: Contrasting Regimes of Historicity in the Upper Amazon." In *Time and Memory in Indigenous Amazonia: Anthropological Perspectives,* ed. Carlos Fausto and M. Heckenberger, 133–168. Gainesville: University Press of Florida.

Tii Ikam, Cesar. 2000. "Toe, Tabaco, y Ayahuasca." In *El Ojo Verde: Cosmovisiones Amazónicos.* AIDESEP and Fundación Telefónica, Programa de Formación de Maestros Bilingues. Lima: Ediciones del Umbral.

Trouillot, Michel-Rolph. 1991. "Anthropology and the Savage Slot." In *Recapturing Anthropology,* ed. R. Fox, 17–44. Santa Fe, NM: School of American Research Press.

———. 1995. *Silencing the Past.* Boston: Beacon.

Turner, Terence. 2003. "Class Projects, Social Consciousness, and the Contradictions of 'Globalization.'" In *Globalization, the State, and Violence,* ed. J. Friedman, 35–66. Walnut Creek, CA: Altamira Press.

Uriarte, Luis. 1985. "Los Nativos y su Territorio: El Caso de los Jivaro Achuara en la Amazonia Peruana." *Amazonía Peruana* 6 (11): 39–64.

Van Cott, Donna Lee. 2000. *The Friendly Liquidation of the Past.* Pittsburgh: University of Pittsburgh Press.

Varese, Stefano. 1972a. *The Forest Indians in the Present Political Situation of Peru.* International Work Group for Indigenous Affairs document. Copenhagen.

———. 1972b. "Inter-ethnic Relations in the Selva of Peru." In *The Situation of the Indian in South America,* ed. Walter Dostal. Geneva: World Council of Churches.

———. 1973. *La Sal de los Cerros*. Lima: Retablo de Papel Ediciones.

———. 1975. "Etnología de Urgencia, Conciencia Etnica y Participación Social en el Peru." *América Indígena* 35 (2): 251–263.

Viveiros de Castro, Eduardo. 1992. *From the Enemy's Point of View*. Chicago: University of Chicago Press.

———. 1998. "Cosmological Deixis and Amerindian Perspectivism." *Journal of the Royal Anthropological Institute* 4 (3): 469–488.

Warren, Kay, and Jean Jackson, eds. 2002. *Indigenous Movements, Self-Representation, and the State in Latin America*. Austin: University of Texas Press.

Winans, Roger. [1955] 1989. *Gospel over the Andes*. Kansas City, MO: Nazarene Publishing House.

Wipio Deicat, Gerardo. 1981. "Education among the Aguaruna." In *Bilingual Education: An Experience in Peruvian Amazonia*, ed. Mildred Larson and Patricia Davis, 67–82. Dallas, TX: Summer Institute of Linguistics.

Wise, Carol. 2003. *Reinventing the State*. Ann Arbor: University of Michigan Press.

Wolf, Eric. 1982. *Europe and the People without History*. Berkeley: University of California Press.

Yashar, Deborah. 2005. *Contesting Citizenship in Latin America*. Cambridge: Cambridge University Press.

Index

Boas, Franz, 18
Bourdieu, Pierre, 18, 65, 67
Bracamoros, 103
Brown, Michael F., 51, 53, 81, 219n1
Buddha, 95
Burden of Dreams (Blank), 186

CAAAP (Centro de Antropología y
    Aplicación Práctica de la Amazonia
    Peruana), 205
cacao, 172
cachi, 62
Cachiyacu, 1–2, 65–66
CAH (Consejo Aguaruna Huambisa), 168,
    170, 173, 179, 181, 183–88, 193–94, 224n9
Cahuaza, Alfonso, 149
Cahuaza, Noé, 85, 147–49, 169, 179, 209
Cahuaza, Pancho, 126, 148
Caicharo, David, 168
Cajamarca, 35
Calhoun, Craig, 206
Camp Wycliffe, 113
Candoshi, 32–33
cannibalism, 91–92
capitalism, 13, 22–24, 112, 139, 162, 194, 201–2;
    and Aguaruna, 25–26, 110, 150–51, 155,
    172–73
Cárdenas, Lázaro, 113
Caretas (Lima), 185
Carneiro da Cunha, Manuela, 62
Carretera Marginal de la Selva, 69–70, 137–38,
    144, 151
Carsons, Esther, 107–8, 220n5
CART (Central Ashaninka del Río Tambo),
    168
Casa Verde, La (Vargas Llosa), 122
Catholic Church, 56, 108, 110–12, 116, 119, 166,
    189, 220n3
Catip, José, 2–3
CCP (Confederación Campesina del Perú),
    142–43, 222n4
CECONSEC (Central de Comunidades Nati-
    vas de la Selva Central), 168, 170
ceja de selva, 31
Chang, Sergio, 72, 148, 189–91, 224–25nn14–15
Chapi Shiwag, 169, 173
Chavez Kuja, Alfonso, 103
Chicáis, 121

Chimpa (Samuel Kasep), 86, 218–19n5
Chiriaco, 64
Chirif, Alberto, 142, 174, 224n6
chuncho, 26–27, 142, 177, 200
Church of the Nazarene, 63–64, 107, 220n6
CIPA (Centro de Investigaciones y Promo-
    ción Amazónica), 174–75, 177–78
citizenship, 63–64, 118–19, 121–22, 127–29
class: and ethnicity, 29, 55, 135, 139, 176; income
    disparity, 36, 161–64, 223n13
Clifford, James, 35
CNA (Confederación Nacional Agraria), 141–42
CNN (Cable News Network), 152
coffee, 153, 155, 158–59
COICA (Coordinadora de Organizaciones
    Indígenas de la Cuenca Amazónica), 167,
    176–77, 189
collective intellectual property, 192–95
Colloredo-Mansfield, Rudi, 162
Comaroff, John and Jean, 13
Comercio, El (Lima), 104, 116
Commission of Cinematic Promotion, 184
commodity-based economy, 110, 112, 162. *See
    also* capitalism
Compañía Industrial del Marañon, 108–9
comunidades campesinas, 55, 135, 139
comunidades indígenas, 55, 135, 139, 176
CONACAMI (Coordinadora Nacional de
    Comunidades Afectadas por la Min-
    ería), 170
CONAM (Consejo Nacional del Ambiente),
    145
CONAP and Affiliates, 194
CONAP (Confederación de Nacionalidades
    Amazónicas del Perú), 5, 167–70, 178–80,
    189, 192–96, 205, 224n8, 225n17
Congreso Amuesha, 168, 170
"Congreso Ipaamamu Jibaro" (CONAP),
    195–96
Congreso-Ipaamamu to Strengthen and Con-
    solidate the Aguaruna and Huambisa
    People and the ICBG Project (1995), 195
Coñivo, Aníbal Francisco, 177
CONOAP (Consejo de Comunidades Nativas
    Nomatsguenga y Asháninka de Pangoa),
    168
Conquista del Perú por los Peruanos, La
    (Belaúnde Terry), 137–38

Work Group on Indigenous Populations, 176
World Bank, 14, 144, 177
Wycliffe Bible Translators, Inc., 113

Yamayakat, 108–9, 172, 220n6
Yarinacocha, 115–16, 121, 126–27, 141
yuca, 62

CPSIA information can be obtained
at www.ICGtesting.com
Printed in the USA
LVHW111739301020
670290LV00004B/293